Sociology in Israel

CONTRIBUTIONS IN SOCIOLOGY

Series Editor: Don Martindale

Sociology in Israel

Leonard Weller

Contributions in Sociology, Number 11

GREENWOOD PRESS

Westport, Connecticut ● London, England

Library of Congress Cataloging in Publication Data

Weller, Leonard.
    Sociology in Israel.

    (Contributions in sociology, no. 11)
    Bibliography: p.
    1. Israel—Social conditions. 2. Sociological
research—Israel. 3. Collective settlements—Israel.
I. Title.
HN761.P32W45   301'.07'205694   72-849
ISBN 0-8371-6417-6

Library of Congress Catalog Card Number: 72-849
ISBN: 0-8371-6417-6

First published in 1974

Greenwood Press, a division of Williamhouse Regency Inc.
51 Riverside Avenue, Westport, Connecticut 06880

Manufactured in the United States of America

Contents

9020

List of Tables

Acknowledgments

I would like to acknowledge my indebtedness to those who helped me in this work. First and foremost, I thank Don Martindale, editor of the series, for his insightful review of the entire manuscript and many helpful criticisms and suggestions. His encouragement and support were such that no acknowledgment can adequately convey my appreciation. Although I profited greatly by his comments, the shortcomings of the work are clearly mine.

I wish to thank those assistants who helped me in various stages: Navah Hanam, Judith Adler, and Ephraim Tabory. I would also like to thank Mrs. Berit Meyers for her secretarial assistance.

And, of course, I am indebted to those sociologists whose work appears in this book. I apologize if an error was inadvertently made in the presentation of their work.

Thanks also go to the Research Committee of Bar-Ilan University whose grant helped in the preparation of the manuscript.

And to my wife and friend, Sonia—just for being.

Introduction

The horror of Nazi terrorism in World War II had taken a heavy toll—
no fewer than six million Jews had perished, many of whom might
have been saved had a place of refuge existed to which they could flee.
In a rare instance of agreement, the United States and Russia supported
a United Nations resolution calling for the establishment of a Jewish
homeland in Palestine. On the very same day that the British withdrew
from Palestine and the new state was proclaimed, seven Arab States
attacked it. The United Nations, after sanctioning the creation of the
new state, would not, or could not, assist in her defense against the
Arab invasion. Instead, the world organization sent truce teams to
arrange a ceasefire. The United States, the first country to recognize
the new state, placed an embargo on American arms to Israel. Out-
numbered by the one hundred million Arabs and at a grave disadvantage
due to their lack of arms, Israel was expected by most military strate-
gists to collapse within a short period of time.

Her ability to survive the 1948 Arab war captured the imagination
of many a writer and historian, but it completely overshadowed the
unique social features which have made her different from other
societies.

There has been, first of all, the remarkable population growth. In
May 1948, there were in Israel 650,000 Jews who had arrived in six
large *aliyot* (waves of immigration). The greatest number came almost
immediately after the creation of the state with the enacting of the
Law of Return, which permitted unrestricted immigration for all the
Jews of the world. The old, the destitute, and the physically broken

3

of the concentration camps—all would be readily accepted into their Homeland. Within two decades the population quadrupled. This would be equivalent to an increase in the population of the United States of six hundred million during a twenty-year period.

The second unique feature has been the extreme ethnic and cultural diversity. Following the proclamation of the new state, Jews had to flee Arab countries, some communities leaving in their entirety. All the Jews of Yemen, Libya, and Iraq, and most of the Syrian and Egyptian Jews, immigrated to Israel. Movement from other African countries, such as Morocco and Tunis, was on a smaller but no less significant scale. Moreover, there was wide heterogeneity among the Eastern Jews. Not only did Yemenite Jews differ from Iraqi Jews, but the Iraqis differed greatly amongst themselves, depending on whether they came from the city or the hinterland. Still, as a group, the Easterners hailed from a fundamentally feudalistic, traditional and patriarchal society, their life-style resembling that of the Moslems. Whether or not this was their first contact with Western society (as in the case of the Yemenites), they discovered Israel differed radically from the old society, in values as well as technology. The European immigrants were pioneers who established the ideology of collectivism and egalitarianism and became the elite of the country. The mass migration from Asian-African countries split Israeli society into two cultural groups, those from the East and those from the West, and decreased the percentage of European Jews from 85 in 1948 to 50 percent today. As this book makes clear, these differences have in many ways sharpened.

Another important factor is the spectacular growth in the number of settlements. In 1961, approximately a quarter of a million Jews lived in areas which less than fifteen years earlier had been totally or almost totally uninhabited. The heavy concentration of the Jewish population on the coastal plain, coupled with the overpopulation of Arabs in the northern and southern regions, was regarded as a dangerous security situation. These factors gave rise to a policy of population distribution, where newcomers, now mostly from Asia and Africa, were directed to areas in need of development. Town planning was not limited to the physical aspects, but involved the economic, institutional, and social spheres. Today twenty-four development towns account for 25 percent of the total Jewish population.

A critical factor distinguishing Israel is the "good neighbor policy" which threatens annihilation by seven Arab countries with a combined population of over one hundred million. The Israelis know that the threat is not an idle one. When the Arabs lose a war they may count it as a battle lost; for the Israelis a lost war could well mean general massacre and the end of the state.

Shortly before the Six Day War, the Arabs announced their intention to inflict such a massacre, and many Arabs were surprised that the victors did not behave in that manner. N. de Shalit, the author of "Children in War," reports her feelings on the eve of the Six Day War:

> We were worried about the children. We put name and address tags on them, and my husband told me that we ought to give the children the addresses of friends in America. But why? Perhaps we would be killed. In which case, why addresses in America, had we no friends and relatives in Israel? Maybe we would all be killed here. Today this sounds irrational. At the time it was a possibility, everything was possible. I am recounting this only to point out the fear of complete annihilation really existed for us.[1]

While Israelis dismiss the possibility of losing a war, the Arab conflict has a number of ramifications affecting many aspects of civilian life. The war is always present and not restricted to the battlefield. Arabs place bombs in supermarkets, terminals, airports, market places, and movie theatres. Not only do Israeli boys serve in the army for three years and girls for two years, but the men are called to active duty for at least forty-five days a year. A soldier who dies may well be a reservist and a father of several children. Settlements in the North which border on Jordan, Syria and Lebanon were shelled before the Six Day War and have still found no peace. After the war, children were hustled into shelters whenever shelling started. However, it soon appeared that this was not a temporary situation. Accordingly, permanent shelters were built, and the children now sleep in them as a matter of routine.

Then there is the *kibbutz*, that unique social experiment found only in Israel. The kibbutz is a cooperative agricultural village where all property, with minor exceptions, is collectively owned. While some *kibbutzim* employ outsiders, most adhere to the original ideology of not using hired help. The complete social and economic equality means that the kibbutz manager and the orange picker receive the same benefits. Since the kibbutz is an organic community based on total equality, all decisions are communal decisions. One of its most interesting features is its method of child rearing, for the children do not live with their parents, but with peers in children's homes supervised by teachers. (The parents visit the children every day for several hours). The kibbutzim were in their heyday in the years 1938-1947, but since 1948 their population increase has been relatively less than that of the rest of the country.

One can see why Israel is an exciting place for the sociologist. In addition to the standard sociological enquiries, the unique social situation arising out of the above factors permits a wide range of additional explorations. The country has justifiably been called a natural social science laboratory.

The primary aim of this book is to present an account of sociological research in Israel, but more than a survey is intended. In each area of sociological research, an attempt has been made not only to present the relevant findings, but to integrate them as well. We ask what the disparate research findings tell of the nature of social class in Israel, the openness of its society, and the degree of upward mobility. Similarly, we review the disparate findings with the aim of evaluating the extent of the educational gap between Jews of Eastern and Western descent.

This, then, is the second objective of the work—an integration of the results of sociological research. At this point we should add that we have employed a loose definition of the term "sociologist." Essentially we have been concerned with the research of the investigator and not with the kind of degree he holds, although in only a relatively small number of cases is the research cited not done by a *bona fide* sociologist. It has been necessary, particularly in the area of education, to include work undertaken by researchers in a number of academic disciplines.

The third objective of the work arises out of the previous two. In reviewing and integrating the research, we have at the same time presented a picture of Israeli society. For example, one can hardly discuss research on religion without discussing the background of the religious cleavage. However, since the prime objective was research, we acknowledge the necessarily limited analysis of Israeli society.

An attempt was made to cover the major studies conducted in the various areas. However, we have not felt compelled to cover a topic which has not stimulated the interest of at least a few sociologists. We ask the indulgence of those whose work we have not included. We hope they understand that some selection was necessary. The studies on social aspects of work, while not reviewed, are included in the bibliography. Furthermore, while we have made use of a number of researches by anthropologists (in Israel the distinction between them and sociologists is blurred), there are some distinctively anthropological researches which have been excluded. Finally, this book is concerned with sociology *in* Israel. Therefore, we have not included contributions made by sociologists to the general theoretical literature. In particular, we have omitted the work of Professor Shmuel Eisenstadt and Professor Louis Gutman whose contributions to general sociology, methodology, social change, and theory are well-known. Nor have we included the important contributions of Elihu Katz on communication, Joseph Ben-David on the role of higher education, science, and the professions, or Jacob Katz on traditional Jewish societies.

This book is divided into two sections. The first deals with immigrant absorption, education, social class and mobility, and intergroup relations. The second treats of family, criminology, religion, and the kibbutz. What distinguishes the two sections is that the first four chapters are integrated by their common analysis—country of origin.

In 1949 and 1950, when the major research on immigration was undertaken, no one foresaw the social cleavage which was to become *the* problem of Israel: the failure of Jews of Eastern origin to "make it." Even those who recognized that Jews from the underdeveloped Asian-African lands would not succeed as well as those from Western countries were unaware that this trend would not abate by the second or third generation. It is not surprising, therefore, that the major unit of sociological analysis became the contrast between Jews of Eastern and Jews of Western descent.

The final chapter discusses factors affecting the immigrants' absorption into Israeli society, and is a baseline for much of the research that follows. The major studies on immigrant absorption, done during the early years of the state, represent a blending of empirical research and high level theorizing. The next two chapters may be considered extensions of the first, for their dominant research theme is the extent of success—or failure—of Jews of Eastern descent in education (chapter 2) and their position in the social class structure (chapter 3). The last chapter (chapter 4) of Section I deals with intergroup relations, which in effect means prejudice towards Jews of Eastern descent. Concomitant with the fact that Jews of Asian-African origin belong to the lower rungs of society there has been a growing prejudice against them and against certain ethnic communities, notably the Moroccans. Most of the research has been concerned with measuring the extent of this prejudice and its effect on the group's self-image. Of late, the attitudes of Eastern Jews towards Western Jews have also been investigated.

The second section concerns family, criminology, religion and the kibbutz. No common theme was found among these chapters. The family (chapter 5), particularly its internal dynamics, has not been well studied, and consequently this chapter presents less of a coherent unit than do the others. Topics such as power relationships in the family, role conflict, mate selection and propinquity, and the three generational family are unfamiliar in Israel. This is due in part to the attention given to the immigrant and kibbutz families. The one topic which has received a considerable amount of attention is intergenerational tension, most likely because it concerns acculturation. Topics studied are family typologies, the ultraorthodox family, the woman's position and demographic changes.

Since the majority of criminals in Israel have been of Eastern descent, it is not surprising that a fair amount of research has utilized the ethnic factor in its analysis. But in spite of a reasonable concern with this factor, most of the research has dealt with a variety of topics, such as the application of theories of culture conflict and differential opportunity in explaining delinquency of Eastern youth, delinquent gangs, social stigma and prostitution, ecological and cultural aspects of delinquency, influence of the judge on sentences, and the evaluation of the effects of suspended sentences. Middle-class delinquency, which has recently made its appearance, has also been studied. Significant theoretical contributions have been made, such as work on the stigma theory of crime and deviation (chapter 6).

The second major social problem is that of religion. In Israel, people define themselves as "religious" or "nonreligious," "religious" meaning orthodox. The third social category, midway between orthodox and nonreligious, is called "traditional." This is a heterogeneous grouping, ranging from those who, in most respects, are orthodox to those who adhere to only a few traditional observances. There is no organized middle of the road religious movement such as Conservative Judaism in the United States.

In view of the importance of this subject, it is surprising that there have been so few pertinent studies. There is the problem of defining who is religious, but it is less difficult in Israel than in the United States. The chapter reports the results of studies which assessed the religious preferences of the population. It furthermore reports on changing behavior in religious observances, and indicates which segments of the population are becoming less observant. Studies on the impact of religiosity on attitudes and behavior are cited. These include the use of contraceptive devices, ethnocentrism, occupational interests, nursing attitudes, authoritarianism, and risk behavior (chapter 7).

The literature of the kibbutz is so extensive that a bibliography for the years 1949 to 1964 covered over 250 items. Owing to my inability to cope with this vast amount of literature, I asked my colleague, Dr. Joseph Shepher, himself a kibbutz member, to write this chapter. Dr. Shepher's thorough familiarity with this subject will be immediately felt by the reader. In his review, Shepher cites vast unpublished research, much of it undertaken by the kibbutz federations, which maintain Institutes of Research. His chapter covers the family, the second generation in the kibbutz, work and public activity, political institutions, stratification, values, and the kibbutz and the surrounding Israeli society (chapter 8).

UNIVERSITY TRAINING AND RESEARCH ACTIVITIES

There are four liberal arts universities in Israel: the Hebrew University in Jerusalem, Bar-Ilan University and Tel Aviv University in the Tel Aviv area, and Haifa University in Haifa.[2] The oldest is the Hebrew University which was founded in 1925 and today has an enrollment of 11,000. Tel Aviv University goes back to 1953-1954 when the Tel Aviv Municipality established two institutes of higher learning with just over one thousand students. Although these institutes became the nucleus of Tel Aviv University in 1956, it was only in 1961 that a special public committee recommended its expansion into a large-scale university; today it has an enrollment of 15,000. Bar-Ilan opened in 1954 with eighty students; today there are 6,000. Haifa University is the youngest. Originally established by agreement between the City of Haifa and the Hebrew University of Jerusalem, it opened its doors in 1963 with a population of 650; less than ten years after its birth it boasts of 5,000 students. Until the 1960s, when both Bar-Ilan and Tel Aviv Universities seriously began to expand, most prospective students had no other course but to enroll at the Hebrew University in Jerusalem. Furthermore, because of the distance from their homes, most of the students had to find lodgings near the university. It is to be noted that most of the students are, on the average, two or three years older than their Western counterparts, having spent two years (in the case of women) and three years (in the case of men) in the army after finishing high school.

Bar-Ilan University

Bar-Ilan offers courses in sociology leading to the B.A. and the M.A. degrees. The purpose of the undergraduate curriculum is to give the student a general knowledge of sociology, in both theory and research. A sociology major is required to attend sixty hours in the discipline (half of his total academic work), while a sociology minor must attend thirty hours.

The following courses are required for the B.A.: Introductory Sociology, The Family, Social Stratification, Social Psychology, Statistics, Research Methods, Sociology of Israeli Society, Research Seminar, and Theoretical Seminar. A number of elective courses are also offered.

In the M.A. program each student is required to take the following courses: Advanced Statistics, Advanced Research Methods, Social Institutions, Social Theory, Israeli Society, Social Psychology, Sociology of Religion or Sociology of Judaism, Thesis Seminar. In addition, the student must take three seminars in one of three areas: Comparative Social Institutions, Sociology of Judaism or Religion, and Social Psychology. A thesis is required.

We list below the full-time members possessing the Ph.D. degree, their academic rank, and their areas of interest:

Member	Rank	Specialization
Chaya Bareli	Lecturer	Education, Values
Akiva Deutsch	Senior Lecturer	Sociology of the Professions, Social Theory
Menachem Friedman	Lecturer	Sociology of Religion
Shulamit Gundrus	Lecturer	Anthropology
Ernest Krausz	Associate Professor	Sociology of Judaism, Research Methods
Carol Liebman	Lecturer	Urbanization
Solomon Poll	Professor	Sociology of Judaism, Sociology of Religion
Leonard Weller	Associate Professor	Social Psychology
Yoel Yinon	Lecturer	Social Psychology

Haifa University

For the B.A. degree, the following courses are required: Introductory Sociology, Introductory Statistics, Methods, Seminar (Research or Theoretical), Social Theory, and Israeli Society. The other courses, approximately 40 percent of the total, are electives. In 1972 the Department received its first M.A. candidates. The following courses are required for the M.A.: Sociological Theory, Research Methods and Statistics, Analysis of Social Problems in Israel, Computer Usage, and a seminar in theory or research. An additional five or six courses are required, part of which must be in the student's area of specialization. A thesis must be submitted.

The Department has twelve full-time members with a Ph.D. degree. The members, their academic rank, and areas of specialization are listed below:

Member	Rank	Specialization
Aaron Ben-Ami	Senior Lecturer	Social Psychology
Jerry Berlin	Associate Professor	Small Groups
Michel Bloom	Lecturer	Systems Theory, Sociology of the Future
Abram Kaplan	Professor	Methods
Maurice Kononitzky	Lecturer	Cooperative Movements
Henry Rosenfeld	Senior Lecturer	Anthropology

Michael Saltman	Lecturer	Anthropology
Joseph Shepher	Lecturer	Kibbutz, Family
Theodore Shanin	Senior Lecturer	Developing Societies
Ovediah Shapira	Lecturer	Sociology of Religion
Zvi Sobel	Associate Professor	Sociology of Religion
Shlomo Swirsley	Lecturer	Social Movements
Gene Weiner	Lecturer	Theory

Tel Aviv University

The B.A. studies in the Faculty·of Social Science were reorganized in 1970-1971. Unlike other universities in Israel, at Tel Aviv the students do not begin majoring during their freshman year, but instead take introductory courses in the Social Sciences, as well as in Mathematics and Statistics. It is in the second year that the student chooses his major. Required courses for the B.A. degree include: Introduction to Sociology and Anthropology, Advanced Anthropology, Research Methods, Social Psychology, Institutions and Organizations, Sociological Theory, Sociology of Israeli Society, Analysis of Selected Social Problems, and two seminars. The student also takes three elective courses.

The M.A. candidate does between eighteen to twenty hours of course work. The following courses are required: Research Methods, Statistics, Computer Usage, Selected Problems in Sociological Theory, Theory and Research of Sociology Today, Thesis Seminar. Three seminar courses are chosen from four areas of specialization: Social Anthropology, Sociology of Organizations and Institutions, Social Psychology, and Methodology. A thesis is required.

The full-time members of the Department, together with their academic rank and areas of specialization, are:

Member	Rank	Specialization
Shlomo Deshen	Senior Lecturer	Sociology of Religion, Political Sociology
Moshe Hartman	Lecturer	Demography, Mathematical Sociology
Ephraim Yuchtman	Senior Lecturer	Social Psychology
Fred Katz	Professor	Social Theory, Organizations

Emanuel Marx	Associate Professor	Anthropology, Non-Jewish Minorities
Chava Etzioni	Lecturer	Social Change, Education
Yohanan Peres	Senior Lecturer	Methods, Ethnic Relations, Religion
Abraham Kordovah	Lecturer	Theory, Sociology of Intellectuals
Isaac Samuel	Lecturer	Social Psychology, Sociology of Institutions
Moshe Shoked	Senior Lecturer	Community Studies, Non-Jewish Minorities
Yohnatan Shapira	Associate Professor	Politics
Rina Shapira	Associate Professor	Education, Youth Cultures
Moshe Shwartz	Lecturer	Sociology of Knowledge
Yisrael Shefer	Lecturer	Anthropology

Hebrew University

The Hebrew University is the oldest and most prestigious of the universities, having been in existence since 1925. Until the 1950s it was the only university in the country which offered a B.A. degree. After the rise of the State of Israel, the University greatly developed its social sciences. In 1953 it founded the Eliezer Kaplan School of Economics and Social Science, which until 1968 was linked to the Faculty of Humanities.

Students may choose a single or dual major program, either in Sociology or Anthropology. Those who have chosen a dual major program must take the required courses, one research seminar and one elective course, a total of twenty-four hours. Students who have chosen a single major program take the same required courses, one elective course, a course entitled "Guided Reading in Groups" and two seminars, a total of twenty-eight hours. They must also take courses outside the department.

The required courses include: Introduction to Sociology, Institutions—Family and Social Stratification, Research Methods, Statistics, Social Structure of Israel, Social Psychology, Introduction to Primitive Societies, Selected Problems in Sociological Theory.

For the M.A. degree, students may choose between two plans. Plan A is designed for students who intend to enroll as doctoral candidates. The student must take at least twenty class hours, divided evenly between required and elective courses. Students of Plan B do not continue for a doctorate. They take twenty-four hours, eight required and sixteen electives.

The full-time members holding the Doctor's degree, their academic rank, and their areas of interest are as follows:

Member	Rank	Specialization
Israel Adler	Lecturer	Methodology
Uri Almagor	Lecturer	Anthropology
Rivkah Bar-Yosef	Senior Lecturer	Comparative Analysis of Institutions, Stratification, Organization and Industry
Joseph Ben-David	Professor	Higher Education, Science, Professions
Eric Cohen	Senior Lecturer	Kibbutz, Non-Jewish Minorities, Power Structure
Shmuel Eisenstadt	Professor	Social Change, Modernization, Israeli Society
Harvey Goldberg	Senior Lecturer	Anthropology
Don Hendelman	Lecturer	Anthropology
Michael Inbar	Lecturer	Group Dynamics
Jacob Katz	Professor	Structure of Types of Traditional Jewish Society
Moshe Lissak	Senior Lecturer	Social Mobility and Social Class
Dov Weintraub	Associate Professor	Agricultural Communities, Modernization
Avraham Zloczower	Senior Lecturer	Sociological Theory

There are also a number of faculty who teach half-time in the Department of Sociology and half-time in another department. These include: Louis Gutman, Elihu Katz, Judah Matras, Ozer Schild,

Chaim Adler, Brenda Denet, Yitzhak Eilan, Dan Horowitz, and Reuben Kahane.

Sociology at the Technion—Israel Institute of Technology

Teaching and research activities at the Technion are administratively located in the Faculty of Industrial and Management Engineering. There is no B.A. program in sociology, but required and elective courses are offered on the undergraduate level. For architects—Urban Sociology and Urban Renewal; for industrial engineers—Industrial Sociology and Labor Relations; for students in the Medical School—General Sociology. Elective courses in sociology are taken by students from various faculties. The main activity, however, is concentrated in graduate studies, where a Master of Behavioral and Management Sciences, and a Master in Personnel Management and Labor Relations draw students with B.A. degrees in sociology.

Research is carried out in the Center for the Study of Man at Work, where studies emphasize social aspects of work, technology, and labor relations. At the Center for Urban and Regional Studies, research is also carried out on the sociological aspects of urban and regional problems.

Member	Rank	Specialization
Albert Goldberg	Lecturer	Complex Organizations, Methods
Amira Galin	Lecturer	Social and Labor Relations
Chanoch Jacobsen	Senior Lecturer	Sociological Theory
Allen Kirschenbaum	Lecturer	Demography, Urbanization
Bilha Mannheim	Associate Professor	Complex Organizations, Industrialization and Urbanization
Eliezer Rosenstein	Senior Lecturer	Industrialization, Labor Relations, Personnel Management

Israeli Institute of Applied Sociology

Professor Louis Gutman (who also has an appointment at the Hebrew

University) is Director of the Israeli Institute of Applied Research. Under a grant from the Israeli Government, the Institute was established in 1949. It is a nonprofit, independent organization which plans and conducts research projects in all areas of social science. While Gutman is best known for the development of the Scalogram Analysis, he has continued to make many valuable contributions, particularly in the field of methodology. In the course of the book, the names of Judith Shuval and Aaron Antonovsky will become known to readers. They have been members of the Institute for many years.

National Organization of Sociology

The national organization of sociology in Israel is the *Israeli Sociological Association,* founded in 1969. Its establishment coincides with the development of sociology departments throughout the country. At the foundation meeting it was decided that only those holding an M.A. degree would be eligible for membership. As of December 1971, 121 members were enrolled. The initiative in founding the organization was taken by Rivkah Bar-Yosef. Professor Joseph Ben-David is the second and current holder of the office.

NOTES

1. In A. Jarus, J. Marcus, J. Oren, C. Rapaport (eds.), *Children and Families in Israel.* (New York: Gordon and Breach, 1970), p. 154.

2. The University of the Negev has just made its appearance; it is currently associated with the Hebrew University.

SECTION I

1

Immigration and Absorption

THE SETTING

Israel's creation, in part, has been the result of the pressing need of the Jewish people of Europe for a haven from persecution. This central tenet of the new nation was enshrined in the Law of Return, which states that every Jew is entitled to settle in Israel. The security problems, economic difficulties, unemployment, and lack of housing which would normally exert pressure on a nation to limit immigration in accordance with what it perceives to be its internal needs have always been shunted aside where the Law of Return is concerned. It has been and continues to be the very *raison d'être* of the state. The early years of statehood saw the survivors of Europe's death camps pour into the country. Shortly thereafter, in the early 1950s, Jews from the ancient communities of North Africa and the Middle East came—equally destitute, equally on the run.

The ingathering of the exiles as a deliberate policy has presented enormous challenges to the fledgling nation. Inundating waves of immigration have quadrupled the population within a period of twenty years. The effect of this ceaseless inflow of newcomers has engaged the attention of sociologists more than any other problem (not excluding the concern with national security) of this hardpressed nation. The bulk of this immigration has consisted not of survivors of concentration camps, but of Jews from Asia and Africa: Turkey, Syria, Lebanon, Iraq, Iran, Yemen, Tunisia, Algeria, Morocco, Libya, Union of South Africa, and other Near Eastern countries.

19

The single most urgent dilemma presented by the large stream of immigrants was housing. Some moved in with relatives; a small number were accepted into kibbutzim. A larger group (some 125,000) were settled in houses abandoned by Arabs during the war of independence, but this was intended only as a stopgap measure. Many of the abandoned houses, some of which had served as workshops and warehouses, were dilapidated, dark structures with no sanitary or heating facilities. Though efforts were made to repair the buildings, the winters brought tragedy to a number of families. There were cases where the buildings literally collapsed. Yet even these houses were insufficient in number. For lack of an alternative, temporary tent-camps were set up. These communities, however, began to develop qualities of permanency as more tents were put up to house the shiploads of immigrants continually arriving and as the building of permanent dwellings fell far behind the growing need.

It soon became clear that the immigrants were growing increasingly dependent on the protected atmosphere of the camps. Aware that they would be fed if they stayed where they were, many lacked the incentive to look for work outside. To remedy this situation, *ma'abarot* (temporary immigrant settlements) were set up near cities, where work could more easily be found. These camps, which at first were composed of tents and canvas huts and later of shacks, frequently turned into slum suburbs, which defeated their original purpose of providing a transition into the economic and cultural life of the country. Furthermore, representatives of the Government continued to be available to whom the immigrant could, and did, turn with all manner of complaints, from leaky shacks to unappetizing European food offensive to Asian stomachs.

As of 1953, the camps were largely inhabited by the immigrants from Afro-Asian countries as the earlier flood of European immigrants had, by and large, succeeded in integrating into the mainstream. The Jews from Africa and Asia were frequently content to remain on welfare and unhappy with the relief work projects arranged by the authorities. Thus, direct forms of aid had to be continued in the camps, despite all attempts at finding and creating employment opportunities.

Some of the difficulties, which at that time were seen solely in the context of the strain put on the country by overwhelming numbers of newcomers, pointed to more profound problems growing out of deep-seated cultural differences. Sanitation, for example, in any case a serious concern in the tightly packed, primitive camp conditions, loomed even larger because many of the immigrants had simply never been exposed to modern facilities. This, of course, was relatively easy to overcome. However, such patterns as the patriarchal family, which relegated wives to subservient roles and kept daughters locked into a rigid family structure, were considerably more difficult to cope with. These were among the reasons why communication between immigrant and veteran settlers was not easily established. Furthermore, the camps were physically isolated from the towns—not necessarily at any great distance from them, yet remote in that none of the services and facilities were shared. The camps thus became self-contained islands, within which different groups of immigrants from different lands, or even different areas of the same land, found it difficult to communicate with each other and with the world outside.

Immigration following 1956 was of another kind. It consisted of groups from widely differing backgrounds. A larger number of these immigrants were people whose move to Israel was motivated not by the need to flee from persecution, but rather by a positive desire to live in Israel. Those from Europe came with academic and technical training, whereas others, from Asia and North Africa, possessed little or no education.

By this time the country had more or less caught up with the need for housing, so that now immigrants were given apartments upon arrival. These apartments, however, were of minimum size, and families were frequently severely overcrowded. Unfortunately, the construction of new apartments could not keep pace with the rate of immigration which was again on the increase and temporary solutions once more had to be found. The new edifices were not tents but asbestos huts, complete with sanitary facilities.

The employment problem was unique to each group of settlers. Many of those with academic training found that their specialities were not needed. Those who had studied humanities had a more difficult time in adapting themselves than did those in the sciences, for the former not only had to learn a new language, but in many cases also needed to be retrained. Lawyers, particularly, had a difficult time, since they had to pass an Israeli bar examination before being allowed to practice. Even medical specialists frequently were forced to general practice. A good deal of effort, however, was devoted to make it possible for academics and professionals to adjust with minimum pain. They received preferential treatment in the retraining opportunities offered and in acquiring residences close to their work. Where necessary, special hostels were erected to accommodate large groups of professionals near areas of employment. Despite all this many academicians still had to work as clerks or in other jobs quite unrelated to their specialities, until such a time as the country developed sufficiently to be able to use their skills. For many, this came too late and they could no longer pick up the profession left behind.[1]

The increasing number of North American immigrants since the Six Day War have also received preferential treatment, such as low interest rates for housing (not available to the native population), tax benefits, and free education in high school and university. At the same time many were faced with employment problems similar to those of the earlier waves of immigrants. A large proportion were professionals, and while engineers and physicists were usually snapped up by the defense industry, those in the humanities and social sciences frequently had more difficulty finding a place for themselves. They, of course, could return to their countries of origin, as earlier immigrants could not.

With this background it is no surprise that the bulk of sociological work done in Israel in the early years was devoted to research and analysis of immigrant absorption. This generally falls into two categories. In the first group are studies of those factors which facilitate absorption to which Professor Shmuel N. Eisenstadt, the distinguished sociologist of the Hebrew University, has made the most valuable contributions in numerous articles, both in Hebrew and English,[2] and in his book *The Absorption of Immigrants*.[3] In the second are anthropological assessments of the quality of life in immigrant communities.

FACTORS INFLUENCING ABSORPTION

Eisenstadt distinguishes between the motivations for immigration to Israel of European Jews and those from the Afro-Asian countries.[4]

Excluding the survivors of the holocaust, the majority of European Jews who came to Israel were motivated by Zionism. This meant a commitment to the establishment of a Jewish community in its historic homeland where Jews would no longer be a permanent minority, and where they would be able to develop fully in their own social and cultural context. Many of the early Zionists were convinced that a viable new society could only be built by rejecting traditional religious values. This seemed particularly crucial because they considered one of their important tasks to be the restructuring of the Diaspora pattern of Jewish employment. Instead of storekeepers, tailors, and merchants, Jews in Israel were to become farmers.

Zionism as an ideology did not exist for Oriental Jews. Their immediate motivations for coming to Israel were economic and political, together with vague religious-messianic aspirations. They did not desire to break with their traditional social structure and culture. They did not see themselves as participants in the creation of a new and better society, but were content to continue their old way of life. Still, there were features in the social structure which favored the assimilation of the Oriental Jew. These included the general social fluidity of the new Jewish community, which saw itself as a melting pot of the far-flung Jewish diaspora, and the absence of any ingrained negative attitude on the part of the European Jew to the Eastern Jew. Nevertheless, these features were not sufficient to counteract the pressures of adjustment on a society based on European values and culture. Thus, as early as 1951, Shmuel Eisenstadt found a good deal of instability, delinquency, and anomie among the Oriental Jews in Israel. These he attributed to the following factors:

(1) Increase in the birth-rate and decrease in the death-rate (a typical phenomenon observed in peasant populations on the verge of being absorbed into an industrial civilization).
(2) Changes in the employment pattern forced by the Israeli economic structure that was radically different from that to which the Oriental Jews were accustomed. Often jobs held in the host country were not needed or were mechanized in Israel, requiring retraining.
(3) Emergence of new goals and disintegration of the elite. As a result of identification with the new society, the old values became questionable. This seriously affected the prestige of the elite.[5]

Eisenstadt was concerned with pinpointing those conditions which
made for successful absorption. He therefore studied carefully the
immigrant family, peer group, reference group, and ego integration
of the individual. He defined "adaptation" as the "effective capacity
to perform successfully those basic roles inherent in the main institutional spheres (i.e., family, economic, political) of the social structure
of the absorbing country," while he saw "integration" as adequate
social participation in the role-expectations and institutional norms
of the absorbing society. The critical determinant of both adaptation
and integration was the immigrant's predisposition to change.

The data are based on field work conducted in 1949 and 1950 in
ten new immigrant settlements. About 1,000 families were studied.
The only factor shown to have a clear influence on positive predisposition to change was age: unmarried people between fifteen and
twenty-two were the most prone to integrate into Israeli society. None
of the other objective, socioeconomic variables, such as country of
origin, occupation, economic status, education, or age at time of
marriage, was related to a positive predisposition to change.

To account for the degree with which an immigrant was equipped
to face challenge, Eisenstadt turned to the family, whose emotional
support during this critical period he regarded as crucial. He distinguished two types of family, the *solidary* and the *non-solidary,* differentiated by the extent of their internal cohesion and collectivity
orientation. The solidary family works as a collective unit and is an
end in itself. Its members evaluate themselves and each other by
measuring their contributions to the perpetuation of the collectivity.
Each member of the family is important because, and insofar as, he is
part of the group. The non-solidary family, by contrast, is characterized by low cohesiveness; it is mainly a base from which each of its
members pursue their separate ends.

Table 1 shows a high correlation between positive predisposition
to change and membership in a solidary family and between negative
predisposition to change and membership in a non-solidary family.
The table also shows that both types of family appear in all ethnic
groups: the traditional extended patriarchal family of the Balkan
and Afro-Asian Jews, and the small nuclear family of the central and
East European Jews may be either solidary or non-solidary.

TABLE 1

DISTRIBUTION OF SOLIDARY AND NON-SOLIDARY FAMILIES ACCORDING TO PREDISPOSITION TO CHANGE AND REGIONAL ORIGIN

Region of Origin	Positive PREDISPOSITION TO CHANGE		Negative PREDISPOSITION TO CHANGE	
	Solidary Families	Non-Solidary Families	Solidary Families	Non-Solidary Families
Yemen	70	16	5	11
North Africa	102	15	25	170
Turkey	45	10	16	20
Bulgaria	—	—	—	—
Yugoslavia	149	13	13	45
Central and Eastern Europe	48	6	78	92
Total	414	60	137	338
Total percentage	87	13	23	77

Source: S. Eisenstadt, "The Process of Absorption of New Immigrants in Israel," *Human Relations* (5, 1952):p. 234.

In his search for the conditions which tend to create the solidary family, Eisenstadt next studied the Jewish identification and diaspora experience of the various immigrant groups. From this vantage point four main groupings emerged:

(1) The traditional, which includes the Yemenite Jews and parts of North African Jewry.
(2) The insecure transitional, comprised of great parts of the North African Jewish communities and most of the Central and Eastern communities which stayed intact after the war.
(3) The secure transitional, comprised of Jewish communities that were well integrated into the Gentile society in which they lived, and limited to Serbian and Bulgarian Jewries.
(4) Ex-inmates of camps for Displaced Persons.

Table 2 clearly shows that the development of the solidary family

is related to the diaspora experience of each community; that solidary
families are found predominantly in the traditional and in the secure
transitional sectors.[6]

TABLE 2
DISTRIBUTION OF FAMILY SOLIDARITY AMONG
SECTORS OF THE JEWISH COMMUNITY

	Solidary Families	Non-Solidary Families	Total
1. Traditional Sector	259 (72%)	73 (28%)	100%
2. Transitional Sector with Status-Anxiety	103 (23%)	311 (77%)	100%
3. Secure Transitional Sector	187 (93%)	14 (7%)	100%

Source: S. Eisenstadt, "The Process of Absorption of New Immigrants to
Israel," *Human Relations* (5, 1952): p. 241.

Eisenstadt also investigated the absorption process from the perspective of the host society, particularly the bureaucracy established
to deal with the influx.[7] Existing agencies were drastically expanded
and new ones hastily organized. Many of the workers pressed into
service were untrained, half-trained or graduates of brief in-service
courses. Most of them were of European background, while the people
they dealt with came chiefly from the Afro-Asian countries. Bureaucratic proliferation is usually marked by increased depersonalization
as expressed in a stringent and universalistic enforcement of rules, as
well as a rigid reliance on the prescribed limitations of the job on the
part of the bureaucrat. In this case, however, quite the contrary situation developed. Officials voluntarily took on more work than was required of them by their organizations and frequently went so far as to
establish personal relations with their clients. The bureaucrats often
assumed the roles of teachers, advising on behavior in the new country.
There were even many instances where bureaucrats sided with their
clients against the parent organization, becoming, in effect, their
leaders.

As the immigrants turned more and more to these officials, and to
the new leaders who were able to deal more effectively with the be-

wildering quantity and quality of information showered on them from all sides, the stature of the traditional leaders began to diminish. A good deal of information was constantly being fed to the immigrants in the *ma'abarot* on such matters as economic opportunities, cultural and educational facilities and the political system, the latter often laden with propaganda. They gradually began to question the traditional leaders' prestige within the new social system and their suitability as interpreters of its values. Attachment to the old elite seemed to stand in the way of their achievement of full status within the new society; the immigrants felt that such attachment cut them off from real participation in it and reduced their sense of belonging.[8]

The single most comprehensive study of immigrant adjustment is Judith Shuval's *Immigrants on the Threshold.*[9] A number of chapters appeared separately as articles before the publication of the book, and one of these earned Shuval the annual prize of the American Society for the Study of Social Problems in 1957.[10]

This study, like Eisenstadt's, was conducted in 1949 and 1950, when approximately 80,000 immigrants were living in thirty-five transit camps. In each of fourteen camps a systematic sample of the adult population was drawn. A total of 1,865 adults were interviewed, 58 percent of whom hailed from Asia and Africa. Forty-nine percent had been in Israel from six to twelve months, 20 percent from four to six months, and 27 percent less than four months, while only 4 percent had been in Israel for more than a year. The questionnaire covered six topics: occupational problems, social relations in the transit camp, morale, attitude toward the host society, acculturation, and amount of information about Israel.

Shuval was primarily concerned with the influence of the several variables on acculturation, specifically: Zionist background, ethnicity, unemployment, level of education, amount of time in Israel, and occupational aspirations. In a separate chapter she also discussed the effects of Nazi concentration camp experiences. Her main findings were:

(1) Zionist immigrants were more receptive to information about Israel than were non-Zionist immigrants.
(2) European immigrants were more disappointed with Israel than were Asian-African immigrants.

(3) European Zionists were less disappointed with Israel than were European non-Zionists. For the non-European immigrant, ideology was not related to acculturation.

(4) Immigrants who were Zionists used new information for constructive planning; additional information for immigrants without such commitment was disfunctional.

(5) Concentration camp survivors proved less optimistic than a control population living under conditions which were not particularly stressful. However, under additional strain, the optimism of the control group dropped while the morale of the concentration camp survivors remained more or less stationary.

(6) Unemployment reduced morale, but not for recent arrivals nor for those with a high level of education. Presumably, the latter group understood the objective difficulties of obtaining jobs.

(7) The highest morale was found among immigrants in transit camps where the relative level of employment was generally low, while lowest morale was found among the unemployed immigrants in camps with relatively high rates of employment. Thus the transit camp of the immigrant served as a reference group.

The next set of variables Shuval dealt with was acculturation, defined as the acceptance of certain norms perceived by the immigrants as representative of Israel, the active search for advice and information from other immigrants or old-timers, and the general attitude toward the host population. The results showed that:

(1) During the one year they had been in the country the Europeans tended to withdraw from Israeli society, while the non-Europeans tended to approach it.

(2) The morale of the Europeans declined with increased stay in the country. This indicated feelings of relative deprivation.

Another set of variables studied was occupational aspirations, particularly immigrants' aspirations for their sons' future occupations. It was found that:

(1) The women held higher aspirations for their sons than did the men. Men preferred the crafts and trades, while women chose the professions and white collar and army jobs.

(2) Non-Europeans harboured greater aspirations for their children than the Europeans.

The relationship of "activity-passivity" to ethnicity and mobility was also studied. This was measured in terms of the individual's degree of acceptance of his overall situation and the extent to which he felt he controlled his own destiny. Two findings emerged:

(1) Active people were more likely to be upwardly mobile than passive people.
(2) European immigrants were more active; non-European immigrants more passive.

Ethnic origin was shown to be the crucial factor determining the attitudes and modes of behavior of this immigrant population, and three elements were seen as distinguishing Europeans from non-Europeans. The first was the differential social and economic conditions that prevailed in their countries of origin and resulted in differing levels of relative deprivation once the immigrant was in Israel. The lower standard of living in the non-European countries led to lower expectations and consequently fewer frustrations and a higher level of morale among the non-Europeans. The second factor was the religious-secular balance that the immigrants brought with them. For the European immigrant, Zionism, an essentially secular ideology, served as a protective device, whereas the traditional religious orientations sustained the non-European immigrant. The third factor, degree of social mobility possible for Jews in the diaspora from which they came, is used by Shuval to explain the greater interest in upward mobility among the non- Europeans, who, frustrated by the limited opportunities in the countries from which they emigrated, wished to take advantage of the occupational opportunities.

AMERICAN JEWS IN ISRAEL

Migration, both forced and voluntary, has been an integral part of Jewish life over the centuries. The last world war brought about a dramatic intensification of the migratory pattern of World Jewry as the remnants of the European communities emigrated to the Western

hemisphere and to Israel, and the Eastern communities moved almost
en masse to Israel. Both of these were "forced" movements of refugees,
the one on the run from the graveyard of Nazi Europe, the other in
flight from Arab persecution in the wake of the declaration of the
state of Israel. In recent years quite a different kind of immigration
of "choice" has been begun by Jews from affluent Western societies. These
are no longer the familiar refugees but people who have, for various
reasons, made the decision to move from conditions of freedom and
comfort to the far less promising economic environment of Israel. In
contrast to the mass movements from Asian and African lands, only a
small number of Jews have come from the United States. As the stream
of refugees has virtually ground to a halt, Israel has become increasingly
concerned about the paucity of Western *aliyah* (the Hebrew term for
immigration to Israel; literally, "ascent"), and has directed a good deal
of energy to encouraging immigration principally from the United
States. Since not until very recently did Russia allow its Jews to leave,
America, with approximately six million Jews, appeared to be the only
major source from which to draw new Israelis. Moreover, there are
more than twice as many Jews in the United States as in Israel and
about as many Jews in New York as in the entire state of Israel.
Furthermore, American Jews represent a desired immigrant group.
While large numbers are not arriving, approximately 50 percent of
those that come (apart from pensioners) are professionals, and this
percentage seems to be increasing.

Only one empirical study has been made of immigration from
North America. This was undertaken several years ago and is
of limited theoretical value. With the awakened interest and
slowly increasing size of American immigration, we can expect
additional studies in the near future. In fact, the Ministry of Absorption, founded in 1968, established a department of research.

Research on American-Jewish immigration is important as it
could illuminate the hitherto unstudied nature of voluntary migration,
and at the same time significantly increase understanding of the
American-Jewish national character. One of the crucial questions
which immediately comes to mind is whether the knowledge that he
can at any time return to America lowers the immigrant's adjustment
potential. Does he more readily throw up his hands in despair and
call it quits at the first sign of difficulty, or, secure in his freedom of

choice, does he face the strains and struggles of adaptation with greater equanimity than those for whom there is no way back? Research is needed to clarify which factors facilitate and which factors hinder the voluntary immigrant's integration into Israeli society, and to uncover the reasons why such a great proportion of those who come with the intention of settling eventually returned to the United States. Until the Six Day War no systematic statistics were kept, but the available evidence points to a figure of 50 percent (a conservative estimate) who returned. Since the Six Day War, immigration from North America has increased from the annual average of 2,000 to 3,000 to somewhere between 6,000 and 8,000. Unlike those who came before 1967, an estimated 40 percent of the new arrivals are orthodox Jews. The proportion who remain in Israel appears to have risen, although exact figures are unavailable.

One of the factors that may exert a positive influence on the adjustment and integration of the American immigrant is the recent ruling of the Supreme Court of the United States by which an American who acquires Israeli citizenship, serves in the Israeli army or votes in the Israeli national elections does not lose his American citizenship. Previously, the American law concerning dual citizenship had been vague and American immigrants frequently had their passports revoked if they served in the Army or voted in the elections. Consequently, until the new ruling, most Americans accepted the status of "permanent residents" but chose not to become Israeli citizens. Harold Isaac's central point in his book, *American Jews in Israel,* is that the American immigrant who retained his American citizenship and neither voted nor entered into government service, or the Army, crucially hindered his own adjustment.[11] The evidence, however, does not really point in this direction, since the most severe problems of adjustment are generally encountered during the immigrant's first few years in the country, and the fateful decision to stay or to leave is usually taken before he is eligible for army service or has to decide whether to accept Israeli citizenship or permanent resident status.

It is possible on the other hand, that the cumbersome bureaucratic structure presents a bigger stumbling block for the voluntary immigrant from North America than it does the forced refugee. Until recently, the handling of the immigrant was shared by both the Jewish Agency and various ministries within the Government. Not only was there a considerable overlap between the two, but the offices dealing with immigration within the Jewish Agency and within the governmental services were rather disorganized. There were frequent instances of contradictory opinions and overlapping authority, as well as unrealistic and inaccurate advice. This often led to despair, particularly as these contacts were among the first that the American had with Israeli society. The Israeli officials were probably equally baffled. They had, after all, many years of experience in settling immigrants, but those of another sort—refugees from persecution or poverty or both. The American accustomed to a relatively efficient bureaucracy, built on the concept of service, found the confusion and his new role as a client almost incomprehensible and even frightening.

The situation has improved considerably since the creation of the Ministry of Absorption in 1968. Once the immigrant arrives in Israel he is theoretically in the hands of the Government of Israel only. This means he has only the one bureaucracy to contend with instead of two. The Association of Americans and Canadians in Israel, the North American immigrant organization, has repeatedly urged that a central address be established within the Ministry to eliminate the need to run to numerous departments where the immigrant is apt to receive conflicting advice. This suggestion has not yet been adopted. At the same time, a number of laws have been passed to ease the newcomer's transition into Israeli life during the critical early years. The most important of these include a considerable reduction in income tax during the first three years, housing allotment (for the first year only) and exemption from a number of miscellaneous taxes. The immigrant is also eligible for a large mortgage at relatively low interest rates and good housing at absorption centers is available at a nominal rent during the first six months in the country. Since Israel has no widespread system of rental housing, this latter service has been most helpful to many families.

How many Americans have emigrated to Israel? Nobody knows; the estimate (before the Six Day War) ranged from 2,000 to 20,000. Aaron Antonovsky and David Katz conducted a survey, which began before the Six Day War, on Americans in Israel.[12] This is the only empirical research on the subject. These investigators coordinated their research with a heart study undertaken by Dr. Ascher J. Segall of the Harvard University School of Public Health. Dr. Segall made an intensive effort to locate *all* Americans and Canadians living in Israel. As there was no central list, Dr. Segall had to do a great deal of searching. His criterion as to who was an American was limited to those Americans and Canadians aged 22 to 65 who had migrated after the age of 18 and had arrived in Israel prior to March 1966. In this classification he located close to 2,400 persons. This criterion excludes children and those over 65. If these are included along with an additional number of Americans whom Segall did not succeed in identifying, a more reasonable total would seem to be between seven to eight thousand. This was the estimate until March 1966. Antonovsky and Katz succeeded in interviewing 82 percent of those examined by Dr. Segall.

The study, as the authors readily admit, is seriously limited by the lack of a control group. We learn about the Americans who came to Israel and stayed, but not about those who left. Nor do we have any basis for comparing these two groups with the majority of American and Canadian Jews who never emigrated to Israel. Nevertheless, within these limitations certain valuable information was uncovered.

Between 1957 and 1966 there was only a slight increase in the number of North Americans who had settled in Israel as opposed to those who had immigrated and returned. Among the settled group the researchers found that women were disproportionately over-represented, particularly among those who had not come to Israel in the wake of active participation in one of the Zionist movements. The greatest number of olim hailed from the metropolitan areas of the United States, particularly New York City. Over the years, the number of persons coming from professional homes increased, as did the average age of the immigrant; the later the period of migration the higher the proportion of those who arrived in Israel aged 30 or over, with a concomitant increase in the number who arrived married and with children. Over the same number of years a decrease was noted in the proportion of kibbutz members and of those who had been active Zionists before they came to Israel.

Zionism and Jewishness were found to be the major motives for coming to live in Israel, although here again a change was noted over the years. The former declined in importance as the latter gained. The desire to lead a fuller religious life and "the sake of the children" were also given as reasons for coming, particularly among the growing number of non-Zionists. Many felt that the country needed them. Negative factors, such as anti-Semitism, disaffection with the general political situation in America, or personal dissatisfactions were minor reasons. Most of those interviewed believed at the time of migration that they would be more contented in Israel than they had been in North America, not so much in terms of friendships as in relation to the nation as a whole.

The later the period of immigration, the higher the proportion of those who had visited Israel before they made the decision to settle permanently. Relatively few of these, however, had made their exploratory trips under any formal auspices. About half of the total group had relatives and friends in Israel before they came to settle. As a whole, the population interviewed showed no symptoms of having been seriously alienated or dissatisfied with work, family relationships and friends. Outside of the personal sphere, however, a marked disaffection emerges. A very substantial number, particularly among kibbutz members, claimed that they did not feel at home in America and were convinced that they would not have been happy had they continued to live there. In fact, as many as one-fourth hardly thought of themselves as Americans at all.

In order to measure the degree of integration into Israeli life the authors asked questions about the respondents' sense of identity as Israelis, their feelings of kinship with people who grew up in Israel, and whether they would again make the move to Israel knowing what they now did about the country. The findings show that those who successfully integrated were more likely to have been in Israel a longer amount of time, had been Zionists in America, received Jewish education, held relatively negative attitudes towards America, anticipated a satisfactory adjustment in Israel and had a fair knowledge about Israel upon arrival in the new country. No relationship was found to exist between past-migration experiences and sex, age at migration, city or country of longest residence before migration, family status, age at interview, father's country of residence, father's education, size of family, and ordinal position in the family.

Two measures of personality were also included: the Cornell Index, composed of 101 brief questions, measuring neuro-psychiatric and psychosomatic symptoms, and the Byrne Scale, consisting of 164 brief statements measuring "sensitization" or the degree to which a person admits unpleasant things about himself. The results show almost no relationship between either of these scales and the level of integration.

The correlation between the Cornell Index and integration was .09, while the correlation between the Byrne Scale and level of integration was .17.

From October to December 1968, a pilot study was undertaken by Leonard Weller. Twenty families were interviewed, all new arrivals from the United States or Canada. Most of those taking part were eager for the chance to "talk about things."[13]

"Zionist convictions" was given by seven families as the main motivation in coming to Israel, while five mentioned "a strong sense of Jewish identity" as the major factor. Other reasons given were: "in order to make a personal contribution" (help build up the country); for "religious fulfillment;" "for the sake of the children;" "in order to belong;" "for professional advancement;" "because of the situation in the United States;" and "feelings of Jewish identity."

The respondents mentioned a variety of irritations with varying degrees of intensity. Some problems were connected with bureaucracy, lack of trust, apartment hunting, high prices, medical services, the attitude towards settlers, and general difficulties.

In the case of twelve families, the initial attitude to Aliyah remained unchanged. As for the remaining eight, the change was in a positive direction in four cases and in a negative direction in the other four.

THE ISRAELI STUDENT IN AMERICA

Research interest has also been directed to the emigre (called in Hebrew *yored,* i.e., "one who goes down," in contrast to the immigrant called *oleh,* i.e., "one who goes up"). Paul Ritterband investigated the factors associated with the Israeli student who goes overseas and fails to return.[14] His study is based on replies to a questionnaire mailed during the summer and fall of 1966, of which some 77 percent were returned—a total of 1,934.

The main reason why a student goes to the United States, Ritterband shows, is because he was not accepted by the school of his choice in Israel. This does not necessarily mean that the student is of poor quality, but it points to the limited space in Israeli universities. This is particularly true in connection with the M.A. and Ph.D. degrees. It is only recently that Bar-Ilan and Tel-Aviv Universities began to develop their graduate programs in a number of departments. Thus for many students there was only one institution where they could undertake

graduate training, namely the Hebrew University. There the departments limited the number of candidates and not all departments had
a developed graduate program. No less important was the fact that
many departments had extremely high standards for the Master's
degree. One student taking his M.A. examinations after eight years of
hard labor reported that the number of pages he was required to read
was 30,000 (thirty thousand). In addition, virtually all of the reading
was in English, which is not his mother tongue. Not unreasonably,
many a student prefers to go abroad in order to study for his advanced
degree. When he returns, now a Ph. D., he often finds his former
fellow students still struggling with their M.A. degrees.

Ritterband was also concerned with factors which predispose
students to return to Israel, particularly familial Zionist background,
social class of the parents, ethnicity, rural-urban residence, and former
participation in youth movement. His results show that parental participation in the Zionist movement was a factor in an individual's
decision to return to Israel. When neither parent belonged to a Zionist
movement, 37 percent of the children wished to return to Israel, in
contrast to 48 percent when both parents were active Zionists. Consistent with other studies of foreign students, students from a higher
social class were more inclined to return home. Thirty-four percent
of the students whose parents had had less than a primary education
indicated a high desire to return, as opposed to 45 percent whose
parents had some university training. Two explanations for this
relationship were suggested by the author. The first (based on differential access to the opportunity structure) holds that the returning
student of middle or upper class background feels he would have
easier access to persons of influence and therefore has a better chance
of securing desired employment. The second explanation sees the
individual of the higher social class as being more committed to his
country.

Ethnic background was discovered to be related to one's intention
of returning to Israel. Among students of Eastern extraction, 31 percent indicated a high desire to return to Israel, compared to 43 percent
of those who were of European extraction. Since families of Eastern
extraction were predominantly found among the lower class and since
Zionism was a European and not an Oriental phenomenon, these

ethnic findings may result from the hidden influence of social class and Zionist background and not ethnicity itself. Ritterband statistically controlled these two factors, and concluded that the differential propensity to return is attributable to country of origin, social class, and the Zionist background of the parents.

It was also suggested that those who had been reared in a rural area would have a stronger commitment to Israel. This expectation was verified when the location of the students' high school was used as an indicator of rural-urban residence. Forty-two percent of those who attended a high school in the city indicated a high interest in returning to Israel, compared to 55 percent of those who went to a high school in a town or a village.

Membership in a youth movement would also be expected to have an effect, insofar as all such organizations, with the exception of the *Tzofim* (equivalent to the Boy and Girl Scouts), are oriented towards pioneering values and nationalism. Surprisingly, participation in a youth movement was unrelated to interest in returning to Israel. The eight youth groups were then classified into three categories, the criterion being whether the ideology was strident, pragmatic or nonideological. When the type of youth movement is examined, it is seen that those who belonged to a pragmatic youth organization manifested a greater willingness to return (49 percent) than did those who belonged to a nonideological (37 percent) or to a strident ideological youth movement (39 percent) or did not belong to any organization at all (40 percent). The same relationship was observed when controlling for parental membership in a Zionist movement.

Finally, a *Background Socialization Characteristic* (BSC) index was constructed, based on the respondent's social class origin, his Zionist background, his participation in a youth movement, and the rural or urban location where he had spent his adolescent years. Table 3 shows the relationship of this index to the proclaimed desire to return to Israel. The index shows rather large differences. Fifty-six percent of those with a high BSC score indicated a high desire to return to Israel as compared with 32 percent of those with a low BSC score. Ritterband also determined whether the student felt the circumstance of being an Israeli affected his desire to return home. Of those who answered in the affirmative, 60 percent were high on the BSC index.

TABLE 3

BACKGROUND SOCIALIZATION CHARACTERISTICS INDEX
ACCORDING TO PROBABILITY OF RETURN

| | BSC INDEX | | |
Probability of Return	High	Medium	Low
High	56%	39%	32%
Medium	18%	19%	19%
Low	23%	41%	46%
No Answer	2%	2%	3%
	(525)	(943)	(446)

Source: Paul Ritterband, *The Non-Returning Foreign Student: The Israeli Case.* (New York: Columbia University, Bureau of Applied Social Research, 1968) (mimeographed).

The Moshav

After the State came into being, *moshav* type settlements were utilized to accommodate many of the new immigrants arriving in Israel. A moshav is composed of about sixty to one hundred families, to whom land is allocated in equal shares. While each family receives its profit according to its production, investment, development policy and purchasing of goods are carried out collectively. The moshav operates as an independent municipality. Its local council, elected by the moshav members, provides the various municipal services. The moshav differs from a purely modern enterprise in that its being solely agricultural has limited its development possibilities. Another restricting factor deriving from ideological considerations is its employment of a minimum of hired help. Its communal identification limits the economic initiatives of each family.[15]

The decision by the Government to foster moshavim (plural of moshav) was based on the necessity of settling the borders and dispersing the population in order to minimize the effects of possible bomb attacks on densely populated areas. Israel also needed to become independent with regard to food production, and it was hoped that these agricultural settlements would make a substantial contribution towards this goal.

The moshav was deemed feasible for a variety of reasons. The country had already had experience with this kind of settlement, and useful advice and knowledgeable personnel were available. Furthermore, independent farming was not deemed feasible for immigrants who were culturally heterogeneous and occupationally untrained. The process of absorption and integration might best be achieved by groups of immigrants living together. All in all, it was thought that the moshav would involve the least amount of change for the nonskilled and agriculturally inexperienced immigrants, as well as assist the State in its development and security.

The new moshavim were set up in various sections of the country. The type of crop grown by a given moshav depends upon the climate and social conditions of the area. In northern and central areas settlements grow vegetables and citrus fruits and also go in for dairy farming. Settlements in the southern part of the country concentrate more on industrial crops, while the hill settlements specialize in orchards, tobacco, and poultry.

Responsibility for the establishment and development of the villages rested largely with the Jewish Agency, which provided most of the requisite capital and furnished agricultural and professional advice. Agricultural instructors and specialists were attached to each moshav, their primary tasks being to teach farming techniques and assume responsibility for the running of the village settlement until the immigrants could take over this responsibility themselves. Social instructors were in charge of economic, social, cultural, and administrative matters. Many of these instructors were recruited from political parties and found themselves in situations of conflict. They had to account for their actions not only to their respective political parties (each of which desired that the settlers be inculcated with its particular values) but also to the Jewish Agency, and of course to the settlers themselves. More important, many of them had insufficient training for this many-sided task, and while expert in specific matters they were unable to deal with the everyday problems arising in the moshav.

The villagers' dependence on the Jewish Agency was so great that the planning authorities could force upon them any change which they wished to introduce. Their directives concerned matters ranging from the type of crops that should be grown to the amount of capital that should be invested in the moshav. Some settlers simply became apathetic as a result of their inability to control their own destiny. Others reacted by seeking the maximum benefits that could be squeezed out of their benevolent patrons.

The elegibility criteria for living in a particular moshav varied. Sometimes kinsmen from the same town were sought, while at other times immigrants who had arrived that very day were introduced into the moshav. When original settlers would leave, new immigrants would immediately be sent to take their places. The movement of immigrants from one moshav to another often weakened the social and cultural character of the moshav, along with its fragile administrative system.

The addition of many non-European immigrants to the moshav created numerous problems. In order to understand the difficulties of adjustment to a modern enterprise such as a moshav that members of a traditional society experienced, it is necessary to delineate the ways in which the latter differs from a modern one. A common characteristic of Oriental immigrants (who not long after 1948 constituted over 60 percent of the population in the moshav settlements) was the wide network of kindred relationships. Authority was in the hands of the elders and collective responsibility rested on the entire family. Occupational structures were rigid and there was little economic specialization or differentiation. The economy was essentially static and occupational roles were inherited. The limited capital available inhibited entrepreneurial initiative. The technological level and the productive output were limited. Social status was based on ascription rather than achievement.

In order to adapt to moshav life, fundamental changes had to be made by these tradition-oriented immigrants. The importance of the extended family became attenuated as the nuclear family was the unit of activity in the moshav. The work required the operation of mechanical appliances and a knowledge of the scientific basis of agricultural procedures, such as when and how to irrigate crops and what formula to use in preparing animal feed. This was easier for the immigrants who came from Western countries to achieve, as they had a tradition of scientific learning that enabled them to grasp the new material without much difficulty. The Eastern immigrants also required a redefinition of sexual roles. In their countries of origin the women had been restricted to matters dealing with the kitchen and the care of the children and had not been an integral part of the productive process proper. Furthermore, the Eastern immigrants had now to learn how to organize their work with the future in mind. Many of their daily activities had no apparent connection with later success. They also had to learn a new governing system with a democratic base. The fact that the moshavim were so dependent on outside sources for help forced their members to negotiate with a bureaucratic system. In some cases the events in a new moshav paradoxically led to a strengthening rather than a weakening of the traditional social structure among Eastern groups.

One factor in the immigrant's success was the cultural predisposition to change. If, for example, in the country of origin there had been a relative flexible pattern of authority and rewards were granted to youngsters for their work, there was more likelihood of accepting the structure of the new country and being receptive to the changes necessary in the economic realm. Other relevant aspects were the elasticity of the status system and the degree of differentiation between the elite and the rest of the population. The emergence within the moshav of new elites with newly acquired skills in the economic and political spheres was yet another factor affecting the success of a moshav. This new elite was more readily accepted by a flexible stratification system in the old country, provided that it worked together with the old one. The probability of success in the moshav increased to the extent that the old social structure provided sufficient psychological support to the immigrant. Both traditional and modern behaviors might coincide within the moshav. This arrangement worked due to the segregation of spheres of living; that is, within the work situation the achievement orientation was prevalent, while after working hours the traditional elite was accorded status. The apparent conflict between the traditional and modern approaches was further mitigated by the fact that most of the immigrants were aware of and accepted both of them.

Many objective factors, however, hindered the success of even those immigrants who had high aspirations. Many moshavim did not have sufficient suitable land for a profitable agricultural enterprise, nor was an adequate supply of water available at low cost. In the early 1950s an incorrect appraisal of the market led to an oversupply of poultry, vegetables and dairy products. Many villagers were discouraged and some sought employment outside the moshav. Immigrants with a relatively high level of education and experience who had consequently learned the requisite agricultural skills had better chances of making arrangements outside the moshav. These immigrants were also influenced by the urban orientation of Israeli society, and were inclined to consider moshav life degrading. Thus, despite low wages on the outside, many grew used to their outside work and preferred their small but steady income to the uncertainty of farm life.

The availability of manpower was an additional and critical factor. In some instances a nuclear family was unable to earn a livelihood from agriculture, as for example a European one composed of relatively old people with small children (a not unfrequent occurrence for families who were survivors of the Holocaust). Sometimes families were too large to be supported by the farm, characteristic of Eastern families with many children. These difficult situations often undermined a whole moshav, for the other members often found it necessary to share their financial assets with unsuccessful families in order to alleviate the latter's plight.

The size and structure of the moshav and its patterns of authority and leadership were all related to its success or failure. Of particular importance was the traditional leadership and the extent to which it was oriented to change and to the needs and interests of the settlers themselves, as well as the degree of legitimization which it received.[16]

In a study of an Israeli moshav settled by Moroccan Jews, Moshe Minkovitz sought to establish the importance of traditional structure and social homogeneity in the adaptation to a new and changing society.[17] Established in 1957, this moshav, named Romema, was composed of thirty-three families divided into three equal groups based primarily upon lineage, called Selag, Biton and Machluf.

Bitter feuds that broke out among the three groups shortly after their settlement caused the village to fail as a cooperative agricultural enterprise. Each of the three groups made a different kind of adjustment, according to their cultural background and the kinship network within the moshav.

In Morocco, the Selag group consisted of rich merchants who had enjoyed high socioeconomic status. The Machluf group was less distinguished. Members of the Biton group had been smiths with low socioeconomic status. The Biton and Machluf groups had hoped the transfer to Romema would reduce the traditional superiority of the Selag group. Among the demands they set forth prior to their settlement in Romema was one to the effect that each group be composed of an equal number of families and that a representative of each group hold one of the three central positions in the moshav. The lack of numbers in the Selag group forced its members to accede to these demands. Shortly after they settled in Romema a feud broke out over the second condition. Only one central position was available, that of the rabbi. The Biton and Machluf groups nominated candidates for that appointment. The Selag group refused to accept a representative of either of the other factions for the one key position. Its refusal, while strictly in accordance with the conditions agreed upon by all concerned prior to their moving to Romema, was construed by Machlufs and Bitons as a manifestation of Selag's resolution to maintain its traditional authority. The ensuing antagonisms and feuds prevented the establishment of a communal enterprise.

Each group made its own adjustment by working outside the moshav. The Selag were most successful in securing the highest paid jobs working in factories. They also had the most stable family situations; none of them moved away from the village. The Bitons followed occupations of lower status as farm workers. The total number of their families in the village remained unchanged as new families resulting from marriage replaced the families who left. The Machlufs were the least successful, being employed in relief work. They left the village in greatest numbers.

A relationship is seen between the structural features of the community and each group's level of success. Selag, the most successful group, had the closest kinship among its members. Biton, less successful than Selag, had looser family relations. Yet these relationships were stronger than those of the unsuccessful Machlufs. Here we witness an apparent paradox. In a modern society where kinship ties are apparently disfunctional as in the case of Romema from its very beginnings, these ties can nevertheless facilitate adjustment to society, as in the case of Romema after the failure of the cooperative venture.

Shlomo Deshen sought to analyze the failure of political modernization in an Israeli moshav.[18] He studied the influence of the particular immigration and settlement processes as well as the specific problems encountered by an immigrant group. The moshav in question, Yatziv, was established in 1955 and was composed of fifty-three families from Djerba (near Tunisia) and ten from Morocco. Since these groups came from underdeveloped countries, it was necessary to alter at least some of their basic value orientations in order for them to succeed in a modern, developing country. The immigrants found they had to learn new and complex marketing and financial arrangements and how to function within a democratic system rather than one based on traditional rules. While the transition to modern society is often fraught with frustrations, Yatziv succeeded in its first years and became a stable enterprise. This was due in large measure to the Djerbans' cultural background and the unique factors affecting their absorption in Israel.

Outside of Israel, Djerban Jews had consisted of two rival communities, known as Hara Kebira and Hara Sghira. Unlike many Eastern Jewish groups, both communities valued learning and adherence to the written rather than the oral tradition. There life had been organized around formalized codes and institutions. The social situation in the transit camp in which the Djerbans resided prior to their final settlement in the moshav also affected their absorption. While still in the transit camp they were taught the basic elements of moshav life by the authorities. This new knowledge was received well, for their particular cultural values had predisposed them towards acceptance of modern technology.

Another feature of life in the transit camp positively affected the cohesiveness of the future Yatziv settlers. Preparing to move to Yatziv were a majority of Djerbans from the Hara Sghira community and some other Tunisian families, including some from the rival Hara Kebira community. The hostility and antagonism among immigrants from different countries within the transit camp had the effect of uniting the various Tunisian factions. This unity started in the transit camp and persisted in the new village, creating a smooth absorption into the moshav.

Settlement in Yatziv went well during the first few years of the moshav. The breakdown in political modernization came at a later date when new settlers, many of them from the Hara Kebira community, joined the moshav. These new settlers were united through traditional kinship ties, but unlike the original Yatziv immigrants these ties were not modified after the newcomers had arrived in Israel. The latter had entered Yatziv shortly after their immigration, thus differing from the veteran settlers who had received some preparation for village life while in the transit camp and had broken their traditional feuds. The new settlers, having entered the moshav with their traditional structure intact, acted in accordance with their old frame of reference.

Frictions soon arose. The new families regarded the veteran settlers as a clique bent on furthering their own familial interests and maintaining their political power. A particularly sore point was the decision by the moshav's leadership (composed of veteran settlers) to curtail jobs (many of which had belonged to the new settlers) in order to reduce expenses. This, naturally enough, embittered the new settlers against the establishment.

The immigration of families from Hara Kebira to Yatziv continued and in due course this group became the majority in the moshav and consequently grew in importance. The traditional frame of reference of the newcomers attracted many of the veteran settlers in Yatziv who hailed from the same place of origin. The result was that the veteran settlers who stemmed from Hara Seghira once again saw themselves as belonging to a separate group rather than as members of an all-encompassing moshav.

Yatziv is thus an example of how traditional orientations can reappear. The absorption experiences of members of the same community assisted only the original settlers in adjusting to modernization. However, when members of their former community joined the moshav at a later date, they reverted to their original patterns of behavior.

CONCLUSION

The extensive research on immigration reflected the social needs of the country, and the researchers not only collected data but reached a high level of theoretization as well. What has happened to research on absorption, so characteristic of work done in the early years of the State? As the rest of the book makes clear, it has remained a dominant theme in Israeli research. As the years passed and the immigrants became "old-timers", the problem of their successful integration into Israeli society remained. Soon the all too sad truth became evident: one distinguishable segment, those from Asian and African countries, did not succeed. This was not surprising, since most of them came from backward countries. In the early years of the state it was felt that if the parents could not "make it," then the children would. The extremely high rate of mobility of second generation Jews in America was a striking example. The evidence collected by researchers in recent years has, however, shattered this hope.

NOTES

1. "Sixteen Years of Immigrant Absorption in Israel," Department of Absorption, Jewish Agency, Jerusalem, 1964. For the early years of immigration, see Moshe Sicron, *Immigration to Israel: 1948-1953* (2 vols. Jerusalem: Israel Central Bureau of Statistics, Special Series No. 60, 1957). Discussion concerning Jewish immigration can be found in S. N. Eisenstadt, *The Absorption of Immigrants*. (London: Routledge and Kegan Paul, 1954), chapters 2, 3, 4; J. Shuval, "Patterns of Intergroup Tension and Affinity," *International Social Science Bulletin* (8, 1956): pp. 75-123; Oscar I. Janowsky, *Foundations of Israel*. (Princeton, N. J.: D. Van Nostrand, 1959); *Government of Israel Yearbook* 1950-51, Jerusalem, 1951; Harry Sacher, *Israel : The Establishment of a State*. (London: George Weidenfeld and Nicolson, 1952); Viscount Samuel, "Where did Israel Put its Million Jewish Immigrants?" *Jewish Journal of Sociology* (8, 1966): pp. 81-91.

2. "Evaluation of the Adjustment of Immigrants," *Megamot* (1, 1950): pp. 335-346 (in Hebrew); "The Social Significance of Education in the Absorption of Immigrants," *Megamot* (3, 1952): pp. 330-341 (in Hebrew); "Problems of Leadership Training among New Immigrants," (4, 1953): pp. 182-191 (in Hebrew); "The Oriental Jews in Israel," *Jewish Social Studies* (12, 1950): pp. 199-222.

3. Eisenstadt, *The Absorption of Immigrants*. (London: Routledge and Kegan Paul, 1954).

4. S. N. Eisenstadt, "The Oriental Jews in Israel," *op. cit.*

5. *Ibid.* Eisenstadt has given particular attention to the elites. This is discussed in his mentioned book and in several articles. See in particular, "The Place of Elites and Primary Groups in the Process of Absorption of New Immigrants," *American Journal of Sociology*

(57, 1951): pp. 222-231; "Communication Processes among Immigrants in Israel," *Public Opinion Quarterly* (16, 1952): pp. 42-58; and "Problems of Leadership Training Among New Immigrants," *Megamot* (4, 1953): pp. 182-191 (in Hebrew).

6. S. N. Eisenstadt, "The Process of Absorption of New Immigrants in Israel," *Human Relations* (5, 1952): pp. 223-246 and "Institutionalization of Immigrant Behavior," *Human Relations* (5, 1952): pp. 373-395.

7. Eliahu Katz and S. N. Eisenstadt, "Some Sociological Observations on the Responses of Israeli Organizations to New Immigrants," *Administrative Quarterly* (1, 1960): pp. 113-133. See also, Elihu Katz and Denet, Brenda, "Petitions and Persuasive Appeals: A Study of Official Client Relations," *American Sociological Review* (31, 1966): pp. 811-822.

8. S. N. Eisenstadt, "Communication Processes among Immigrants in Israel," *op. cit.*

9. Judith Shuval, *Immigrants on the Threshold.* (New York: Atherton Press, 1963).

10. "Some Persistent Effects of Trauma: Five Years After the Nazi Concentration Camps," *Social Problems* (5, 1957-1958): pp. 230-243; "The Role of Ideology as a Predisposing Frame of Reference for Immigrants," *Human Relations* (12, 1959): pp. 51-63.

11. Harold Isaac, *American Jews in Israel.* (New York: John Jay, 1967). The material first appeared in two issues of the *New Yorker.*

12. Aaron Antonovsky and David Katz, "Factors in the Adjustment to Israel; Life of American and Canadian Immigrants," *Jewish Journal of Sociology* (12, 1970): pp. 77-87. Many essays appear in Israeli newspapers bemoaning the relative lack of immigration from Western countries. For example, Hayim Yaari, "Unsuccess in Absorption from Affluent Countries," *Davar* (January 1, 1966) (in Hebrew); and by the same author, "Why do American Immigrants Fail in Business?" *Davar*

(February 4, 1966) (in Hebrew). On psychological adjustment of Americans in Israel see, Abraham Albert Weinberg, *A Study of Mental Health and Personal Adjustment in Israel, Migration and Belonging.* (The Hague: Martinus Nijhoff, 1961).

13. Leonard Weller, "The Adjustment of American Jews in Israel: First Phase of a Longitudinal Study," Dept. of Sociology, Bar-Ilan University, 1968 (mimeographed).

14. Paul Ritterband, *The Non-Returning Foreign Student: The Israeli Case.* (New York: Columbia University, Bureau of Applied Social Research, 1968) (mimeographed).

15. A general description of the moshav may be found in Joseph Ben-David (ed.), *Agricultural Planning and Village Community in Israel.* (Paris: UNESCO, 1964); Yonina Talmon-Garber, "Social Differentiation in Cooperative Communities," *British Journal of Sociology* (3, 1952): pp 339-357; A. Weingrod, "Administered Communities: Some Characteristics of New Immigrant Villages in Israel, *Economic Development and Cultural Change* (11, 1962): pp. 69-84; Alex Weingrod, "Reciprocal Change: A Case Study of a Moroccan Immigrant Village in Israel," *American Anthropologist* (64, 1962): pp. 115-131; Shmuel Dayan, *Moshav Ovdim in the Land of Israel.* (Tel Aviv: Palestine Pioneer Library, No. 6 in Hebrew). For the effects of various demographic policies on populating moshavim, see Weintraub, *op. cit.;* S. N. Eisenstadt, *op. cit.;* M. Minkovitz (Shokeid), *Nevatim: A Village in Crisis* (Jewish Agency Settlement Department, Beersheba, 1963 (mimeographed in Hebrew).

16. Studies of factors influencing adaptation to the moshav are found in: Dov Weintraub, "A Study of New Farmers in Israel," *Sociologia Ruralis* (4, 1964): pp. 3-51; J. Ben-David, *op. cit.;* Dov Weintraub, "Patterns of Social Change in New Immigrants' Smallholders' Cooperative Settlements," unpublished Ph.D. dissertation, Hebrew University, Jerusalem, 1962 (in Hebrew); S. N. Eisenstadt, "Sociological Aspects of the Economic Adaptation of Oriental Immigrants in Israel: A Case Study in the Process of

Modernization," *Economic Development and Cultural Change* (4, 1956): pp. 269-278; S. N. Eisenstadt, *The Absorption of Immigrants, op.cit.;* D. Weintraub and Moshe Lissak, "The Absorption of North African Immigrants in Agricultural Settlements in Israel, " *Jewish Journal of Sociology* (3, 1961): pp. 29-54; Alex Weingrod, "Moroccan Jewry in Transition," *Megamot* (10, 1960): pp. 193-208 (in Hebrew); Alex Weingrod, "Change and Continuity in a Moroccan Immigrant Village in Israel," *Middle East Journal,* (14, 1960): pp. 277-291 (also appears in Hebrew: *Megamot* [10, 1960] : pp. 322-335); Dorothy Willner, "Politics and Change in Israel: The Case of Land Settlement," *Human Organization* (24, 1965): pp. 65-72.

17. Moshe Minkovitz (Shokeid), "Old Conflicts in a New Environment: A Study of a Moroccan Atlas Community Transplanted to Israel," *Jewish Journal of Sociology* (9, 1967): pp. 191-208; In a somewhat different form this paper appears in "The Adjustment of the Extended Family to the Moshav," *Megamot* (12, 1963): pp. 281-284 (in Hebrew).

18. Shlomo A. Deshen, "A Case of Breakdown of Modernization in an Israeli Immigrant Community," *Jewish Journal of Sociology* (7, 1965): pp. 63-91. Additional analysis of the same community may be found in: Shlomo A. Deshen, "Conflict and Social Change, The Case of an Israeli Village," *Sociologia Ruralis* (6, 1966): pp. 31-35; Shlomo A. Deshen, "Non-Conformists in an Israeli Immigrant Community," *The Mankind Quarterly* (9, 1969): pp. 166-177.

2

Education

Failure among school children of Eastern descent has troubled Israeli educators for almost two decades. Particularly distressing is the finding that the inferior educational performance of Eastern children is not attributable to their being new immigrants, for second and third generation Israeli children of Eastern descent still perform more poorly than the native-born child whose parents or grandparents are of European origin.

The ethnic difference in educational attainment is in large measure one of social class, for families of Eastern extraction are predominantly lower social class while families of Western origin are predominantly middle class. The middle class (Western) family provides a richer school oriented home environment than does the lower class (Eastern) family. Moreover, the income differential between the families of Eastern and Western extraction appears to be widening despite a general rise in the standard of living. One vital aspect of social class is the ecological factor. Faced simultaneously with the overwhelming problems of housing thousands of immigrants and securing its borders against Arab attack, Israel decided to build new towns and develop old ones in unsettled areas. Immigrants, even those straight off the boat, were sent to these places, many of which were far from metropolitan areas. Since, as of 1953, over 75 percent of the immigrants to Israel have come from Asian-African countries, the majority who live in these towns are of Eastern descent. Many development towns did not succeed, with the school adding its part to the total picture of failure. Despite the special concern and financial assistance of the Department of Education these schools enjoy, they often lack a capable and stable teaching staff. Their distance from the large metropolitan areas reduced their appeal for the elite educators and newly married couples. The teaching, therefore, often rests with young, inexperienced teachers who are only too happy to leave at the first opportunity.

Yet a number of research studies support the conclusion that the differential school success of Eastern children cannot be completely explained by social class. When comparing children of the same social class, it is still the children of Eastern background who are the least successful, and not necessarily newly arrived immigrants. Studies on thinking, abstraction, perception, and delayed gratification—factors which would seem to be related to school success—indicate an ethnic effect beyond that of social class.

Whatever the effects of social class and the impact of country of origin, a large part of the blame rests with the school system itself for neglecting to cope with the specific educational problem of the Eastern children. The curriculum was constructed by educators of European origin for students of Western background, and was not compatible with the psychological view and grasp of children whose parents came from Asia and Africa. Owing to the lack of educational progress of Eastern children, educators proposed the abandonment of a uniform curriculum and the implementation of a special educational program aimed at Eastern students. Due to the prevailing ideology of equality these suggestions were for the most part unheeded.

SCHOOL ATTENDANCE—BEFORE AND AFTER 1948

The education gap between those of Eastern and Western origin did not stem from the social upheavals caused by the mass migration from Moslem countries after the establishment of Israel. In 1938 Moses Brill found that there were two and a half times as many pupils of Eastern extraction who failed to be promoted than there were of Western origin.[1]

Ten years later Chanan Enoch collected data showing identical trends among elementary school children in Tel Aviv.[2] Seventy-five percent of the children not promoted were of Eastern descent.

In areas characterized by the lowest socioeconomic layer of the Eastern population, those left back totalled almost 22 percent of the total registration, in contrast to a 3.2 percent failure rate in the middle class neighborhood of Western origin.

In 1960 Michael Chen undertook a followup of graduates from elementary schools in Tel Aviv.[3] While the absolute number of pupils applying for admission to high school had increased, the percentage of applications for each ethnic group remained constant. There was, however, a decrease in the proportion of applicants to academic high schools and a rise in the proportion of Eastern applicants to vocational schools. One factor determining the nature of the applications to high school was their success at the elementary school level. In elementary schools in lower class southern Tel Aviv the proportion of pupils who failed a grade was 20 percent, while in middle class northern Tel Aviv the proportion of such students was less than 9 percent.[4]

Chen, writing in 1961, examined whether there was an increase in the number of applicants to high schools from poorer families since 1948 (high school in Israel was neither compulsory nor free, although numerous scholarships were available.)[5] To this end he compared the proportion of high school applicants who came from the poorer areas of Tel Aviv to those who lived in the better areas. Table 4 shows that despite the moderate growth in the number of applicants for high school in the southern section of the city, the hiatus between the neighborhoods was not reduced. In 1949 the difference between them stood at 34 percent, in 1956 at 35 percent, and in 1960 at 34.6 percent. There is no reason to believe that these findings are atypical of other urban areas.

Another notable aspect of the selective process in education is the kind of high school Eastern and Western children choose. The data of Table 5 show that Eastern students were poorly represented in the post-elementary institutions which serve as preparatory schools for higher education. A larger percentage was found in high schools that combined academic learning and vocational training and in those allowing students to enter the labor market during the course of studies through evening, agricultural and commercial schools.

Although the Department of Education has encouraged the entry

of children of Oriental descent into the high schools by means of
scholarships and preferential selection, it is not yet clear whether
this policy has had significant effect on the number of Easterners
who have completed secondary school. When a pupil of Eastern extraction reaches secondary school, his ability to compete with his
Eastern counterpart is marred by his inferior elementary school education, particularly if he lives in a development town. His inability
to pay for tutorial help may also be significant. For example, both
the compulsory examinations at the end of the eighth grade and at
the end of high school include English tests. These tests in large
measure determine the child's eligibility for high school and college.
Since English is often poorly taught, many parents who have the
means provide tutors for their children.

TABLE 4

**PERCENTAGES OF EIGHTH-GRADE GRADUATES LIVING IN
TEL AVIV WHO CONTINUE STUDYING, ACCORDING TO
SEX AND RESIDENTIAL AREA IN TEL AVIV**

Year	NORTH TEL AVIV			SOUTH TEL AVIV		
	Boys	Girls	Total	Boys	Girls	Total
1949	86.8	90.6	88.7	47.5	61.2	54.7
1951	88.7	89.8	89.3	46.2	65.2	62.4
1953	89.4	91.3	90.3	51.6	58.7	52.8
1956	91.7	97.7	90.1	55.5	54.5	55.1
1957	91.4	92.4	91.9	52.3	55.8	54.5
1959	89.9	92.0	91.0	54.3	61.9	58.2
1960	91.0	93.6	92.3	57.4	58.3	57.7

Source: M. Chen, "Patterns of Applications to High School Among
Tel Aviv Elementary School Graduates," *Megamot* (11, 1961): p. 394.

The pattern of university attendance is similar. The absolute
number of Easterners in higher education since the 1950s has
increased, yet this growth is negligible as compared to the increase
in the number of students of Western origin. Thus the gap between
the percentage of Easterners and Westerners in higher education has
widened.[6] In 1963-1964 the distribution of students studying for

the B.A. consisted of 15 percent students of Western birth, 7.5 percent of Asian-African birth, and the remainder born in Israel. In 1966, 80 percent of the students in institutions of higher learning were of Western birth, 6 percent of Asian-African birth, and 14 percent were of Israeli birth. While the latter group contained both children of Eastern and Western extraction, it can be safely assumed that children of Western origin were in the majority.[7]

TABLE 5

**PUPILS AGED 14 TO 17 IN THE HEBREW
SECONDARY SCHOOLS, ACCORDING TO CONTINENT
OF BIRTH, SEX, AND TYPE OF SCHOOL
(RATES PER 1,000 IN THE JEWISH POPULATION: 1964/1965)**

STUDENT BORN ABROAD   STUDENT BORN IN ISRAEL

	Born in:			Father Born in:			
	Asia-Africa	Europe-America	Israel	Asia-Africa	Europe-America	Total	All Pupils
Total	262.9	486.8	571.5	383.3	700.5	603.8	468.8
Boys	246.2	451.4	558.6	354.8	649.8	565.4	437.9
Girls	280.9	525.3	584.1	412.4	756.4	644.7	502.1
High School	81.8	275.6	273.2	147.6	374.5	304.3	226.0
Seminaries for School and Kindergarten Teachers	9.9	16.0	38.5	12.5	31.2	27.3	19.3
Evening High School	13.2	9.7	21.3	22.2	8.9	13.8	12.7
Extension Courses	13.4	27.3	47.3	29.4	98.0	74.3	44.8
Commercial Schools	98.9	123.8	139.4	129.0	142.6	138.7	122.7
Agricultural Schools	32.9	30.8	47.9	34.1	42.9	41.3	36.4
Evening High Schools (part-time)	12.9	3.7	4.0	8.5	2.3	4.1	6.9

Source: Central Bureau of Statistics, Israel Statistical Yearbook, 1965 (No. 16, p. 585). Adapted from M. Lissak, *Social Mobility in Israel* (Jerusalem: Hebrew Universities Press, 1969): p. 41.

A discernible increase is seen in the absolute number of children of Eastern descent who are interested in attending high school and college, but this group is overshadowed by a similar increase among children of Western extraction. Thus the educational gap between the Asian-African and European populations is not substantially reduced. Pupils of Western extraction tend to select a college preparatory program while in high school, whereas pupils of Eastern extraction whose approach to post-elementary schooling is more pragmatic tend to choose a vocational program.

SCHOOL ACHIEVEMENT–AFTER 1948

We cite further on a number of studies dealing with the school achievement of children of Eastern origin as against children of Western origin. These researches generally dealt with success in elementary schools, particularly at the early grades, and focused their attention on the population segment which had migrated from Moslem countries. An important discovery showed that the school success of new immigrants from Moslem countries was not essentially different from that of the Israeli-born child of Eastern parents. Data on the socioeconomic status of heads of Eastern immigrant families and of Eastern families with prolonged residence in Israel showed no significant variation. This may be the reason for the lack of difference in school success between Eastern children born abroad and born in Israel. Or, it may be that adaptation to a culture which differs markedly from one's country of origin requires a prolonged period of adjustment.

The work of Sara Smilansky, "Children who Fail in the First Elementary Grades and Their Parents,"[8] deals with the home setting of the child, the ethnicity of the parents, their attitudes towards school, and the association between intelligence and school achievement. The research, conducted in a Jerusalem neighborhood, involved two years of observation in kindergartens and lower grades in school. Reports by the teachers on the pupils' standing in the class were gathered, and achievement and intelligence tests were administered. The sample consisted of 446 children—233 from the kindergarten and 213 elementary school children.

The tests showed a wide divergence in school achievement, with

the parents' country of origin being the primary factor accounting
for this variation. At the end of grade 1 only 6 percent of children of
Eastern origin read fluently, as against 54 percent of the children of
European origin. The gap in reading continued in grade 2, where 29
percent of the children of Eastern descent had at this stage not yet
mastered reading, as compared to 2 percent of the children of European descent. The tests also showed a discernible difference between
the two ethnic communities in the area of arithmetic. The proportion of children of Eastern origin who had successfully learned arithmetic in grade 1 was 35 percent, in contrast to 70 percent of the
children of European stock. The influence of their father's country
of origin did not lose its effect despite the increasing length of residence
in Israel by those of Oriental origin. This finding coincides with the
results of other researchers who found that backwardness in learning
was not a temporary phenomenon connected with the problems of
absorption by new immigrants. The factor common to new Eastern
immigrants as well as those who had been in the country a long time
was their low socioeconomic status manifested by less expenditure
on education and cultural activities. (Not all Eastern ethnic communities necessarily follow the same pattern; see, for example, the study
by Leonard Weller and Shlomo Sharan.)[9]

The study also explored the effect of the children's intelligence on
their success in school. Table 6 shows that children with high intellectual ability read well, while those whose intelligence level was not
particularly high performed poorly in the reading tests.

By means of a scale of adaptability consisting of one hundred
sentences describing various areas of behavior, Smilansky compared
the children's adaptation at the end of grade 1 with their adaptation
at the end of kindergarten. She found that after one year in school
there was a decline in the adaptation of children of Eastern origin.
The behavioral reactions characterizing children who failed
educationally were also studied. These children compensated by
disturbing, aggressive and derisive behavior towards others, showed
loss of attention to and interest in school material, worsened their
relations with their teachers, whom they blamed and with whom they
cooperated less, and accepted the image of the "poor student," "the
dunce," and "the slow one" that was incorporated into other areas of life.

The parents' reactions to their child's failure were studied in order to understand the factors that turned school failure into an experience charged with negative emotion. The features which frequently appeared in families whose children failed were an inconsistent pattern of reward and punishment for school accomplishments, a lack of encouragement of intellectual curiosity, less money spent on cultural items such as books, and a low level of verbal communication.

TABLE 6
RELATIONSHIP BETWEEN LEVEL OF READING ACHIEVEMENT AND INTELLIGENCE ACCORDING TO FATHER'S AREA OF ORIGIN

Area of Origin of Father	Kind of Intelligence	Level of Reading Achievement		
		1*	2	3
Europe	Verbal Test	109.5	108.6	100.1
	Performance Test	109.0	105.2	95.9
Asia-Africa	Verbal Test	97.0	96.8	90.4
	Performance Test	94.5	98.8	87.6

*1=Highest level of reading achievement.

Source: S. Smijansky, "Children Who Fail in the First Elementary Grades and their Parents," *Megamot* (8, 1951): p. 435.

Three types of parental reaction to the child's failures at school were isolated: blaming the child, blaming the school, and blaming themselves. In the group that blamed the child, the parents criticized him for matters which were not even remotely connected with school, and in turn the child became aggressive. In the group which blamed the school, the parents viewed the approach of the school as opposed to their traditional outlook. In the group which blamed itself, the child's failure was considered by the family to have resulted from its own failure. These parents had placed great hopes on the child's progress, and his failure undermined their own weak self-image.

Dina Feitelson studied twelve first grade classes from schools in Jerusalem where the children were chiefly lower class and of Eastern origin.[10] Her control group consisted of children selected from schools where most of the pupils were of middle-class Western origin. The total number in both groups was 243 boys and girls.

The child's store of elementary knowledge was measured through such questions as, "What is the man who makes clothes called?" and "What are shoes made of?" Western children mastered the elementary facts to a much larger degree than did Eastern children. The use of comprehensive terms, very common among children from the control group, was rare among those from the research group. For example, a much larger percentage of the former group had no difficulty in answering the question, "What is the general name for tomatoes and green peppers?"

Differences between the achievements of children from the control group and those from the research group also emerged in the field of vocabulary. The average grade in the control group was 13.8 points, while that in the research group was 8.2 points. All the children from the research group had difficulty in the verbal field, although this failure was not intrinsic to children in whose home-environment a foreign language was spoken. Of special importance were the findings that children of Western origin who were in the country for only two or three years had higher achievements than children of Eastern origin from veteran families. Whereas the Western children seemed to be organizing and enlarging acquired knowledge at home, Eastern children had first to acquire this basic knowledge.

The teaching method was shown to affect the child's success. In classes where the free teaching method (learning of general topics but not according to defined subjects; drill not emphasized) was practiced school achievement was low compared with classes using a systematic teaching method (emphasis on systematic drill in each subject). Furthermore, the method of teaching had different effects on children depending on their level of intelligence. Table 7 shows that talented children overcame the negative effects of poor teaching, while average and weak pupils were most vulnerable to inadequate teaching. Feitelson also studied the importance of the kind of home (whether it be stimulating or unstimulating) and the kind of teaching method on the reading success of children of average intelligence. Thus we learn that in spite of the relative importance of a stimulating home, the method of teaching is weighty. It can, to a considerable extent, overcome a poor home environment manifested by an absence of cultural content and lack of encouragement in the direction of academic achievement (Table 8).

TABLE 7
SUCCESS IN READING ACCORDING TO THE LEVEL OF INTELLIGENCE AND TEACHING METHOD

	Weak (I.Q. -89)	Average (I.Q. 90-110)	Talented (I.Q. 111)
Systematic Teaching	45%	76%	100%
Free Teaching	—	49%	89%

Source: D. Feitelson, "Factors of Scholastic Failure Among First Grade
Pupils," *Megamot* (4, 1953): p. 161.

TABLE 8
SUCCESS OF AVERAGE CHILDREN ACCORDING TO TEACHING METHOD AND HOME STIMULUS

	UNSTIMULATING HOMES		STIMULATING HOMES	
	Free Teaching	Systematic Teaching	Free Teaching	Systematic Teaching
Succeeded	15%	65.4%	50%	88.2%
Failed	85%	34.6%	50%	11.8%

Source: D. Feitelson, "Factors of School Failure Among First Grade
Pupils," *Megamot* (4, 1952): p. 163.

In 1951, Aryeh Simon[11] studied the effects of ethnicity, socioeconomic status, and type of settlement on achievement in elementary
school. The pupils included in this study were in grades two, three
and four. Schools were chosen which represented four types of settlement: city (populated predominantly by new immigrants), town
(populated predominantly by new immigrants), village and moshav.
The survey covered 780 pupils from six schools and seventeen classes.
The research group (Oriental pupils) consisted of 480 students and
the control group (European students) of 300.

The investigator constructed an achievement test in Hebrew,
Arithmetic and Bible and tested the children on material studied
in the past school year. The pupils were then classified according to
three levels of achievement:

(1) Those who answered more than 80 percent of the questions correctly, defined as exceptional achievement.

(2) Those who answered 50 to 80 percent of the questions correctly, defined as intermediate achievement.

(3) Those who answered 50 percent or less of the questions correctly, defined as failing.

Some 50 percent of the Oriental pupils were classified as failing, in contrast to 13 percent of the Western pupils. Almost 53 percent of the Western children were considered to have exceptional ability, in contrast to 16 percent of the Oriental children.

A comparison of the achievement level of the Eastern and Western pupils in the various subjects showed that the former group was relatively more successful in arithmetic than in Hebrew (Table 9). The reason for their difficulty in mastering the language did not seem to be lack of knowledge arising from the short period of residence in Israel, for a high proportion of failures in Hebrew was also found among Israeli-born students of Eastern origin. Language difficulties appear to be characteristic of children of Eastern extraction, regardless of their length of stay in Israel. It is noted that Gina Ortar found in a study discussed at greater length further on that when Eastern and Western children were of the *same* level of intelligence the former showed superior arithmetic ability.[12]

TABLE 9
PERCENTAGE OF FAILING AND EXCEPTIONAL STUDENTS ACCORDING TO SUBJECT

	PERCENTAGE FAILING		
	Hebrew	Arithmetic	Bible
Research Group	55	44	54
Control Group	11	13	13
	PERCENTAGE PASSING		
Research Group	15	22	10
Control Group	60	48	41

Source: Adapted from A. Simon, "On The Scholastic Achievement of Immigrant Children in the Negev," *Megamot* (8, 1957): p. 348.

A comparison of the achievement of various schools showed that the type of settlement affected the level of achievement. Pupils of the village school performed better than pupils of other schools. Indeed, their achievement level approached that of the children in the control group. An analysis of the composition of the village school showed that it did not differ from the other schools in the research group either in terms of the country of origin of the students or their socioeconomic level. It would seem that the reason for the relative success of the pupils lay in the nature of the school's small classes. The average number of students per class was 17.5, in contrast to 40.7 in the city schools.

Leah Adar attempted to clarify the relative importance of the school *per se* and the influence of the child's home environment on his success at school.[13] Her sample was comprised of nine fourth-grade classes from Jerusalem schools. The 255 pupils were children of immigrants from Moslem countries and pupils with long residence (mostly of Western origin) whose families were in the middle and higher income levels.

The research was conducted over the period of a complete school year. It included classroom observation, the administering of questionnaires and the assessment of achievement in three subjects. The children were asked questions on the contents of stories they had learned in class. The stories which were not comprehended by the majority of children were analyzed since no more than 45 percent of the answers were correct. The analysis disclosed that lack of comprehension was often caused by an emotional block. In other instances situations were presented which either conflicted with the accepted views of good and evil in the children's cultural background or contained material foreign to their experience.

The following is an example of a story which created opposition on the part of the children. A Yemenite lad who lives in a ma'abara is brought to a hospital. There he meets a boy from a long-settled Western family living in a big city. A deep friendship develops between the two boys and when their stay in hospital is over they are reluctant to part. The parents of the Western boy agree to adopt the Yemenite boy, and thus the two of them remain together. The ending of the story aroused feelings of rejection and ambivalence in the Eastern child whose reactions were of conflict, repression, and avoidance of the story's contents.

During the course of the study, the author noted numerous occasions where immigrant children did not understand the contents of a simple story. To examine the extent of this lack of comprehension, the children were told to read a short story and were then asked questions on its contents. Of the 174 children tested, 67 entirely understood the story, while an identical number did not at all comprehend its contents and 40 others only partially understood it. It was further found that many children did not understand words of average difficulty that appeared in stories they had read in class. These discouraging results are consistent with the results of other investigators. Thus, in his work discussed above, Aryeh Simon found that in the third grade (composed of immigrant children from the Eastern communities), 31 percent could not read at all, while in the second grade, 43 percent of the pupils read faultily.[14] Sara Smilansky found that 29 percent of the pupils of Asian-African origin in grade 2 had not yet mastered the art of reading.[15] It would seem that the lack of reading technique typifies the marginal nature of a large group of Eastern children in the schools. The fact that a large number drops out of the school system at an early age makes this an acute problem.

Additional data on the distinction between the school achievement of children of Eastern and Western extraction were presented by Gina Ortar in a study of pupil achievement in the *seker*.[16] The seker (which means "survey" in Hebrew) is a combined intelligence and achievement test that, until its discontinuation in 1972, was given to all eighth grade pupils. The student's success in this test determined in large part whether he will attend a high school and which kind of school it will be. Ortar examined the data of the seker over a period of thirteen years from 1955 (when it was instituted) to 1967.

This study population was grouped according to national origin, as follows:

(1) Born in Israel, of Israeli-born parents.
(2) Born in Israel, of Asian-African parents.
(3) Born in Israel, of European parents.
(4) Born in Asia or Africa.
(5) Born in Europe.

An examination of the students' age showed that children of European extraction tended to start first grade at an earlier age and consequently completed elementary school at an earlier age than those of Eastern origin. Pupils whose parents came from Europe did better on the seker than did pupils whose parents emigrated from Asia and Africa. Country of origin of the father had a larger impact on the child's success in language and on subject matter not studied at school than on topics studied at school.

Table 10 illustrates the influence of the father's country of origin and his level of education on the pupil's achievement on the seker. The table shows that regardless of the educational level of the father, the achievement of Eastern children was lower than that of Western children. The level of achievement of Eastern pupils born outside of Israel was especially low.

TABLE 10
AVERAGE GRADE IN SEKER ACCORDING TO COUNTRY
OF ORIGIN AND LEVEL OF FATHER'S EDUCATION

Father's Educational Level	All Students	PUPILS BORN IN ISRAEL			OUTSIDE ISRAEL	
		of Israeli Parents	of Eastern Parents	of Western Parents	of Eastern Parents	of Western Parents
No School	89	88	89	92	89	94
Elementary School	97	96	93	104	92	100
High School	105	106	1Q2	107	96	103
College	109	110	107	101	100	107

Source: G. Ortar, "Thirteen Years of the Seker," *Megamot* (15, 1967): p. 227.

The effect of the home on the student's academic achievement was measured by answers to the question, "When the homework is difficult, who helps you?" As shown in Table 11 Eastern students received less help from their parents than did Western children: Thirty-three percent of the Eastern children had no one to help with their lessons when they needed it, as compared to 12 percent of the Western children. The significance of this help is made clear in Table 12 which shows large differences in the level of achievement between students who received help with their studies by family members and

those who did not receive such assistance. Parents' help with their
children's studies would seem to reflect more than mere technical
aid; it very likely offered an incentive to the child.

TABLE 11

**SOURCE OF HELP WITH HOMEWORK ACCORDING TO MOTHER'S
COUNTRY OF ORIGIN (PERCENTAGES)**

Who helps?	Born in Israel	Eastern born	Western born
Total	100	100	100
No help needed	43	35	49
Mother or Father	17	5	12
Private teacher	11	6	12
Friend or relative	16	20	11
No one	11	33	12
No answer	2	3	4

Source: G. Ortar, "Thirteen years of the Sekar," *Megamot* (15, 1967): p. 228.

TABLE 12

SOURCE OF HELP WITH LESSON BY SEKER GRADE

Who helps?	Pct. Answering	Mean Seker Score
No help is needed	43	111
Father or Mother	10	107
Private teacher	6	100
Group leader	4	99
Friend or relative	15	94
No one	19	89
No answer	3	95

Source: G. Ortar, "Thirteen Years of the Seker," *Megamot* (15, 1967): p. 227.

Gina Ortar studied differences in intellectual functioning when the
general level of intelligence is equal.[17] By means of paired compari-

son in intelligence tests, the investigator compared children of European origin to children of Eastern origin, holding length of stay in the country constant. The sample included the following three groups: a) Israeli-born children of Western descent, or children of Western descent who were in the country no more than three years; b) native-born children of Eastern descent; and c) recent immigrants of Eastern descent.

The current assumption, based on daily experience in educational institutions, is that children of Eastern descent have difficulties in their capacity to abstract. By comparing the achievements of Western and Eastern children of the same I.Q., Ortar found virtually no difference in the field of verbal abstraction, although there were considerable differences in the richness of vocabulary and in the capacity for verbal orientation under hypothetical conditions. In the field of vocabulary the consistent difference between the two ethnic groups stemmed from conceptual rigidity among Asian-Africans, expressed chiefly in lack of linguistic flexibility. In arithmetic tests, Eastern children were superior to their Western counterparts. Ortar attributes this relative advantage to an inclination for numbers by pupils with a conceptual rigidity. This does not necessarily imply a talent for mathematics; it is rather evidence of strict and definite conceptual performances.

Tests of picture meaning, assembly, motorial flexibility and mechanical concentration revealed no differences between the two groups. The equal achievements in the fields of picture completion and cubes gave rise to problems of interpretation. Although Western children are known to have more opportunities to experiment with games, no differences emerged in the subtests which should reflect such experiences. Presumably the actual intellectual level of children of Eastern extraction was fully displayed only in the arithmetic subtests. The evidence presented by Ortar confirms the general impression of the difficulties experienced by Oriental children.

The study by R. Feuerstein and M. Richelle on the intellectual level of North African children[18] supports the contention that varying cultural and economic conditions are the major causes of deficient abstract thinking. This research was carried out in a transit camp of the Jewish Agency to which North African children had been brought before their departure for Israel. The difficulties of these children on the eve of their immigration elucidated problems in the cultural and

intellectual background of the North African child. The whole issue
is of great importance, since North African Jews are the most problematic Eastern group.

The school children came from the ghettoes of North African cities
and a poverty-stricken class with shattered social foundations. The
lower class urban Jewish population in North Africa was concentrated
in narrow and overcrowded streets in the big cities of Morocco, Tunisia
and Algeria. The population density in the Jewish quarters was very
high. Services in the Jewish ghetto were poor; there was no running
water and several families had to share a toilet. Epidemics, chronic
ailments, syphilis and alcoholism were widespread. Children were
undernourished and suffered from neurological disturbances. People
married at a very early age and had many children. The father was an
authoritarian whose threats were often violent. The mother-child
relationship was the closest of any, but no moral or educational
influence was exerted by the mother.

The rate of one-parent families was high—14 percent. Only a small
percentage of the children received formal education and classes were
overcrowded. Twenty-six percent of the children in the sample had
never gone to school. Even the teachers had never enjoyed a formal
education, and teaching methods were outmoded. Mechanical mem-
orizing was practiced with no concern for the need to understand or
think creatively. Instead of stimulation and encouragement the children
were given traditional explanations for all phenomena. The lack of
sexual curiosity was attributed to the fact that children lived in such
crowded circumstances that no intimate experience was concealed
from them.

Examination of difficulties in linguistic expression showed that
these children were unable to give precise terminology for objects,
or to indicate the differences between articles, thoughts, emotions
or their interrelations. Language served as a mere social tool and
was characterized by an extremely limited vocabulary, a lack of
precise terms, few prepositions, and poor language. When a North
African child was angry at somebody, he would echo his father saying, "I'll kill you." While the many hand gestures which accompanied
the child's conversation compensated for his poor language, his lack
of linguistic tools left him unable to express complex situations in
a precise, organized way. The researchers inferred that, for the North

African child, Hebrew was not merely a new language to be learned but involved the acquiring of basic habits of linguistic expression, hitherto strange to him, and the formation of new terms, relations, and definitions.

Linguistic difficulties were not unique to these children. Most of the researchers, comparing the level of intelligence and the vocabulary of children of Eastern origin with those of their Western counterparts, claimed that the former faced considerable difficulties in the field of language. We have cited Gina Ortar's findings showing that, even when the level of intelligence of an Eastern child was the same as that of a Western one, there nevertheless existed a difference in the components of intelligence, particularly in vocabulary.[19] And Dina Feitelson pointed to the far-reaching implications of these difficulties with regard to the children's capacity to study and to acquire habits of thinking and a vocabulary of terms.[20]

SOCIAL-PSYCHOLOGICAL STUDIES

To complete the picture we present a series of studies, conducted in recent years by several social psychologists, dealing with the effects of ethnicity on perception. In a sense they are more revealing than other kinds of research, for they examine fundamental psychological processes. Moreover, several of them are counted among the few that took into consideration the mutual effect of social class and ethnicity.

To determine whether the perceptual style of Easterners differs from that of Westerners, Ilana Preale, Yehudah Amir and Shlomo Sharan examined 88 male students of Eastern ethnic background and 112 male students of Western origin.[21] They were all nineteen or twenty years old and had similar I.Q.s. The first of the four tests was the Embedded Figures Test (EFT), consisting of sixteen geometrical designs, each embedded in a larger complex figure. The subject was asked to locate the designated figure within a specific time limit. The second was the Human Figure Drawing (HFD), in which the subject was asked to draw a male and a female figure. The degree of primitivity-sophistication of the drawing, i.e., the relative degree of sophistication with which the individual perceives the human body, was assessed according to Helen Marlen's scoring method. The third and fourth tests consisted of the Block Design (BD), and the Picture Completion (PC), taken from the Wechsler Intelligence Test.

The prediction that subjects of Western origin would display a higher level of field independence (degree to which figures are distinguished from their backgrounds) than would subjects of Eastern origin was confirmed by all of the four tests (Table 13). That is, the cognitive development of the child is affected by the ethnic group to which he belongs.

TABLE 13
LEVEL OF PERCEPTUAL ARTICULATION IN WESTERN AND EASTERN ETHNIC GROUPS

Test	Western	Eastern	t
Embedded Figures[1]	Mean 8.21	Mean 6.59	2.55*
Block Design[1]	Mean 33.14	Mean 30.07	3.01**
Picture Completion[1]	Mean 14.73	Mean 13.55	2.78**
Figure Drawing[2]	Mean 2.64	Mean 2.99	2.23***

*p = .02; **p = .01; ***p = .05

[1] Larger means indicate higher level of articulation.

[2] Smaller means indicate higher level of articulation.

Source: Preale, Yehudah Amir and Shlomo Sharan, "Perceptual Articulation, Socialization Patterns and Task Effectiveness," *Journal of Personality and Social Psychology* (15, 1970): pp. 190-195.

Baruch Zadik was also concerned with field dependence and independence, and hypothesized that Eastern children would be more field-dependent than Western children.[22] His sample consisted of ten Eastern boys matched with ten Western boys and ten Eastern girls matched with ten Western girls on the basis of I.Q. The children were all thirteen years old. In addition to the Embedded Figures Test and the Human Figure Drawing used in the previous study, the rod and the frame test was employed. The hypothesis was confirmed in each of the three measures.

Neither of these studies held social class constant. However, another study by Leonard Weller and Shlomo Sharan examined influence of ethnicity and social class on the human figure drawing of first grade children.[23] With a more elaborate theoretical framework, the authors predicted that children of Oriental parents would show less body sophistication than children of Western parents. They also hypothesized that superior body sophistication would be demonstrated by middle-class rather than lower-class children. The sample consisted of 357 first grade children of Western and Eastern ethnic background from both the lower and the middle classes. As in the two previous studies, these results showed that children of Eastern origin manifested less body sophistication than children of Western ethnic origin. Lower-class children, however, did not differ from middle-class children on body sophistication. Since the previous studies did not examine the mutual influence of social class and ethnicity on field-dependence, it was likely that the reported findings on ethnicity reflected the hidden impact of social class. The Weller-Sharan study suggests that the findings on body sophistication truly represent an ethnic influence.

In another paper Shlomo Sharan and Leonard Weller reported additional findings based on the sample of 357 school children.[24] Here the concern was with cognitive style and delayed gratification. This was one of the few studies which simultaneously studied the effects of class and ethnicity (together with sex).

The major part of the study concerned the children's ability to classify objects by level of abstraction. The Seigel Sorting Task, comprised of an Active and Passive condition, was employed. In the Active condition twelve items (e.g., notebook, crayons, cup) were placed on the table one at a time while the child named them. The examiner then selected one object from the array, put it on one side, and said to the child, "Look at all these things and put over here the ones that are like this one or go with it." The same procedure was followed with each of the twelve objects. After each sort, the child was asked to give his reasons for placing these objects together. In the Passive condition the child was presented with a grouping selected by the examiner from the array. The child was asked to explain why these objects are alike or go together.

The responses were scored according to two major dimensions. The first concerned the child's ability to explain why the objects

belonged together. The hypothesis, that lower-class and Eastern
children would be less able to give a rationale for grouping objects
together than would middle-class and Western children respectively,
was confirmed. The second dimension concerned level of abstraction.
The hypothesis was that lower-class and Eastern children would cate-
gorize objects on the basis of a lower level of abstraction than would
middle-class and Western children. The results showed a different
pattern for ethnicity and social class. Lower-class children were less
able to employ the most abstract, categorical style of grouping than
were middle-class children. Eastern children were less able than Western
children to employ the Descriptive category, which was the style most
prevalent among all children in this sample. Their lower ability for con-
ceptualizing groups of stimuli was interpreted as an inability to cope
with the basic task of formulating a conceptual rationale for grouping.
Thus they avoided the task *per se.*

Leonard Weller examined the effects of class and ethnicity on delayed gratification.[25] First to fifth grade children chose between a
small candy which they would receive immediately or a larger candy
which they would get in a week. They were also asked to draw a vertical line as *slowly* as possible from the top of a sheet of paper to a
horizontal line drawn across the center of the sheet. Preference for
the larger candy over the smaller was indicative of delayed gratification. Taking a long time to draw the line signified motoric restraint
and perhaps was also indicative of delayed gratification.

The results show absolutely no correlation between the two measures.
Those children who preferred the small candy took the same amount of
time to draw the line as did those children who chose the larger candy.
There were, however, ethnic and class differences. Western and middle-
class children took longer to draw the line than did Eastern and lower-
class children, respectively. On candy choice, middle-class in contrast
to lower-class children were more willing to wait a week in order to
get the larger candy, but there were no ethnic differences. Thus class
seems to be a more important determinant of delayed gratification
than ethnicity.

In sum, this set of studies complements the earlier findings, showing
that the perceptual articulation (which is also associated with school
success) of Easterners is poorer than that of Westerners. Furthermore,
these studies support the contention that the observed ethnic differ-

ences are not hidden social-class influences, although clearly social class is an important element. Furthermore, these studies again demonstrate that the East-West differences are manifested in the first grade, if not before.

CONCLUSION

The similarities in evidence emerging from the research carried out among the various Eastern ethnic communities suggests that the educational difficulties spring from factors common to all children of Asian and African countries. More recent researches have demonstrated the effect of the father's country of origin on the children's perception and ways of thinking—factors which are considered to be associated with poor school performance. Moreover, ethnic differences in the standard of achievement and level of intelligence are apparently not attributable solely to the process of immigration and absorption that the children undergo; among children of veteran settlers of Oriental origin a similar tendency is discernible. Those children perform less well than their Western counterparts at all levels of schooling.

While numerous differences between the two ethnic communities can of course be cited, little research has been done on the nature of these ethnic groups in order to discover what predisposes them to poorer performance. With the exception of several excellent studies of the socialization patterns of specific ethnic communities—conducted for the most part in the early 1950s—virtually all of the studies have been concerned with ascertaining the extent of the ethnic differences and not their causes. This is true even of the more sophisticated social-psychological research of recent years.

A critical issue is the extent to which Eastern children born in Israel, or born abroad but raised in Israel for the better part of their life, perpetuate the values and socialization patterns of their ethnic communities. The Yemenites who arrived in Israel *en masse* less than twenty-five years ago had for centuries lived in a situation *vis-à-vis* the Arabs similar to that of the Negroes in the Deep South. Yet today they are not only the most respected Eastern group, but they do not reveal the slightest sign of centuries of servitude. The army, where service is compulsory for both sexes, has an extensive educational program of its own and undoubtedly serves as a great democratizing influence.

One would think that the ethnic influence would be weaker for men and women who have returned from the army, but there is no research on this subject.

When we consider that the state of Israel is merely a quarter of a century old and that much of the research was conducted on first-generation Jews of Eastern extraction who had been under old-world influences, their failure and that of their children to achieve rapid advancement should perhaps not be viewed in such a discouraging light.

Without a doubt, the structure of the Israeli school must share a goodly part of the blame for the scholastic failure of Eastern children. Brill, Simon, Adar, and Smilansky[26] contend that Israeli teaching methods make little allowance for the specific needs of Asian-African children. The problems peculiar to Eastern children were neglected by educators with a Western background who constructed a curriculum Western-oriented both psychologically and in terms of content. To succeed in school a child needed to have a Western background, or, if he were a child of Eastern extraction, to possess unusual ability.

It cannot be argued that educators were unaware of the situation. Reforms suggested as far back as 1956 were not accepted with alacrity. Perhaps, at that time, the gravity of the problem was not generally realized, but today it is glaring. Thus, unfortunately for the "People of the Book," many Eastern Jews have reading difficulties. One aspect of this problem is demographic. A large number of Jews of Eastern extraction live in development towns which are for the most part situated in rural areas. These towns do not produce their own teachers, and those already holding positions elsewhere are loathe to accept appointments there. Those who do teach there are usually newly qualified or are teachers who have been secunded by the army. The teacher turnover is understandably high.

Several words of caution on the above discussion are in order. First, American research literature reports that members of the lower class, unlike those of the middle class, are less likely to defer present satisfactions, less intellectually alert, and perform less well in school. Since social class was held constant in all but a few of the researches in Israel, we are not in a position to state with certainty that the observed differences derive from ethnic and not social class influences. Undoubtedly, differences between the two ethnic groups are in part attributable to differential class membership, but the extent of the independent effects of ethnicity and of social class is not known.

Second, most of the researches lump the Asian-African ethnic groups into one category, Eastern, overlooking the character, tradition and specific conditions unique to each of them. Whenever possible we have in this book emphasized intraethnic differences among the Jews of Asian-African origin. Unfortunately we have scanty data. It is probably true that the variance between the two major ethnic communities is larger than the variance within the Eastern communities. It is this assumption that justifies the lumping together of all the Jews of African-Asian extraction. Nevertheless, there are large ethnic differences within the Eastern community (some are cited in the next chapter), and these have not received sufficient attention. (For example, a higher percentage of Jews of Iraqi descent go on to higher education than do Jews from other Eastern ethnic communities.)

Third, the measurement of intelligence by standard instruments, such as the Wechsler Test, raises the legitimate but almost insoluble problem of a culture-free test. Though designed to measure a general factor in intelligence, it is likely that the contents of intelligence tests are geared to the conceptions and previous experiences of Western culture. A question as yet unanswered is to what extent does the superior performance of the Western group reflect the cultural bias of the test.

Finally, we repeat, many of the studies of the values and socialization patterns of the various Eastern communities were conducted in the early fifties, not long after the arrival of the immigrants. There is now a generation of children who were born in Israel, have served in the army, and are of marriageable age. It is not known to what extent these children who spent all or the major part of their lives in Israel will perpetuate the cultural values of the old country.

NOTES

1. Moses Brill, "Retarded Children and Adult Learning," *Education* (11): pp. 110-122 (in Hebrew).

2. Chanan Enoch, "Early School Leavers in the Municipal Schools of Tel-Aviv," *Megamot* (2, 1950): pp. 34-51 (in Hebrew).

3. Michael Chen, "Patterns of Applications to High School From Tel-Aviv Elementary School Graduates," *Megamot* (11, 1961): pp. 388-396 (in Hebrew).

4. *Ibid.*

5. See also: Emanual Jaffe and Moshe Smilansky, "The Extent and Causes of Early School Leaving," *Megamot* (9, 1958): pp. 275-285 (in Hebrew).

6. *Population and Housing Census* (Jerusalem: Central Bureau of Statistics, 1961) (in Hebrew); Haim I. Cohen, "A Look at the Education of Oriental Communities," *Molad* (23, 1966): pp. 208-210 (in Hebrew).

7. Moshe Lissak, *Social Mobility in Israeli Society* (Jerusalem: Israel Universities Press, 1969), p. 37.

8. Sarah Smilansky, "Children Who Fail in the First Elementary Grades and Their Parents," *Megamot* (8, 1957): pp. 430-445 (in Hebrew). See also: "The Effect of Certain Learning Conditions on the Progress of Disadvantaged Children of Pre-school Age," *Megamot* (14, 1966): pp. 213-224 (in Hebrew); "The Kindergarten as a Means of Promoting Intellectual Development in Underprivileged Children," *Megamot* (9, 1958): pp. 165-180 (in Hebrew).

9. Leonard Weller and Shlomo Sharan, "Articulation of the Body Concept Among First-Grade Children," *Child Development* (4, 1971): pp. 1553-1559.

10. Dina Feitelson, "Causes of Scholastic Failure in First Graders," *Megamot* (4, 1952): pp. 37-63 (in Hebrew) and "Causes of Scholastic Failure in First Graders—Part Two," *Megamot* (4, 1953): pp. 123-173 (in Hebrew). For another relevant article of hers see: "Education of Pre-school Children in Kurdistan Communities," *Megamot* (5, 1954): pp. 95-109 (in Hebrew).

11. Aryeh Simon, "On the Scholastic Achievements of Immigrant Children in the Lower Elementary Grades," *Megamot* (8, 1957): pp. 343-368 (in Hebrew).

12. Gina Ortar, "Differences in the Structure of Intelligence—A Comparative Analysis of Ethnic Sub-Groups," *Megamot* (4, 1953): pp. 107-122.

13. Leah Adar, "A Study on the Scholastic Difficulties of Immigrant Children," *Megamot* (7, 1956): pp. 139-180 (in Hebrew).

14. Aryeh Simon, *op. cit.*

15. Sarah Smilansky, *op. cit.*

16. Gina Ortar, "Thirteen Years of the Seker," *Megamot* (15, 1967): pp. 220-230 (in Hebrew).

17. Gina Ortar, *ibid.* For her other studies on intelligence, with particular reference to immigrant children see: "The Validity in Israel of Certain Intelligence Tests for Children at the Age of Six," *Megamot* (1, 1950): pp. 206-223 (in Hebrew); "Standardization in Israel of the Wechsler Test for Children," *Megamot* (4, 1952): pp. 87-100 (in Hebrew); "Differences in the Structure of Intelligence-A Comparative Analysis of Ethnic Sub-Groups," *Megamot* (4, 1953): pp. 107-122 (in Hebrew); "The Diagnostic Significance of the Wechsler-Bellevue Test at Different Intelligence Levels," *Megamot* (4, 1953): pp. 199-216 (in Hebrew); "The Eighth Grade Survey of 1955," *Megamot* (7, 1956): pp. 77-85 (in Hebrew); "The Influence of Some Environment Factors on Bible Study in Elementary School," *Megamot* (7, 1956): pp. 265-273 (in Hebrew); "Elementary School Graduates: Their Scholastic Aspirations and Achievements," *Megamot* (8, 1957): pp. 56-70 (in Hebrew); "The Predictive Value of the 'Eighth Grade Survey' Tests: A Follow-up Study," *Megamot* (10, 1960): pp. 209-221 (in Hebrew); "Educational Achievements as Related to Socio-Cultural Background of Primary School Graduates in Israel," *Megamot* (15, 1967): pp. 220-230 (in Hebrew); (with C. Frankenstein), "How to Develop Abstract Thinking in Immigrant Children from Oriental Countries," *Megamot* (2, 1951): pp. 361-384 (in Hebrew).

18. R. Feuerstein and M. Richelle, *Children of the Mellah* (Jerusalem: Jewish Agency and Szold Foundation, 1953); see also F. Feuerstein

and M. Richelle, "Perception and Drawing Ability Among North African Jewish Children," *Megamot* (9, 1958): pp. 156-162 (in Hebrew).

19. Gina Ortar, "Differences in the Structure of Intelligence—A Comparative Analysis of Ethnic Sub-Groups," *Megamot* (4, 1953): pp. 107-122 (in Hebrew); Ortar has also discussed the problems of using Western-designed tests on children from Western backgrounds; see: G. Ortar, "Verbal and Performance Tests: Their Relative Value as Tools for Inter-cultural Comparison," *Megamot* (9, 1958): pp. 207-227 (in Hebrew); G. Ortar, "Improving Test Validity by Coaching," *Megamot* (11, 1960): pp. 33-37 (in Hebrew); G. Ortar, "Principles of Transfer of Psychological Tests from One Culture to Another," *Megamot* (11, 1961): pp. 338-344 (in Hebrew); G. Ortar, "On the Validity of Certain School Entrance Tests—A Follow-up Study," *Megamot* (3, 1951): pp. 375-379 (in Hebrew); G. Ortar, "The Validity in Israel of Certain Intelligence Tests for Children at the Age of Six," *Megamot* (1, 1950): pp. 206-223 (in Hebrew).

20. Dina Feitelson, *op. cit.*

21. Ilana Preale, Yehudah Amir and Shlomo Sharan, "Perceptual Articulation and Task Effectiveness in Several Subcultures," *Journal of Personality and Social Psychology* (15, 1970): pp. 190-195.

22. Baruch Zadik, "Field Dependence-Independence Among Oriental and Western School Children," *Megamot* (16, 1968): pp. 51-58 (in Hebrew).

23. Leonard Weller and Shlomo Sharan, "Articulation of the Body Concept Among First-Grade Israeli Children," *Child Development* (42, 1971): pp. 1553-1559.

24. Shlomo Sharan and Leonard Weller, "Classification Patterns in Underprivileged Children in Israel," *Child Development* (42, 1971): pp. 581-594.

25. Leonard Weller, "The Effects of Class, Ethnicity, Age and Sex on Delayed Gratification of Israeli School Children" (1972, mimeographed).

26. Moshe Smilansky, "The Social Implications of the Educational Structure in Israel," *Megamot* (8, 1957): pp. 227-238 (in Hebrew). See his other articles: "Outlines for a Reform in Secondary Education," *Megamot* (11, 1961): pp. 364-372 (in Hebrew); (with B. Burg and T. Kreiger), "Regional Enrichment Centers for Disadvantaged Children in the Grades of Elementary School," *Megamot* (14, 1966): pp. 200-212 (in Hebrew); (with T. Parnas), "Educational and Vocational Guidance in Israel: a Follow-up Study," *Megamot* (10, 1960): pp. 242-270 (in Hebrew); (with Y. Yam), "The Relationship Between Family Size, Ethnic Origin, Father's Education and Student's Achievements," *Megamot* (16, 1966): pp. 248-273 (in Hebrew).

3

Social Class and Mobility

Zionist ideology before the establishment of the state of Israel envisioned a new society, essentially socialistic, with relative economic equality and a fair division of labor. Ideally, the pioneer subordinated his own interests to the national need. The absence of an aristocracy and the fact that much land belonged to public organizations buttressed the strong egalitarianism of Israel before 1948. However, even before 1948, the development of the economy had begun to produce changes which were at variance with the pioneering ideology. Manual labor was no longer highly valued, and prestige was accorded to occupations in an ordering somewhat like that of Western society. Research on social class addresses itself to those problems arising out of a fluid social situation: the degree of class crystallization, occupational ranking and the criteria for such ordering, and an assessment of the extent to which Israel's class structure is open or closed.

Two kinds of mobility studies make up the greater portion of social class research. One is a comparison of the overall mobility rates for the entire Israeli population to those of other countries. The other, an analysis of mobility rates according to ethnicity, occupation and education, also serves as a measure of integration. Today, with the East-West problem as the focal issue of Israeli society, intra- and inter-generational mobility analysis permits an assessment of the exact nature of the ethnic gap.

SOCIAL CLASS

Rivkah Bar-Yosef and Dorit Padan compared the income structure of Israel with that of other countries.[1] As shown in Table 14, the top tenth percentile of wage earners in Israel received 1.6 percent of the total income, or fifteen times more than the bottom tenth percentile, who received 24.2 percent of the total income. This difference shows Israel to be more egalitarian than Holland, Britain or the United States.

TABLE 14
PERSONAL INCOME DISTRIBUTION IN ISRAEL AND OTHER COUNTRIES (PERCENTAGES)

	Israel 1957/58 Urban pop.	Holland 1950	England 1952	America 1952
Total	100.0	100.0	100.0	100.0
Top tenth percentile	1.6	1.3	2.0	1.0
Bottom tenth percentile	24.2	35.0	30.0	31.0
Income difference between top and bottom percentiles	22.6	33.7	28.0	30.0
Top half	25.8	21.0	25.0	23.0
Bottom half	74.2	79.0	75.0	77.0
Income difference between top and bottom	48.4	58.0	50.0	54.0

Source: R. Bar-Yosef and D. Padan, "Eastern Ethnic Communities in the Class Structure of Israel," *Molad* (22, 1964): p. 505.

The Israeli and American populations were grouped in four social classes (lower, lower-middle, upper-middle, upper) on the basis of income, employment, and education. Comparisons between the two countries revealed a striking similarity in income but great differences in occupation and education (Table 15). Moreover, in America there was a marked congruence of income and education, while in Israel no such correspondence was found.

Occupational Ranking

Various occupations have been ranked according to prestige. Moshe Lissak[2] asked 419 youths between the ages of 16 and 25 to rate twenty-

seven occupations on the basis of an objective or "public hierarchy"—
the order of importance attributed by the general public—and according
to a "subjective hierarchy"—how they themselves felt. These data are
presented in Tables 16 and 17. Among the first fourteen occupations
there is a high correspondence between both sets of ratings. The most
highly esteemed are the academic professions and those in the political
sphere. Manual labor is accorded low status, as are unskilled jobs. Of
special interest are the ratings of kibbutz and moshav members. Both
are accorded low prestige, particularly in the "public hierarchy."

TABLE 15
CLASS CRYSTALLIZATION (PERCENTAGES)

	Income	Employment	Education
U.S.A.			
Lower	38.5	56.0	38.6
Lower-Middle	39.6	19.0	43.2
Upper-Middle	18.1	21.2	–
Upper	3.8	3.8	18.2
ISRAEL			
Lower	33.2	25.5	51.1
Lower-Middle	43.4	24.7	35.1
Upper-Middle	19.5	34.0	–
Upper	3.9	10.5*	12.2**

*There is an error in the original article. These figures do not equal 100.
**An additional 66 were classified as "other kinds of education."

Source: R. Bar-Yosef and D. Padan, "Eastern Ethnic Communities in the
Class Structure of Israel," *Molad* (22, 1964): p. 510.

Subjective Class Identification

Another investigator, Aaron Antonovsky, has provided us with one
of the few studies in Israel on subjective class affiliation.[3] He drew a
representative sample of 1,170 adults, excluding members of the kibbutz.
Each interviewee was asked to select the social class to which he belonged:
upper, upper-middle ("upper-middle" was introduced by Antonovsky;
it was not included in the American studies), middle, worker, or lower.

Table 18 presents the findings, along with comparative results from the United States. The similarity between the two countries is seen in the small percentage of respondents who considered themselves "lower-class." However, whereas the majority of Israelis (52 percent) saw themselves as "middle class," the majority of Americans regarded themselves as "workers." Objectively, 70 percent of the Israeli population were hired laborers, a higher percentage than in the United States.

TABLE 16
HIERARCHY OF OCCUPATIONS AS PERCEIVED BY SAMPLE POPULATION
(PUBLIC HIERARCHY)

Rank	Occupation	Rank	Occupation
1	Scientist	16	Public Servant
2	Diplomat	17	Trader (businessman)
3	Physician	18	Party Functionary
4	Member of Parliament	19	Clerk (in a private firm)
5	Flight Officer	20	Farmer in a Moshav (private ownership)
6	Engineer		
7	Author	21	Mechanic
8	Lawyer	22	Locksmith
9	High School Teacher	23	Member of a Kibbutz (collective settlement)
10	Banker	24	Member of a Moshav (cooperative settlement)
11	Army Officer		
12	Industrialist	25	Teamster
13	Artist (painter, musician)	26	Waiter
14	Rabbi	27	Usher
15	Athlete		

Source: M. Lissak, "Patterns of Change in Ideology and Class Structure in Israel," *Jewish Journal of Sociology* (7, 1965): p. 58.

There was a high association between objective measures of social class and subjective class affiliation. The smallest difference between objective and subjective class identification was seen among the professionals and big businessmen; 90 percent regarded themselves as

belonging to the middle class (31 percent of these said they belonged
to the upper-middle class). The largest gap was found among white and
blue collar workers: only 20 percent of the former and 48 percent
of the latter said that they were workers.

TABLE 17
HIERARCHY OF OCCUPATIONS AS PERCEIVED BY
SAMPLE POPULATION
(SUBJECTIVE HIERARCHY)

Rank	Occupation	Rank	Occupation
1	Scientist	15	Banker
2	Physician	16	Member of a Kibbutz
3	Diplomat	17	Farmer in a Moshav
4	Engineer	18	Member of a Moshav
5	Author	19	Locksmith
6	Member of Parliament	20	Athlete
7	Flight Officer	21	Clerk
8	High School Teacher	22	Public Servant
9	Artist (painter, musician)	23	Trader (businessman)
10	Lawyer	24	Teamster
11	Army Officer	25	Party Functionary
12	Rabbi	26	Waiter
13	Industrialist	27	Usher
14	Mechanic		

Source: M. Lissak. "Patterns of Change in Ideology and Class Structure in
Israel," *Jewish Journal of Sociology* (7, 1965): p. 58.

A large gap was noted between objective and subjective class identification when education instead of occupation was used as the objective
index of class. Thirty percent of those with an eighth grade education
identified themselves as middle class, in contrast to 55 percent who had
some college education. Immigrants from North Africa were least likely
to consider themselves middle class (29 percent), followed by immigrants
from Asia (48 percent). Eighty-three percent of the "sabras" (born in
Isarel) of Western descent saw themselves as belonging to the middle
class, and indeed most of them were engaged in middle-class occupations.

Still, European immigrants who held the same occupations as did sabras of European descent were less prone to identify themselves as middle-class.

TABLE 18
SUBJECTIVE CLASS IDENTIFICATION IN
ISRAEL AND AMERICA (PERCENTAGES)

Social Class	Israel 1962 (Both sexes)	U.S.A. 1946 (Masculine, white)
Upper	1	4
Upper-Middle	7	—
Middle	52	36
Working	29	52
Lower	5	5
No Answer	6	3
Total	100	100
N	(1170)	(1337)

Source: A. Antonovsky, "Socio-Political Attitudes in Israel," *Amot* (June-July, 1963): p. 14.

Subjective aspects of class interested Eric Cohen in research concerning perception of the stratification system which he conducted in Kiryat Gat, a development town.[4] Noneducated and low-income people among the new immigrants were predisposed to see the stratification system as conflicting, whereas groups with higher income and education were more likely to perceive it as harmonic.

In a similar study conducted on a large sample of urban youth aged sixteen to twenty-five, the youngsters were asked questions aimed at eliciting their perception of the class structure.[5] Essentially, Moshe Lissak was concerned with the number of social classes the youth thought existed, their criteria of differentiation, and the degree of rigidity with which they perceived the stratification system. Table 19 presents data revealing whether the youth saw society as consisting of two distinct classes (referred to as "dichotomous model") or of three or more classes (referred to as "trichotomous model"). Table 20 presents the results of the youths' perception of their chances for mobility. The results show differential perception between youth of

TABLE 19

**DISTRIBUTION OF YOUTHS AGED 16-25 ACCORDING TO
ETHNIC ORIGIN AND TO ESTIMATES ABOUT NUMBER OF
CLASSES IN STRATIFICATION SYSTEM IN ISRAEL
(IN ABSOLUTE NUMBERS AND PERCENTAGES)**

Continent of Birth	Dichotomous Model (2 Dimensions)	Trichotomous Model (3 Dimensions)	Multi-dimensional Model (More than 3 Dimensions)	No Answer or Could Not Decide	Total
Youth of European Origin	(15) 8.0%	(48) 25.5%	(91) 48%	(35) 18.5%	(189) 100%
Youth of Asian-African Origin	(54) 23.5%	(56) 24.5%	(75) 32.0%	(46) 20.0%	(230) 100%
All the Population	(69) 16.5%	(104) 25.0%	(166) 39.5%	(81) 19.0%	(419) 100%

Source: M. Lissak, "Expectations of Social Mobility and Occupational Choice
Amongst Urban Youth in Israel," *Bahistadrut* (1965-1966). Cited in M. Lissak,
Social Mobility in Israeli Society, 1969, p. 65.

TABLE 20

**DISTRIBUTION OF YOUTH ACCORDING TO ETHNIC ORIGIN
AND DYNAMISM OF STRATIFICATION MODEL
(IN ABSOLUTE NUMBERS AND PERCENTAGES)**

Ethnic Origin	POSSIBILITIES OF MOBILITY					
	Limitless	Many	Few	No	No Answer	Total
European Origin	6 11.7%	31 60.8%	10 20.0%	1 2.0%	3 5.5%	51 100%
Asian-African	3 5.0%	19 36.5%	14 27.0%	15 29.0%	1 1.8%	52 100%
Total	9 8.7%	50 48.5%	24 23.3%	16 15.5%	4 4.0%	103 100%

Source: M. Lissak, "Expectations of Social Mobility and Occupational Choice
Amongst Urban Youth in Israel," *Bahistadrut* (1965-1966). Cited in M. Lissak,
Social Mobility in Israeli Society, 1969, p. 66.

European and of Asian-African origins. The former saw the stratification system as more complex. There were more classes, the criteria of class placement were numerous, and their chances of mobility were high.

Influence of Social Class on Attitudes and Values

There have been virtually no studies on the effect of class on attitudes and values nor on the interaction patterns within the family as influenced by social class. The one large-scale study on the topic is that of Aaron Antonovsky,[6] who examined the relationship of class to religiosity, political affiliation, and ideology, according to both subjective and objective indices.

A negative correlation was found between social class (as defined subjectively) and religiosity. Twenty-two percent of the subjects who considered themselves part of the upper or upper-middle class said they were religious as compared to 25 percent of the middle class, 34 percent of the working class and 46 percent of the lower class. Similarly, there was a decidedly negative correlation between education and religiosity. Forty-eight percent of those with less than an eighth grade education said they were religious, in contrast to 29 percent of those who had finished elementary school, and 16 to 20 percent of those who had a partial high-school education or better.

To the question: "With which political party are you affiliated?" the percentage of indifferent replies grew as one went down the occupational ladder from 22 to 42 percent. The subjective measure of social class yielded a higher association with political ideology than did the objective measures. Both kinds of measures of social class testified to a preference on the part of the middle and upper socioeconomic groups for a rightist ideology. Between the levels of education and pro-capitalism quite a positive relationship was indicated , from 19 percent among the least educated, to 36 percent among the highest educated. There was also a positive association between higher socioeconomic status and the desire to limit the Histadrut (Labor Federation). Fifty percent of the respondents were very much in favor of limiting the Histadrut, while another 25 percent favored limiting it with reservations.

Education was also associated with attitudes towards the Arab countries, although differences were less noticeable than in the

previous questions. Forty percent of those who did not complete
eighth grade were against a more active policy, in comparison with
66 percent of those who had attended a university.

Since medical services in Israel tend to be uniform, a study of
longevity rates in different ethnic groups provides an excellent
opportunity to examine the effects of both ethnicity and social
class on health and morbidity.

H. V. Muhsam[7] classified the population into the following
groups:

  I Born in Israel.
 II Born in Europe, immigrated before 1947.
III Born in Europe, immigrated during 1948-1954.
 IV Born in Europe, immigrated 1955 or later.
  V Born in Africa and Asia (excluding Israel), immigrated before 1947.
 VI Born in Africa and Asia (excluding Israel), immigrated during 1948-1954.
VII Born in Africa and Asia (excluding Israel), immigrated 1955 or later.

The results shown in Table 21 were altogether unanticipated. The
veteran settlers from Europe (II), because of their high socioeconomic
status and their Western culture, had been expected to show the best
record, but they had almost the lowest life expectancy. In general, those
born in Asia and Africa had a longer expectation of life than those born
in Europe. On the other hand, as was predicted, persons born in Israel (I)
had the most favorable record, while the most recently-arrived Asian-
African immigrants (VII) had the worst.

TABLE 21
EXPECTATION OF LIFE (AT AGE 15) OF SOCIAL STRATA IN ISRAEL

	I	V	IV	VI	III	II	VII
Males	61.6	60.9	59.6	59.2	58.5	57.5	54.6
Females	62.7	60.5	60.3	60.5	59.2	59.3	58.9
Both sexes combined	62.2	60.7	60.0	59.9	58.9	58.4	56.8

Source: H.V. Muhsam, "Mode of Life and Longevity in Israel," *Jewish Journal
of Sociology* (8, 1966): p. 41.

A number of factors were examined in an attempt to find an explanation for these surprising results. Since the author's own rank-order was based on socioeconomic status, this variable was no explanation. Socio-economic status did, however, coincide with life expectancies for Jews born in Asia and Africa for newcomers as well as old settlers. Another possible factor, differential environmental sanitation and preventive medicine, was ruled out. The fact that hospitalization rates were high for veteran settlers helped to explain the longevity of such immigrants from Asia and Africa but did not account for the lower life expectancy of their counterparts from Europe.

The author raised the simple question whether "survival of the fittest" could explain his results. Since non-Western immigrants received at best very poor medical services while living in Asia and Africa, the survivors would be the physically fit. However, while certain hereditary diseases are known to be more frequent among given ethnic groups and while the causes of death have been shown to differ according to national origin, there is no evidence that hereditary factors affect longevity among the groups under discussion. Varying dietary habits may account for differential incidence of some diseases, but they still do not explain the general pattern of morbidity. Interestingly, a larger percentage of persons of European origin were engaged in occupations which are essentially sedentary.

With no evidence to support any of the above explanations, the author is at a loss to explain his findings. Whatever the reasons, ethnicity, and not socioeconomic status, is highly correlated with longevity. The poorer groups among those of Asian-African origin actually live longer than do those placed higher financially who are of European origin.

MOBILITY

The basic cleavage in Israeli society is clearly seen in the class struc-ture where, due to their low level of education, Jews of Asian and African origin have little access to white-collar and professional jobs. Moreover, most of the Eastern Jews emigrated from backward coun-tries, where they had worked as small tradesmen or craftsmen. Since these occupations did not suit the need of the new country, the immigrants were directed to new jobs, many of which were dependent on seasonal and economic fluctuations. Lacking basic training, they were unable to secure clerical or skilled work, not to speak of the professions. Furthermore, these desirable jobs had already been manned by veterans of European origin.

The low work status of immigrants of Eastern origin naturally had an impact on their income, which still is considerably lower than that of Westerners.[8] The relationship between ethnicity and the level of occupation and income is illustrated by data published by the Israel Central Bureau of Statistics in 1970. It is seen that, in 1969, of all those holding professional positions only 15.8 percent were of Oriental origin, as opposed to 50.2 percent of European origin and 21.4 percent of the native-born. (The latter group consists of Jews of both Asian-African and European extraction.) Of all those working in business, the ethnic distribution of employees was: Asian and African origin, 30.4 percent; European origin, 57.1 percent; native-born, 12.4 percent. In jobs ranked at the bottom of the occupational hierarchy (construction, industry and the trades), Jews of Asian and African origin were overrepresented. For example, of all those in construction, 45 percent were of Eastern extraction compared to 32 percent of European extraction and 13 percent of the native-born.

Occupational Mobility

In studying inter-group differences, we need to make two comparisons: old-timers should be compared with newcomers, and Asian-African residents should be compared with those of Western origin. Due to the overlap of geographic origin and time of arrival in the country, the best analysis involves holding constant one of the two variables. Thus, we should compare Asian-African new immigrants to Asian-African old-timers and European new immigrants to European old-timers, and Asian-African new immigrants to Western new immigrants and Asian-African old-timers to Western old-timers.

Changes in the occupational distribution of Asian-African immigrants indicate the degree of success of absorption, yet it is of limited value in predicting long term change. This is because the immigrants of Asian-African origin are of a lower educational level than any other group in the population. The critical test is a comparison between the Israeli-born children whose parents immigrated from Europe with those whose parents came from Asia or Africa.

Virtually all the information on mobility comes from census data, which have been intensively analyzed by Judah Matras[9] and Moshe Lissak.[10]

Before examining mobility rates, the change in the pattern of labor force should be noted. If one looks at Table 22, it will be seen that during the years 1954-1961 the rate of labor force participation for new immigrants was lower than that of veteran residents, and that the rate of labor force participation of Asians and Africans was lower than that of the Europeans. There was a high rate of participation for women born in Israel.

Matras asked why there was little difference between women veteran residents and women immigrants of Asian-African descent. The most plausible explanation is that in these ethnic communities the women still do not go out to work. Since nonparticipation in the labor force is presumably related to the low level of education and high level of fertility, it is likely that girls of Eastern descent, who are becoming better educated nowadays, will bear fewer children and will not be content to be completely bound to the home.[11]

Moshe Lissak presents data on what he calls "class mobility on the occupational level."[12] As seen in Tables 23 and 24, there were changes between 1954 and 1965 in the occupational structure according to ethnicity and length of residence. Among the new Asian and African immigrants, a gradual and consistent abandonment of agricultural jobs was accompanied with an increased involvement in construction, industry and trades. For Asian-African old-timers, there was a decrease in agricultural work, an abandonment of sales and business jobs, and an increase in service occupations. In addition, European new immigrants abandoned agricultural jobs and moved into the professions and the low-grade white-collar jobs. A rather stable pattern for the European veterans was seen.

To complete his analysis, Lissak examined changes in the ethnic composition of occupational categories for the years 1954-1965. The criterion of change was an increase or decrease of 5 percent or more in the employment of a given ethnic group in an occupational category. As shown in the general schematic summary presented in Table 25, the Israeli-born increased their participation in agriculture and the professions. Fewer Asian-African old-timers were found in business, while the number of new Asian-African immigrants increased in all occupational categories except agriculture. The percentage of

TABLE 22

JEWISH POPULATION OF ISRAEL AGED 14+ BY SEX, PLACE OF BIRTH, AND DURATION OF RESIDENCE: LABOR FORCE PARTICIPATION RATES (PERCENT IN THE LABOR FORCE), 1954-1961

Place of Birth, and Duration of Residence	June 1954	Nov. 1955	June 1956	Average 1957	Average 1958	Average 1959	Average 1960	Average 1961
BOTH SEXES:								
Total-All Places of Birth	49.4	54.4	52.2	55.3	54.5	53.9	54.1	54.4
Born in Israel	43.5	51.8	47.5	53.1	50.5	50.7	49.7	52.7
Born in Europe-America								
Veteran Residents	60.3	61.7	60.6	62.7	61.7	61.8	62.8	61.6
New Immigrants	51.6	54.4	52.6	56.2	56.3	55.7	55.1	54.7
Born in Asia-Africa								
Veteran Residents	50.2	52.9	49.4	56.3	52.5	50.2	53.6	53.9
New Immigrants	43.8	47.9	46.5	48.0	48.6	48.8	49.2	50.2
MALES:								
Total-All Places of Birth	76.6	80.3	78.5	79.9	79.3	79.5	73.4	79.0
Born in Israel	59.1	64.9	61.5	66.1	62.9	64.2	62.5	67.1
Born in Europe-America								
Veteran Residents	91.5	91.0	89.5	90.5	89.3	89.5	89.1	88.9
New Immigrants	83.8	81.2	81.6	82.8	82.4	82.4	80.3	79.5
Born in Asia-Africa								
Veteran Residents	83.2	81.6	79.8	86.0	84.6	83.4	85.2	82.8
New Immigrants	74.5	76.3	73.9	73.9	75.7	77.0	76.0	77.4

TABLE 22 (cont.)

JEWISH POPULATION OF ISRAEL AGED 14+ BY SEX, PLACE OF BIRTH, AND DURATION OF RESIDENCE: LABOR FORCE PARTICIPATION RATES (PERCENT IN THE LABOR FORCE), 1954-1961

Place of Birth, and Duration of Residence	DATE							
	June 1954	Nov. 1955	June 1956	Average 1957	Average 1958	Average 1959	Average 1960	Average 1961
FEMALES:								
Total-All Places of Birth	21.7	27.9	25.3	30.4	29.4	28.0	29.5	29.4
Born in Israel	27.4	37.4	32.6	39.3	37.8	36.2	36.8	38.2
Born in Europe-America								
Veteran Residents	27.9	31.2	29.6	33.9	32.7	32.9	34.1	32.8
New Immigrants	21.5	28.3	25.5	31.2	30.9	29.7	32.0	30.6
Born in Asia-Africa								
Veteran Residents	15.2	21.9	18.2	22.9	(18.0)	17.8	19.2	21.5
New Immigrants	14.8	19.9	18.6	21.4	21.3	20.5	22.2	22.7

Source: 1955, 1957, 1958, 1959, 1960, 1961-Israel Central Bureau of Statistics, *Statistical Abstracts* (No. 10, 11, 1954); *LF Survey* (June, 1954): Table 7, p. 13; *LF Survey* (June, 1956): Table 11, pp. 22-23. Adopted from Judah Matras, *Social Change in Israel*. (Chicago: Aldine, 1965), p. 144.

TABLE 23

PERCENTAGE DISTRIBUTION OF ASIAN-AFRICAN BORN EMPLOYED PERSONS ACCORDING TO LENGTH OF RESIDENCE AND OCCUPATION, 1954-1965

	ASIAN-AFRICAN-BORN NEW IMMIGRANTS					ASIAN-AFRICAN-BORN OLD-TIMERS				
Year	Agriculture	Construction, Industry and Trades	Liberal professions and Bureaucracy	Business	Services	Agriculture	Construction, Industry and Trades	Liberal professions and Bureaucracy	Business	Services
1954	27.4	*19.5 +23.0 42.5	**9.7 (3.4)	7.1	11.8	7.4	*24.5 +21.0 45.5	13.6 (3.5)	15.7	12.6
1958	26.9	38.6	11.4 (3.9)	5.9	15.3	8.5	32.7	20.0 (6.2)	17.1	8.5
1961	22.3	41.0	10.3 (3.9)	5.9	17.7	11.6	32.8	18.0 (6.2)	16.0	11.1
1963	20.8	42.5	11.1 (4.2)	5.6	16.4	6.8	33.6	19.2 (4.1)	13.8	18.8
1965	20.9	45.1	14.7 (5.4)	5.8	16.1	5.1	35.7	24.5 (5.6)	9.3	19.0

Note: The figures do not add up to 100% since we chose only specific occupational categories.

*The upper number refers to skilled workers and the lower number refers to unskilled workers who partly (and it is not clear to what extent) did not work in this category; therefore we have to refer to this figure with care.

**The figure in parenthesis refers to the liberal professions while the upper number refers both to the liberal professions and the bureaucracy.

Source: Taken from M. Lissak, *Social Mobility in Israeli Society*. (Jerusalem: Israel Universities Press, 1969), p. 10.

TABLE 24

PERCENTAGE DISTRIBUTION OF EUROPEAN-AMERICAN EMPLOYED PERSONS ACCORDING TO LENGTH OF RESIDENCE AND OCCUPATION, 1954-1965

| | EUROPEAN-AMERICAN NEW IMMIGRANTS | | | | | EUROPEAN-AMERICAN OLD-TIMERS | | | | |
Year	Agriculture	Construction, Industry and Trades	Liberal professions and Bureaucracy	Business	Services	Agriculture	Construction, Industry and Trades	Liberal professions and Bureaucracy	Business	Services
1954	20.7	*27.1 +15.1 42.2	**21.9 (8.5)	11.4	10.0	9.5	23.4 +6.3 29.7	38.4 (15.4)	12.0	5.6
1958	12.7	33.9	24.8 (11.1)	10.7	13.2	10.4	26.0	37.9 (14.3)	10.9	9.0
1961	11.1	35.4	23.8 (12.0)	11.8	13.7	9.3	25.4	39.7 (17.4)	11.8	8.7
1963	9.5	32.6	31.4 (16.5)	8.8	13.5	8.3	24.1	38.8 (16.6)	10.9	9.3
1965	7.3	34.8	31.5 (15.2)	10.8	12.4	8.0	22.2	46.4 (18.7)	10.6	7.8

*The upper number refers to skilled workers and the lower number refers to unskilled workers who partly (and it is not clear to what extent) did not work in this category; therefore we have to refer to this figure with care.

**The figure in parenthesis refers to the liberal professions while the upper number refers both to the liberal professions and the bureaucracy.

Source: M. Lissak, *Social Mobility in Israeli Society*. (Jerusalem: Israel Universities Press, 1969), p. 11.

European-born old-timers decreased in all the occupations, while
European-born new immigrants increased their participation in
business and the professions.

TABLE 25
CHANGES AND STABILITY IN ETHNIC COMPOSITION OF
OCCUPATIONAL CATEGORIES, 1954-1965

	Agriculture	Industry	Business	Services	Liberal Professions
Israel Born	+	0	0	0	+
Asian-African born Old-timers	0	0	−	0	0
Asian-African born New Immigrants	0	+	+	+	+
European-American born Old Timers	−	−	−	−	−
European-American born New Immigrants	0	0	+	0	+

Note: + Indicates increase in the percentage of employed
      − Indicates decrease and drop-out
      0 Indicates stability
      Only increases or decreases of over or under 5% were recorded.

Source: M. Lissak, *Social Mobility in Israel.* (Jerusalem: Israel Universities
Press, 1969), p. 20.

Intergenerational Occupational Mobility

Matras' study of intergenerational mobility is based on information
supplied in 1955 by bridegrooms on their occupations and those of
their fathers (Table 26). These data reveal a relatively low proportion
of sons who followed the fathers' occupations. Fifty-seven percent
of the sons chose occupations different from that of their fathers,
while 43 percent followed the same occupations. The correspondance
between father and son was greater among the skilled and semi-skilled
categories (68 percent) and farmers (63 percent), and lower for professional (34 percent), clerical and sales (21 percent), and unskilled
(36 percent) occupations.

The analysis revealed that ethnicity and duration of residence had
little effect on the amount of intergenerational mobility. The greatest

TABLE 26

PERCENTAGE DISTRIBUTION OF JEWISH GROOMS, ISRAEL, 1955, BY FATHERS' AND OWN OCCUPATION GROUPS

Fathers' Occupation Groups	SONS' (GROOMS') OCCUPATION GROUPS					
	Prof., Tech., Management	Clerical, Sales	Skilled, Semi-Skilled	Unskilled	Farm	Total	Number
Professional, Technical, Management	33.82	15.43	32.16	5.39	13.20	100.0	538
Clerical, Sales	13.56	21.18	42.20	8.82	14.24	100.0	1,917
Skilled, Semi-skilled	4.42	8.25	67.57	9.23	10.53	100.0	1,539
Unskilled	1.95	6.44	47.91	35.80	7.90	100.0	1,025
Farm	3.82	5.03	23.96	4.51	62.68	100.0	576
Number	552	711	2,651	753	948		5,595
Occupational Distributions:							
Fathers	9.62	34.26	27.51	18.32	10.29	100.0	
Sons (Grooms)	9.87	12.71	47.38	13.10	16.94	100.0	

Source: Israel Central Bureau of Statistics, unpublished data for 1955. Taken from Judah Matras, *Social Change in Israel.* (Chicago: Aldine, 1965), p. 15.

ethnic change was found among children born to Western new immigrants (63 percent) and the least change among Asian-African new immigrants (57 percent). However, there were decided effects of ethnicity and duration of residence on the *direction* of intergenerational change. Western-born sons were more prone to enter the professions and technical occupations than were Asian-African sons. They also moved directly from low prestige to high prestige occupations. In contrast, sons of new Asian-African immigrants were more likely to be found among the unskilled than were sons from any other group.[13]

It should be noted that this study was conducted in 1955, seven years after the creation of the state. Thus not only is there no recent information on intergenerational mobility, but the research is limited to sons who had obviously been born abroad. The crucial comparison of Israeli-born sons of Western parents with Israeli-born sons of Asian-African parents is yet to be done.

The extent of intergenerational mobility in Israel was compared to that of other countries. Matras consolidated his data into three categories (manual, non-manual and farm), computed the proportion mobile according to these three categories, and (based on data given by Lipset and Bendix)[14] compared Israel's mobility rates to those of other countries (Table 27).[15] The conclusion is evident: among the countries cited, Israel has the highest proportion mobile. An unusual trend was also indicated, in that unlike other countries, the proportion in agriculture did not decrease as it did in white-collar occupations.

Economic Mobility

Family incomes between the years 1951-1960 have been analyzed by Giora Hanoch.[16] As shown in Table 28, the income of Asian-African families was consistently lower than that of Western families; it would appear that the income gap between Easterners and Westerners is increasing rather than decreasing. Since the average number of children among Asian-African families was greater than in Western families, mean per capita income might be a more sensitive index of income differential. Such a comparison did indeed disclose a more marked income difference.

Educational Mobility

The National Census of Nevember 1948 determined that 94 percent

TABLE 27

INTERGENERATIONAL OCCUPATIONAL MOBILITY IN
ISRAEL AND SELECTED INDUSTRIALIZED COUNTRIES:
OCCUPATIONAL DISTRIBUTIONS (PERCENT) OF SONS,
BY FATHERS' OCCUPATION GROUPS

Country and Fathers' Occupation Groups	SONS' OCCUPATION GROUPS			
	Non-Manual	Manual	Farm	Proportion Mobile
ISRAEL:				
Non-manual	38.0	48.0	14.0	
Manual	10.9	79.6	9.5	.579
Farm	8.8	28.5	62.7	
FRANCE:				
Non-manual	73.0	18.0	9.0	
Manual	35.0	55.0	10.0	.316
Farm	16.0	13.0	71.0	
GERMANY:				
Non-manual	58.0	38.0	4.0	
Manual	27.0	68.0	5.0	.349
Farm	19.0	28.0	54.0	
SWEDEN:				
Non-manual	74.0	23.0	3.0	
Manual	29.0	64.0	7.0	.439
Farm	23.0	42.0	35.0	
SWITZERLAND:				
Non-manual	84.0	13.0	3.0	
Manual	44.0	54.0	2.0	.307
Farm	27.0	19.0	54.0	
U.S.A.:				
Non-manual	64.0	34.0	1.0	
Manual	31.0	67.0	2.0	.464
Farm	24.0	46.0	30.0	
JAPAN:				
Non-manual	74.0	21.0	5.0	
Manual	33.0	59.0	8.0	.398
Farm	28.0	22.0	50.0	

Source: Israel Central Bureau of Statistics, unpublished marriage data
for 1955; other countries—S.M. Lipset and R. Bendix, *Social Mobility in
Industrial Society,* pp. 19-21. Taken from Judah Matras, *Social Change in
Israel.* (Chicago, Aldine, 1965), p. 159.

of the Jewish population was literate in at least one language, including Hebrew (Table 29). This high literacy rate was attributable to the large number of European-born; for while the Asian-African-born had approximately a 60 percent literacy rate, they comprised no more than 15 percent of the Jewish population.

While questions concerning literacy were not considered again until the 1961 census, a national sample survey in 1957 included such questions. It was seen that during the period of mass migration (1948-1954) the percentage of literates had declined. However, a comparison of the 1954 data with those of 1961 revealed a decrease in illiteracy among Asian-African-born boys, from 18.4 percent to 13.3 percent, and an increase in number of Asian-African-born studying in institutions of higher learning, from 0.5 to 3.5 percent. Still, the illiteracy rate of African-Asian-born remained high at 31 percent.

While there is evidence of educational mobility by the Oriental-born, there was clearly greater mobility among the European-born. In 1954, 1.8 percent of the new immigrants from the West received a higher education; by 1961 there was a rise to 11.6 percent. These statistics show that while children of Asian-African parents were becoming more successful in school, the difference between the Eastern and Western groups was not narrowing.

Unlike the United States, high school education is not compulsory beyond the second year, nor is it completely free.[17] Numerous scholarships are awarded, however, and a good but needy student is always helped to complete the four year course. Therefore, an increase in high school attendance on the part of Eastern children would be a good indication of mobility. Over the years there has been a marked growth in pupil enrollment in high school for children of both Eastern and of Western descent. For example, the percentage of youth aged fourteen to seventeen attending school increased from 43 percent in 1951-1952 to 61 percent in 1961-1962.

Table 30 presents high school attendance for the years 1956-1957, 1958-1959, and 1961-1962, according to the birthplace of the student. In each of these years there was an over-representation of Israeli-born (mainly of Western origin) and of European-born, and an under-representation of the Asian-African-born. On the other hand, comparisons between the years 1956-1957 and 1961-1962 revealed that the percentage of Israeli-born attending high school increased by less than

TABLE 28

FAMILY INCOMES ACCORDING TO COUNTRY OF BIRTH; FAMILIES OF SALARIED URBAN WORKERS, 1951-1960

Country of birth	AVERAGE INCOME (I.L. per month)				INDEXES (Total: 100)			
	March 1951	1954	1956/57	October 1959-March 1960	March 1951	1954	1956/57	October 1959-March 1960
National average	78.0	216.0	274.2	373.3	100	100	100	100
Asia-Africa: Total	69.3	164.7	214.9	282.6	88.8	76.2	78.4	75.7
Iraq, Iran	76.1	181.8	218.4	—	97.6	84.2	79.6	—
Yemen, Aden	61.7	147.5	191.8	—	79.1	68.3	69.9	—
North Africa	69.5	162.7	199.9	—	89.1	75.3	72.9	—
Other countries in Asia-Africa	—	175.3	230.6	—	81.1	81.1	84.1	—
Europe-America: Total	78.9	233.0	294.5	418.4	101.2	107.9	107.4	112.1
Poland, Russia	80.7	238.5	306.3	—	103.5	110.4	111.7	—
Rumania, Bulgaria, Yugoslavia, Greece	69.5	200.4	258.0	—	89.1	92.8	94.1	—
Other countries in Europe-America	84.8	265.8	310.3	—	108.7	123.1	113.2	—
Israel-born: Total	80.3	223.9	288.5	416.2	102.9	103.7	105.2	111.5
Father Asian-African born	—	—	261.7	—	—	—	95.4	—
Father European-American born	—	—	324.7	—	—	—	118.4	—
Gap: Asia-Africa/Europe-America (in percentages)					88	71	73	68
Cost of living index (100: IX/1951)	93	220	254	280				

Source: Giora Hanoch, "Hevdeley Haknasot be Israel" (Income differences in Israel), Falk Center Report No. 5, Table 4, p. 47

3 percent, while the percentage of Asian-African-born increased by 12 percent. These figures, then, point to a relative improvement in the educational mobility of the Asian-African-born. However, it should also be kept in mind that the relative number of fourteen to seventeen year-olds of Asian-African origin attending high school was low. Although Eastern children constituted 35 percent of the population in 1961, only 13 percent of them were attending post-primary school.

TABLE 29
PERCENTAGE OF LITERATES IN JEWISH POPULATION
(1948, 1954, 1957)

	Total	Males	Females
JEWS			
1948 (aged 15 and over)	93.7	96.8	90.4
1954 (aged 15 and over)[1]	85.0	91.8	78.3
Old-timers[2]	92.0	95.9	88.2
Israel born	95.2	98.0	92.7
Asian-African born	62.9	78.2	46.8
European-American born	97.1	99.0	95.2
New Immigrants	78.6	88.0	69.7
Asian-African born	59.3	77.5	42.2
European-American born	95.5	97.4	93.7
1957 (aged 14 and over)	85.6	90.9	80.4
Old-timers[2]	93.8	96.2	91.3
Israel born	96.1	97.4	94.8
Asian-African born	68.5	81.7	53.3
European-American born	97.4	98.6	96.4
New Immigrants	78.3	86.0	71.0
Asian-African born	60.6	74.8	46.9
European-American born	95.0	97.2	93.0
OTHERS			
1954 (aged 15 and over)[1]	42.8	64.1	21.0
1957 (aged 14 and over)	46.9	70.1	23.4

[1] Percentage of those who attended school
[2] Israel born and immigrants until 1947
Source: *Israel Statistieal Yearbook.* (No. 1957-1958), Table 21, p. 364.

Data on the background of students studying for a bachelor's degree in 1963-1964 showed that 7.5 percent were Asian-African-born, 15 percent European-born, and the rest Israeli-born. The percentage

TABLE 30
SECONDARY SCHOOL STUDENTS ACCORDING TO BIRTHPLACE:
PERCENTAGE DISTRIBUTION ACCORDING TO TYPE OF SCHOOL, 1956-57, 1958-59, 1961-62

CONTINENT OF BIRTH AND YEAR OF STUDY

Type of School	All birthplaces			Israel born			Asian-African born			European-American born		
	1956/57	1958/59	1961/62	1956/57	1958/59	1961/62	1956/57	1958/59	1961/62	1956/57	1958/59	1961/62
Total number of students in secondary schools	100.0	100.0	100.0	100.0	100.0	100.0	100.0	100.0	100.0	100.0	100.0	100.0
General high schools (day)	42.3	45.2	48.1	45.7	48.8	48.0	25.0	30.9	32.2	46.6	46.6	58.2
Secondary schools (night)	7.1	6.6	5.8	5.6	5.2	5.0	11.9	12.2	10.8	8.3	6.3	3.9
Continuation classes	16.2	13.8	10.5	17.7	15.3	15.2	12.1	10.5	6.0	14.1	11.6	5.5
Trade schools	16.8	19.0	17.6	17.0	18.2	17.0	16.9	21.7	19.6	16.2	19.2	17.5
Agricultural schools	13.3	9.5	8.0	9.2	6.0	7.1	31.5	19.1	12.3	11.2	12.0	7.2
Teachers seminars	4.3	5.9	4.1	4.8	6.5	5.3	2.6	5.6	3.3	3.6	4.3	2.5
Other secondary schools	—	—	5.9	—	—	2.4	—	—	15.8	—	—	5.2

Source: M. Lissak, *Social Mobility in Israeli Society*. (Jerusalem: Israel Universities Press, 1969), p. 40.

of the latter group of Asian-African descent is not known. According to a survey of the Central Bureau of Statistics in 1966, of those being awarded academic degrees, 80.4 percent were European-born, 13.5 percent Israeli-born, and 6.1 percent Asian-African-born.[18]

In summary, these data on ethnic mobility show that children of Asian-African parents are improving their status in each of the three areas discussed: occupation, income and education. However, the mobility of youths of Western origin is considerably more pronounced than that of youths of Eastern origin. The ethnic gap seems to be widening.

Mobility in Development Towns

The development towns are of special interest for several reasons. First of all, these towns were established after the mass immigration of the 1950s. They are populated almost exclusively by Asian-African immigrants. Due to controlled planning and organization by the absorption authorities, the towns have similar conditions of employment, services and educational facilities. In this relatively homogeneous context, differences in the adaptability of various Eastern ethnic groups are noteworthy. Moreover, since Jews of European extraction as well as some native-born Israelis are also found there (albeit in smaller numbers), a comparison between groups of different geographic origins is possible. Finally, one should keep in mind that the population in these towns is about one quarter of the total Jewish population of Israel.

In October 1965 a survey of the development town Kiryat Malachi was published.[19] The majority of the population had immigrated to Israel after 1948. Since 1964 its population distribution according to country of origin was as follows: Africa—56.2 percent; Asia—36.3 percent; Europe— 6.7 percent. Twenty-eight percent of the total population was illiterate, 55 percent had received an elementary education only, and a mere 15 percent were high school graduates.

There was virtually no upward mobility in Kiryat Malachi. Only a few of the workers had acquired specific training, and there were but few who thought they had a chance for occupational advancement. The greatest satisfactions with one's work was found among the skilled workers; the unskilled workers were the least satisfied (Table 31). A remarkably low rate of occupational aspiration was found for the town as a whole. Only 22 percent evinced an interest in job advancement, 15 percent were apathetic, and 63 percent showed no concern whatsoever in occupational training. The highest hopes for occupational mobility were found among the workers who had been brought up and educated in Israel. Attitude toward job advancement was found to be related to occupational status; those better off were more optimistic.

TABLE 31
PERCENTAGE DISTRIBUTION OF SATISFACTION WITH
WORK ACCORDING TO OCCUPATION

	Pct.
Skilled workers in industry and craft	68
Skilled workers in building	68
Unskilled workers in building	59
Unskilled workers in services	61
Unskilled workers in industry and crafts	56
Unskilled workers in agriculture	39

Source: *Adjustment to the Physical and Social Environment in a Development Settlement — Kiryat Malachi.* (Jerusalem: Ministry of Housing, 1965), p. 23, mimeographed.

Dimona, another development town, was studied in 1969.[20] Many of the 19,250 residents were immigrants who had been brought there by the absorption authorities immediately upon their arrival in Israel. The group which had not chosen to live in Dimona actually remained there longer than those who had voluntarily gone to live there. Three-quarters of the families were of Eastern origin (half of the population came from Morocco), 20 percent were of European origin, and 5 percent were native-born.

The average family in Dimona was larger than the average Israeli family: a quarter of the town's families consisted of more than seven members each. There were twice as many illiterates in Dimona as there were in the total Jewish population. The low standard of education was a major factor in the constant unemployment, as 90 percent of those seeking jobs were unskilled workers. Downward mobility was experienced by no fewer than 40 percent of Dimona's population.

The adolescents, who for the most part were without occupational training, suffered a high rate of unemployment. Seventeen percent of the boys between the ages of fourteen and seventeen were unemployed and did not attend school. Among girls the rate was an even higher 22.4 percent (Table 32). In spite of the trend to drop out from the labor market and to continue the father's pattern of unemployment, there was a tendency (although limited) towards upward mobility among members of the second generation. As many as 69 percent of the boys and 64 percent of the girls were studying, the majority receiving occupational training within the framework of the schools. Still, the secondary education which these young people received was geared more to the acquisition of essential training for skilled work, rather than to general education. (This trend existed among youth brought up in the cities as well; Michael Chen in his research on the choice of high schools among Tel Aviv elementary school graduates disclosed a similar trend among lower-class children of Eastern origin.)[21]

TABLE 32
PERCENTAGE DISTRIBUTION OF ADOLESCENTS (AGED 14-17) IN DIMONA ACCORDING TO OCCUPATION AND SEX

Sex	Percent	Studying	Working or Seeking Work	Neither Studying nor Working
Boys	100	69	13.9	17.1
Girls	100	64	13.6	22.4

Source: Dimona, *Social-Economic Development.* (Jerusalem: Ministry of Housing, 1969), p. 45.

Aspirations for their children's higher education was directly related to the parents' own level of education; the higher it was the greater their interest in their children's learning. However, the attitudes varied according to country of origin. All of the native-born parents wished their children to attend college, in comparison to 67 percent of the European parents. Expression of interest in education was especially low among parents of Asian-African origin.

A readiness to leave one's town and move to a more highly developed area would signify interest in upward mobility. The rate of those wishing to leave Dimona was highest among the younger segment of European

extraction. Residents with a higher standard of education and a higher
level of income indicated greater readiness to leave the town. Those
of Asian-African descent, although earning less, were not inclined to
leave, probably because of the uncertainty as to their chances for
economic improvement in another place. Attachment to the extended
family group also prevented many from moving; i.e., kinship relations
were preferred to chances of upward mobility outside the town. In
fact, many of the residents of Eastern extraction who had come to
live in Dimona of their own free will had done so not because of
economic motives but for family reasons.

Conditions of social and economic adjustment in small development towns were explored in a study conducted in 1968 by Yehudah
Don, Hagit Hovav, and Leonard Weller.[22] The towns included in the
sample were chosen as representatives of ecological regions. Or Akiva
and Yavneh are in the central part of the country, while Netivot is
in the south and Shlomi in the north. The populations of Shlomi
and Netivot were ethnically homogeneous, while those of Or Akiva
and Yavneh were heterogeneous.

The participants in the study, over 1,000 heads of households,
were selected at random. The interview touched upon several problems
relating to attitudes and ambitions in the occupational field, evaluation
of present occupation, desired occupational status, perceived chances
for promotion, relative economic level, resources for consumption,
and spending patterns.

The majority of the inhabitants of these towns were of North
African or Asian extraction; in Shlomi this group constituted 97
percent of the population, in Yavneh 90 percent, in Netivot 94 percent,
and in Or Akiva 61 percent. Fifty-six percent of the breadwinners were
Moroccan Jews, 15 percent were from other North African countries,
13 percent were of Middle Eastern or Asian extraction, and 16 percent
were of European origin or had been born in Israel. In the areas remote
from the center of Israel, the North African element constituted the
majority of the population, 94 percent in Shlomi and 93 percent in
Netivot. An average of ten years had passed since these families had
immigrated to Israel. While most of the Moroccan and European
families settled in these towns immediately or soon after immigration,
the Tunisian, Libyan, Persian and Egyptian immigrants moved there
quite some time after they had immigrated.

The average age of breadwinners was a relatively high forty-six
years of age. Only 8 percent of the heads of households had reached
Israel when under fourteen years of age. The fact that the majority of
men immigrated at a fairly advanced age must have added to their
social problems.

The residents of these towns had received little formal education,
an average of four years, which fell far below the average for the Jewish
population in Israel, which in 1968 (the time of the study) was eight
years. Furthermore, the percentage of illiteracy among the populations
studied was six times as great as the average of the Israeli population.
Even among the younger heads of households the educational level
was low, although somewhat higher than that of their elders.

The age as well as the low educational standard of these interviewees affected their occupational level and income. In the twenty-
nine-and-under age-group the percentage of nonskilled workers reached
34 percent, compared with 60 percent in the sixty-plus age group.

The residents of these four development towns failed to merge into
the modern occupational system of Israel. The lack of any specific
vocational training among the majority of the breadwinners forced
them into nonskilled migratory labor. A sudden decline in the country's
economy could turn them into unemployed persons on welfare. It is
not surprising that they displayed little economic initiative and tended
to become dependent on relief.

Distinct differences were revealed between the occupations previously
held by immigrants in their countries of origin and those held in Israel.
The most pronounced changes were felt by those from Iran, Iraq and
Morocco. Approximately one-third of the Moroccan group had been
employed in some form of commerce in their country of origin as compared to 5 percent in Israel. Moreover, 3 percent of the Moroccan immigrants had been formerly employed in agriculture, as compared with 40
percent currently so engaged in Israel. Since the status of the agricultural
worker in Morocco was extremely low, this change of occupation caused
many Moroccan immigrants to feel that their social status had been lowered.
This anti-agriculture ethic was opposed to the outlook of the early pioneers
who had immigrated to Israel with the ideal of working the land.

The change in the immigrant's occupation was obviously affected by
his educational level. The uneducated group, which had been employed
in trade in its country of origin, was now employed in relief work. The

number of illiterates absorbed in industrial work, manual labor, and building in Israel was small in comparison with the number employed in these fields abroad. The percentage of factory, building, and manual workers with a background of postelementary schooling had increased in comparison with the rate in their country of origin. The percentage of white-collar workers in this group had decreased in Israel.

These findings demonstrate a condition typical of immigrants from Moslem countries, where a person of average education was able to attain a fairly high occupational and social status. In Israel his abilities and educational level did not measure up to the standard in many occupational categories.

The participants compared their individual economic situation in Israel with that of their country of origin. Fifty-four percent indicated that they had lowered their economic status following immigration. For 19 percent the economic status had not changed, while 27 percent had improved their situation. Variables which did affect changes in the immigrants' occupational status were length of residence in Israel and income. The more recent immigrants to Israel claimed that their economic status had declined in this country, where the hardships of economic and social adjustment were still particularly acute.

Having ascertained that the majority of workers were employed in nonskilled or semi-skilled jobs, the investigators turned their attention to job satisfaction. Forty-seven percent of the participants declared that they were satisfied with their jobs, an additional 9 percent were satisfied with reservations, and 44 percent claimed no job satisfaction whatsoever.

Job satisfaction was found to be lowest in the Moroccan group. Only 40 percent of the Moroccans were satisfied as compared with 50 percent in the Tunisian, Libyan, Yemenite, Iraqi and Persian groups. The highest rate of job satisfaction was found among European immigrants (60 percent) and was probably related to their higher wages.

Job preference was also studied. The question posed in this connection was: "Taking your skill and experience into consideration, which job would you prefer if you could choose your occupation?" The responses varied according to age, educational level, national origin and time elapsed since immigration. In the 40-50 age-group a tendency existed to prefer business and white-collar work, while in the younger 20-30 age-group the majority preferred building and factory work, which were the main occupational branches in the development towns. These realistic and modest desires on the part of the younger men were not confined to Orientals in development towns. As studies of Leah Adar and Chaim Adler[23] and of Moshe Lissak[24] have shown, moderate, realistic aspirations are typical of youth in the big cities as well. It was as if, in the determination of occupational ambitions, the younger age-group feels part of Israeli society while the parents still think in terms of their country of origin.

The responses to the question of job preference according to country of origin is of special interest (Table 33). While all the ethnic

TABLE 33
OCCUPATIONAL ASPIRATIONS ACCORDING
TO COUNTRY OF ORIGIN

Desired Occupation	Total	Morocco	Tunisia Libya	Yemen	Iraq Iran	Europe
Total	100.0	100.0	100.0	100.0	100.0	100.0
Services	7.9	7.8	6.6	5.3	9.7	9.2
Building and Factory Work	40.2	36.7	46.7	39.5	45.2	45.0
Selling	29.4	34.2	26.2	18.4	29.0	18.3
Agriculture and Afforestation	8.8	10.3	7.4	15.8	3.2	5.0
White-Collar Jobs	13.7	11.0	13.1	21.1	12.9	22.5

x^2 = 38.82 df. = 20 p $<$.001

Source: Y. Don, H. Hovav and L. Weller, *Social and Economic Adjustment in Small Development Towns.* (Ramat-Gan: Bar-Ilan University, 1970), p. 185, mimeographed.

groups rejected low-status service jobs in favor of vocational work, industry, and building, the Yemenites and the Europeans showed the greatest interest in white-collar jobs. A similar trend was observed among school children by Adar and Adler in their study on occupational values among immigrant children. They also found that boys of Eastern extraction selected vocational occupations, whereas those of European extraction chose the professions. Their summary statement describes the present findings as well: "The selection of occupation in the group studied (boys of Oriental extraction) is more realistic than that of the control group (boys from Western families). The focus on the skilled vocational worker reflects a degree of social mobility well within the bounds of a concrete and logical level of ambition."[25]

Mobility in Urban Areas

At the request of the Prime Minister's office, several sociologists and educators prepared a report in January 1965 dealing with the youth problem of the Morasha district in the center of Jerusalem.[26] This area was distinguished by the low level of its housing, income, and education. Almost 80 percent of the inhabitants were of Asian or African extraction. Two-thirds had immigrated to Israel between 1948 and 1952 and were considered settled immigrants, the majority belonging to the working class.

The study was mainly concerned with the young people who grew up in the district and constituted some 10 percent of its 4,000 inhabitants. These youths were educated for the main part in Israel, but they still belonged to a marginal society retaining values and guiding principles of their countries of origin. Their proximity to the urban centers, the investigators believed, would lead to a high and unrealistic level of ambition. A state of conflict would ensue because of the clash between ambitions engendered by this contact and the youths' poor potential for realizing them. Frustration and deviant behavior were therefore anticipated.

Half of the youth of the Morasha district were engaged in non-skilled work. A number of questions were put to these young people for the purpose of examining attitudes and conceptions of their future occupational and social status. The results were similar to those reached in studies of mobility aspirations among Oriental youths in development towns. They too saw their social status as similar to that of their parents. Despite the many years before them, these youths had no anticipation for any significant change in occupational level; as nonskilled workers they regarded their work as permanent, not as a transitory phase of

their occupational career. Nevertheless, within their designated level
they anticipated a small degree of progress. This tendency towards a
low and realistic level of ambition could also be discerned from the
fact that 85 percent of the youths preferred a low-income permanent
position to a higher-income temporary job.

Sixty percent of the youths saw their lack of education and ability
as most obstructive to progress and success, while another 15 percent blamed discrimination, short period of residence in Israel, or the
low prestige of their country of origin. Thus it would appear that most
of the youth seemed to have accepted the values of the wider Israeli
society, regarding individual ability and education as the prerequisites
of mobility. They failed to realize these and were quite resigned to
the marginal position they occupied. Thirty percent of the youths
attended high school for only a short period of time. The dropout
was highest among those attending academic high schools and less
among those attending vocational high schools. A large portion of
the students attended night or vocational schools, spending most of
their time at work. They barely exploited available facilities for
vocational training in spite of the fact that they knew that therein
lay their chief means of mobility.

In south Tel Aviv there is a quarter named Kfar Shalem that
resembles the Morasha district in its demographic, economic, and
social structure. The district was studied by Abraham Nadad in
1955.[27] Over 90 percent of the inhabitants were of Asian and African
extraction. Sixty percent immigrated to Israel before 1948. The housing
situation in the district was extremely bad and the density of living
quarters reached a rate of 3.5 persons to a room. Some 60 percent of
the men, 70 percent of their wives, and 25 percent of the youth aged
14-20 had completed four years or less of formal education. Forty
percent of the inhabitants were nonskilled workers and 20 percent
of the heads of families were unemployed.

The 14-20 age-group accounted for some 10 percent of the overall population of Kfar Shalem. The relatively long period of residence
of the population in Israel provided a basis for the assumption that
the youth would value education as an avenue to mobility, and that
they would willingly make use of vocational training facilities and
proficiency courses. Thus it was expected that intergenerational
mobility would be high.

A slight improvement had in fact occurred in the educational level of the youths aged 14-20 as compared with a group that was ten years older (20-30), but the difference was insignificant (Table 34).

TABLE 34
EDUCATIONAL LEVEL OF MORASHA YOUTH
ACCORDING TO AGE (PERCENTAGES)

	AGE	
Education	14-20	20-30
No Schooling	6.0	12.2
1-4 yrs.	18.7	26.6
5 or 6 yrs.	10.0	12.2
7 yrs.	5.6	10.0
Completed Elementary School	21.7	31.3
Agricultural High School	—	—
Vocational High School	1.0	1.1
Academic High School	2.4	3.3
Other	1.6	3.3
Still Learning	22.6	—
No Answer	10.4	—

Source: A. Nadad, "The Village of Shalem—Image of a Poor Neighborhood," *Megamot* (7, 1956): pp. 15, 16.

Among the 20-30 year-old group, 38.8 percent did not finish the fourth grade, compared to 24.7 among the 14-20 age-group. One conclusion to be drawn from these data, therefore, is that over one quarter of these youths lacked basic prerequisites for advancement. They could not rise even within a limited range of mobility.

The educational facilities were definitely not suited to the elementary school graduates, and this is a special source of concern. Most of the youths in both age-groups had no vocational training whatsoever. The high rate of unemployment was striking, reaching to one-third of the local youth.

In summarizing his findings, Nadad writes: "The youths fail to break through the poverty cycle, and are bound by their parental heritage. These youths are the breadwinners of the future. If no serious steps are taken towards their vocational training we shall have no basis to suppose that their occupational situation will be better than is that of their parents today."[28]

As an ecological unit, Kfar Shalem is fairly typical of the other poverty areas in the big cities in Israel, although it may be somewhat more problematical. Nonetheless, both the data of Kfar Shalem and those of the Morasha district (collected a decade after the Kfar Shalem study) testify to the lack of intergenerational mobility among the lower class youth of Oriental extraction. The youths did not adequately utilize educational institutions, neither to attain a proper education nor to acquire a vocation. The level of ambition and expectation was extremely low and, one is tempted to say, too realistic. There were no signs of mobility beyond the level of non-skilled workers. The youths in these slums were resigned to their marginal status and lack of prestige and influence in Israeli society.

The exploration of the manner of imparting values in schools for immigrant children was the aim of Leah Adar and Chaim Adler in a study conducted during the years of 1960-1964.[29] The research was carried out among 533 eighth grade students, chiefly immigrants from Islamic countries, who attended secular and religious schools in large cities, development towns and immigrant settlements. A control group was included consisting of six eighth-grade classes from schools in which most pupils were native-born and of Western origin. The economic status of the children's families showed that the majority of the fathers in the research group were unskilled workers (only 1 percent were professionals) compared with 20 percent of the control group. The educators' values were likewise assessed to determine to what extent the values which were taught reflected their own goals. The teachers, moreover, ranked the same values as did the students. The affinity between the parents' attitudes and those of their children was also studied by interviewing a hundred parents of children from the research group. Attitudes toward interpersonal behavior, nationality, work, religion, citizenship, study, education, and leisure were studied. The relative emphasis given by the school to the values in their different areas was examined by calculating the number of times a particular value was mentioned by the teacher or the student during class proceedings (Table 35).

TABLE 35
PERCENTAGE DISTRIBUTION OF VALUES ACCORDING TO AREA AND AVERAGE NUMBER OF RECURRENCES IN ONE LESSON

	Sum Total of Elements	Percentage Distribution			Average No. of Elements per Lesson	
		Rel. Schools	Non-Rel. Schools	Sum Total	Rel. Schools	Non-Rel. Schools
Nationality	186	34	34	34	0.82	1.00
Citizenship	99	16	20	18	0.38	0.58
Interpersonal Relationship	90	15	18	16	0.36	0.51
Religion	81	22	8	15	0.54	0.24
Study and Education	44	7	9	8	0.17	0.26
Work	21	2	5	4	0.05	0.15
Personal Characteristics	20	3	5	4	0.06	0.13
Leisure and Nature	7	1·	1	1	0.04	0.03
Total	548	100.0	100.0	100.0	2.42	2.90

Source: Leah Adar and Chaim Adler, *Education for Values in Schools for Immigrant Children.* (Jerusalem: School of Education of the Hebrew University, 1965), p. 38.

As shown, the schools emphasized the importance of nationalism, but were less concerned with the value of work and the importance of personality characteristics (such as will power, the ability to overcome difficulties, dedication, and the use of leisure time). The schools' disregard for the inculcation of values concerning education and work severely affected children of Eastern extraction. These pupils were mostly sons of unskilled workers whose homes did not encourage or direct them towards the acquisition of knowledge and the search for occupational satisfaction. No guidance in choosing a course of further studies and work was available for such youths, so they reached the labor market without incentives.

A number of questions were asked of the students in order to obtain their attitude toward work and occupation. "A young man has won a lottery and now has a considerable sum of money, sufficient for the rest of his life. Should he stop working? Why?" Table 36 shows the differences in the attitudes of the research and control groups. Almost 35 percent of the research group approved of work on the grounds that "his money will be exhausted," the same reason given by 28 percent of the children of the control group. That work is a preventive measure against social degeneration was most often cited by the control group (42.6 percent) and least often by the research group (21.9 percent).

TABLE 36
"THE LOTTERY WINNER"—
PERCENTAGE DISTRIBUTION OF ANSWERS

Answers	RESEARCH GROUP		CONTROL GROUP
	Easterners	Westerners	
1. He should continue to work, because:			
a) his money will be exhausted	34.9	34.4	27.7
b) idleness breeds degeneration or crime	21.9	34.3	42.6
c) idleness and sin weaken the body	17.2	11.2	8.4
d) work is more interesting, idleness is dull	7.5	8.4	15.3
2. Miscellaneous	12.3	10.3	5.7
3. There is nothing wrong in his stopping to work	6.2	1.4	0.4
Total	100.0	100.0	100.0

Source: Leah Adar and Chaim Adler, *Education for Values in Schools for Immigrant Children.* (Jerusalem: School of Education of the Hebrew University, 1965), p. 87.

Work for reasons of satisfaction and interest was most frequently cited by children from the control group: 15.3 percent approved of work for this reason, compared with 7.5 percent of the children from the research group. Denying the need for work for its own sake was more common in the group of Eastern children, accounting for 6.2 percent of their answers compared with 1.4 percent in the control group.

Parents of Eastern origin held more intrinsic attitudes towards work than did their children. Sixty-two percent approved of work for moral reasons (corresponding to 30.7 percent of the children) and 22 percent gave instrumental reasons for working (corresponding to 35.5 percent of the children). Only 2 percent of the parents denied the need for work (compared with 11.7 percent of the children).

The students were asked to give their reasons for choosing a particular occupation. We learn from Table 37 that those of Western origin in both groups tended to disregard external and materialistic factors when considering their future occupation, stressing rather satisfaction and personal inclination for the work. Children of Eastern origin consistently referred to income, status and permanency in work as the focal factors determining occupational choice; they were little concerned with satisfaction and personal inclination.

The different approach to mobility was illustrated by occupational preference. The children of the control group held an unrealistically high level of aspirations. Seventy-five percent chose the professions, whereas only 19 percent of their parents were professionals (Table 38). Children in the research group, on the other hand, tended to choose skilled labor, which was also symptomatic of social mobility, since 68.5 percent of their parents were unskilled workers. Clearly, this mobility was restricted, determined as it was by realistic, moderate considerations.

The children's attitude to the prestige attached to each of the occupations was studied by means of the following question: "Here is a list of several professions: bank clerk, teacher, kibbutz member, soldier, mechanic, merchant, engineer. Underline the two most respected." The distribution of answers to this question is given in Table 39.

An important finding concerns the children of the research group who were of Eastern origin. Most ranked mechanic very low in the order of prestige, although more than 50 percent saw skilled work as their future occupation. Thus the youth of Eastern extraction had no illusions concerning their future: they saw themselves working on the same level as their parents throughout their lives.

TABLE 37
OCCUPATIONAL CHOICE AND WORK SATISFACTION

Questions and Answers	RESEARCH GROUP		CONTROL GROUP
	Easterners	Westerners	
Open question (explanation for occupational choice)			
a) Interested in, or fond of, the occupation	38.0	52.5	63.4
b) Reasons related to the contents of the occupation	12.9	17.9	23.4
c) External reasons: the occupation is respectable, paying, permanent, easy, convenient, etc.	45.9	26.4	10.9
d) National reasons	3.2	3.2	2.3
Total	100.0	100.0	100.0
Closed question (the work the child chooses should be:)			
a) Satisfying	31.4	50.0	81.5
b) Respectable and important	61.9	40.0	15.2
Total	93.3	90.0	96.7
Closed question (when are people satisfied with work)			
a) When it is interesting and appeals to them	47.8	60.0	81.5
b) When it is lucrative	44.4	37.5	18.5
Total	92.2	97.5	100.0

Source: Leah Adar and Chaim Adler, *Education for Values in Schools for Immigrant Children.* (Jerusalem: School of Education of the Hebrew University, 1965), p. 90.

TABLE 38
OCCUPATIONAL CHOICES OF BOYS AND GIRLS (PERCENTAGES)

Desired Occupation	RESEARCH GROUP		CONTROL GROUP
	Easterners	Westerners	
Boys:			
Professions, Management	10.9	28.1	75.7
Teaching	12.0	11.0	2.4
Clerical Work, Commerce	7.4	4.7	3.6
Skilled Work	53.2	50.0	17.1
Pilot, Officer	3.4	4.7	1.2
Agriculturist	5.1	1.5	—
Miscellaneous	8.0	—	—
Total	100.0	100.0	100.0
N	(175)	(64)	(82)
Girls:			
Professions, Management	3.7	19.9	35.3
Teaching	29.7	37.2	47.2
Clerical Work	17.9	13.9	8.0
Handiwork (dressmaker)	20.0	17.9	1.1
Nurse	15.0	10.0	6.0
Agriculturist, Miscellaneous	3.7	2.0	2.4
Total	100.0	100.0	100.0
N	(134)	(51)	(88)

Source: Leah Adar and Chaim Adler, *Education for Values in Schools for Immigrant Children.* (Jerusalem: School of Education of the Hebrew University, 1965), p. 91.

TABLE 39
OCCUPATIONAL PRESTIGE (PERCENTAGES)

Occupation	RESEARCH GROUP Easterners	Westerners	CONTROL GROUP
Teacher	40.5	36.0	28.5
Soldier	28.7	30.7	38.9
Engineer	19.9	24.1	19.6
Bank clerk	6.6	2.2	1.4
Kibbutz member	3.9	7.0	11.2
Merchant	0.3	0.0	0.3
Mechanic	0.0	0.0	0.0
Total	100.0	100.0	100.0

Source: Leah Adar and Chaim Adler, *Education for Values in Schools for Immigrant Children.* (Jerusalem: School of Education of the Hebrew University, 1965), p. 93.

CONCLUSION

As Eisenstadt shows in his seminal analysis of Israeli society, the establishment of the state brought major changes in social organizations: the growth in manpower, the arrival of new immigrants of varied social backgrounds, continuous economic development which led to social and economic differentiation and gave rise to new patterns of mobility, and the use of political power as a source of social status. The new social reality could not mesh with the pioneering ideology.

The research in this chapter relates to the question of the class situation in Israel today. Unfortunately, while a fair amount of research has been conducted on this topic, much of it is not new. Studies carried out in the mid-1950s and even those in the mid-1960s, may already be outdated. Nevertheless, several patterns seem to emerge from the various findings.

Israel is not the classless society it had once hoped to become. There is a growing interest in consumption, and a growing concern with raising the standard of living. The percentage of the population owning refrigerators and washing machines has increased considerably. This statistic has much more significance here than in America, for it must be noted that in this country the high "luxury" tax on all electrical apparatus is often over 200 percent of the retail price. The Government is compelled to impose such taxes because of its heavy defense budget. (A personal note: a soldier interviewed by the writer at the Suez Canal said, "I used to complain about the heavy taxes; but now that I see how much it costs to keep us here, I won't complain any more."). Percentage of income spent on food has declined, while expenditures for health and education have increased. Certainly the economic situation has improved for the whole population in spite of the burdensome taxes.

Given the increased desire for material goods, coupled with an increase in the standard of living, it is not startling to learn that the former societal values of pioneering and agriculture have weakened.

Surprisingly little empirical research has been undertaken to disclose the new values. Moshe Lissak's research, in which urban youth rated numerous occupations, is the most informative. The most highly esteemed occupations were academic and political (on the national level), while manual labor was accorded low status. His data were collected in 1957-1958, but it is reasonable to assume that these perceptions have become hardened with time.

The professions, too, have changed. Joseph Ben-David has shown that the position of the professional before 1948 was one of the worst in the world, a result of the poor supply and demand as well as the employment of a large percentage of professionals by public bureaucracies. While the growth of the economy resulted in a need for more professionals, and the decline in pioneering values boosted their status, their financial position is still not favorable.[30]

Until recently class crystallization was minimal. One demonstration of this is the Rivkah Bar-Yosef and Dorit Padan study, which showed that 51 percent of the population belonged to the lowest educational level and 33 percent were on the lowest income level. The school situation is also illustrative of the lack of status crystallization. Many school principals do not hold a B.A. degree. At the elementary school level a minority of teachers has graduated from college, although a B.A. degree is required at the high school level. However, the stiuation is rapidly improving as a B.A. degree is now required for teaching in the junior and high schools. This is a reasonable requirement today, as it is now possible for relatively large numbers to attend any of the four universities offering a B.A.

degree. When the state was founded in 1948 there was only one institution of higher education which granted an undergraduate degree in the liberal arts. Due to the relatively smaller proportion of Israelis who study for a college degree, the B.A. is of higher value here than it is in America. It is becoming a requirement for most higher echelon, nonmanual jobs, and, as in America, it is giving way to the M.A. It seems, then, that in the near future there will be a convergence of the occupational, educational and income spheres, and that education and occupation will be the major components of the stratification system.

Whether it be income, occupation, or education, the basic cleavage is always according to the country of origin. Persons of Eastern descent have lower incomes than persons of Western descent. Since they have larger families as well, the gap in the standard of living between the two ethnic communities is even greater. It has also been shown that the number of Jews of Eastern origin practicing a profession is disproportionately low, as is the number attending high school and college. The basic contradiction is that in absolute numbers the position of Jews of Eastern origin is improving. They are earning more, a larger number are entering the better jobs, and more are proceeding to higher education; yet because of the concomitant mobility of Jews of Western descent the *relative* difference between the two main ethnic communities is not narrowing. This is *the* problem of Israeli society.

The studies cited in the previous chapter, revealing the lack of academic success of Eastern children in the kindergarten and first grades and throughout the educational system, are sadly complemented by the findings of this chapter.

NOTES

1. Rivkah Bar-Yosef and Dorit Padan, "Eastern Ethnic Communities in the Class Structure of Israel," *Molad* (22, 1964): pp. 504-516 (in Hebrew).

2. Moshe Lissak, "Patterns of Change in Ideology and Class Structure in Israel," *Jewish Journal of Sociology* (7, 1965): pp. 46-62. See also

Moshe Lissak, "Factors in Occupational Preferences: Theoretical Model and Hypotheses for Research," *Megamot* (11, 1965): pp. 321-330 (in Hebrew).

3. Aaron Antonovsky, "Israeli Social-Political Attitudes in Israel," *Amot* (6, 1963): pp. 11-22 (in Hebrew).

4. Eric Cohen, "Social Images in an Israeli Development Town," *Human Relations* (21, 1968): pp. 163-176.

5. Moshe Lissak, "Expectations of Social Mobility and Occupational Choice Amongst Urban Youth in Israel," *Bahistadrut* (4, 1965-1966): pp. 2-40 (in Hebrew).

6. Aaron Antonovsky, *op. cit.*

7. H. V. Muhsam, "Mode of Life and Longevity in Israel," *Jewish Journal of Sociology* (8, 1966): pp. 39-48.

8. Giora Hanoch, "Income Differences in Israel," *Falk Center for Economic Research in Israel* (Report No. 5 for the year 1959-1960) Jerusalem, 1961.

9. Judah Matras, *Social Change in Israel.* (Chicago: Aldine, 1965).

10. Moshe Lissak, *Social Mobility in Israeli Society.* (Jerusalem: Israel Universities Press, 1969).

11. Matras, *op. cit.*, p. 147.

12. Lissak, *op. cit.*, pp. 8-21.

13. Matras, *op. cit.*, p. 158.

14. Seymour M. Lipset and Reinhard Bendix, *Social Mobility in Industrial Society.* (Berkeley: University of California Press, 1959), pp. 19-21.

15. Matras, *op. cit.*, pp. 158-159.

16. Hanoch, *op. cit.*, p. 47.

17. As of September 1970, high school education in the first year has been both free and compulsory. This is soon to be extended to the second year of high school.

18. Moshe Lissak, *op. cit.*, pp. 36-37.

19. *Adjustment to the Physical and Social Environment in a Development Settlement–Kiryat Malachi.* (Jerusalem: Ministry of Housing, 1965) (mimeographed in Hebrew).

20. *Dimona: Social-Economic Development.* (Jerusalem: Ministry of Housing, 1969) (mimeographed).

21. Michael Chen, "Patterns of Application to High School from Tel Aviv Elementary School Graduates," *Megamot* (11, 1961): pp. 388-396 (in Hebrew).

22. Yehuda Don, Hagit Hovav and Leonard Weller, *Social and Economic Adjustment in Towns in Israel.* (Ramat-Gan: Bar-Ilan University, 1970) (mimeographed in Hebrew). See also, Kirschenbaum, Allen and Cumay, Y., "Components of Attraction to New Towns: Preliminary Results," *Environmental Planning* (19, 1972): pp. 85-92.

23. Leah Adar and Chaim Adler, *Education for Values in Schools for Immigrant Children in Israel.* (Jerusalem: School of Education of the Hebrew University, 1965) (in Hebrew).

24. Moshe Lissak, "Expectations of Social Mobility and Occupational Choice Amongst Urban Youth in Israel," *Bahistadrut* (1965-1966) (in Hebrew); Moshe Lissak, "Stratification Models and Mobility Aspiration: Sources of Mobility Motivation," *Megamot* (15, 1967): pp. 66-82 (in Hebrew).

25. Adar and Adler, *op. cit.*, p. 91.

26. Chaim Adler, *et al., Youth in the Morasha District,* Report submitted to the Prime Minister's office, 1965 (mimeographed in Hebrew).

27. Abraham Nadad, "The Village of Shalem—Image of a Poor Neighborhood," *Megamot* (7, 1956): pp. 5-40 (in Hebrew).

28. *Ibid.,* p. 19.

29. Adar and Adler, *op. cit.*

30. Joseph Ben-David, "Professions and Unions in Israel," *Industrial Relations* (5, 1965-66): pp. 48-66. See also two other articles of his: "Scientific Endeavor in Israel and the United States," *American Behavioral Scientist* (9, 1962): pp. 12-16; "Social Factors in the Origins of a New Science; The Case of Psychology," *American Sociological Review* (31,1966): pp. 451-465.

4

Interethnic Relations

Before the state was established the Jewish population consisted almost entirely of immigrants from European countries. Only 15 percent were from Oriental countries. With the establishment of the state and the ensuing mass immigration, large numbers emigrated from Islamic countries. The organizations that dealt with absorption were committed to an equalitarian ideology and were not always tolerant of ethnic differences. At the same time, the adaptation of Eastern immigrants to Israeli society and its economic system was particularly difficult. A comparison between their level of occupation and social status in their countries of origin and those which they attained in Israel reveals that many suffered a decline. Moreover, whereas among Westerners the standard of living improved with length of residence in the country, Easterners were not likewise affected.[1]

Research pertinent to the issue of prejudice and ethnic tension is discussed below. While the starting points of these studies vary, they give a rather comprehensive picture of the situation. The main work in this area has been done by two investigators, Judith Shuval and Yohanan Peres.

GROUP REJECTION

Attempting to explain the emergence of interethnic tension Judith Shuval investigated the impact of two independent variables, ethnic origin and social class.[2] Four hundred and fifty families living in Bet-Mazmil, an immigrant quarter on the outskirts of Jerusalem, were studied. This neighborhood comprised a heterogeneous population of immigrants, under acute economic and social pressures. The research was carried out in 1953 when mass immigration had reached its climax. Most of the immigrants were still in a state of transition and there was austerity in the country.

It was established that 25 percent of the European families in the sample belonged to the lower class, as compared with 53 percent of the Oriental families. There were notable differences in class distribution, particularly among the groups from Asia and Africa. Thus, Jews from Morocco and Iraq were found in greatest numbers among the lower class, while Jews from Yemen were found more frequently in the middle class (Table 40). By ranking the various origin groups according to negative sentiment directed against them, one can ascertain the relationship between the position of an ethnic group in the stratification system and the extent of its rejection.

The families were asked with which ethnic group they least sympathized. Half of those interviewed refused to comment—a reaction indicative of acceptance of egalitarian values. As shown in Table 41, the Moroccan and Iraqi groups were most disliked: 39 percent singled out the Moroccans and 26 percent the Iraqis as the least likeable. It is recalled that these two groups were highly concentrated within the lower social class. A relationship is then observed between high level of enmity and low socioeconomic status.

Since the Moroccans had little education and were mostly unskilled, they could not easily be absorbed into urban areas. The absorption authorities therefore directed them to development towns. In Kiryat Malachi, for instance, a third of the residents are of Moroccan origin and a fifth are from Iraq. Jews from North Africa total almost half of the local population. In Dimona, half of the local population is of Moroccan origin, and in other development town such as Kiryat Gat and Kfar Yerucham this group is found in even higher concentrations.

In 1959 Shuval interviewed 1,511 settlers from four development towns, Kiryat Gat, Ashkelon, Beer Sheva and Kiryat Shmona.[3] The question asked was: "On the basis of your experience in living here, which ethnic group would you most or least prefer as neighbors?"

TABLE 40
SOCIOECONOMIC STATUS OF ETHNIC GROUPS

| Country of Origin | PERCENTAGE OF ETHNIC GROUPS IN THE THREE CLASSES | | | |
	High %	Middle %	Low %	Total %
Rumania	41	31	28	100 (40)
Poland	24	50	26	100 (70)
Hungary	42	32	26	100 (38)
Other European countries	54	28	18	100 (54)
Morocco	8	30	62	100 (192)
Other North Africans	12	32	56	100 (59)
Egypt	17	33	50	100 (40)
Iraq	4	28	68	200 (25)
Yemen	16	45	39	100 (38)
Other non-European countries	35	39	26	100 (65)
Average	25	34	41	100 (721)

Source: J. Shuval, "Patterns of Inter-group Tension and Affinity,"
International Social Science Bulletin. (8 1956):p. 89.

Table 42 shows that North Africans were rejected by all groups,
including those most similar to them, the Near Easterners. The
European was the neighbor preferred by all groups. The table also
points to a tendency towards self-hatred, as North Africans did not
necessarily choose other North Africans as the most desired neighbor.

Shuval has also shown that the North African group was increasingly
rejected over the period of a decade. The same questions were asked
in the years 1950, 1953, and 1959. Table 43 shows increased rejection
towards the North African group. By 1959, the group's low position
within the social structure of the absorbing society had been established,
which, according to the author, invited further rejection.

Shuval's studies dealt with the connection between social status and
ethnic enmity but did not concentrate on the sociopsychological pro-

cesses determining the intensity of the dislike, nor their impact on the individual member of the ethnic group.

TABLE 41
PERCENTAGE OF RESPONDENTS[1] WHO SELECTED A GIVEN ETHNIC GROUP AS MOST DISLIKED

Country of Origin	Percentage	Country of Origin	Percentage
Rumania	3	Morocco	39
Poland	4	Tunisia	2
Hungary	4	Algeria	—
Czechoslovakia	—	Tripolitania	1
Germany	—	Egypt	—
Austria	—	Iraq	26
Yugoslavia	—	Turkey	—
Bulgaria	—	Yemen	2
Russia	—	Persia	2
Other European countries	—	Other countries	4
Askenazim[2]	3	Sepharadim[3]	10

[1] Percentage calculated out of a total of 367 cases which answered this question.
[2] A generalized term for Jews of European origin.
[3] A generalized term for Jews of non-European origin.
Source: J. Shuval, "Patterns of Inter-group Tension and Affinity."
International Social Science Bulletin (8, 1956):p. 93.

Yohanan Peres in his research entitled, *Ethnic Identity and Inter-Ethnic Relations,* utilizes a sociopsychological orientation in analyzing interethnic relations.[4] His research is the most complete study to date of ethnic prejudice in Israel. It also is notable for analyzing the attitudes not only of Westerners to Easterners but also of Easterners to Westerners and the difference to intensity between the two. His sample consisted of 675 high school boys and girls aged sixteen and seventeen. The parents of fifty-one of the students were also interviewed to permit a comparison between the generations. The youth came from the middle and lower-middle social classes.

TABLE 42
REJECTION OF ETHNIC GROUPS AS NEIGHBORS IN TERMS
OF ETHNIC ORIGIN OF RESPONDENTS

Country of Origin of Respondents	PERCENTAGE INDICATING DISLIKE OF NEIGHBORS FROM THE FOLLOWING COUNTRIES OF ORIGIN			
	Europe	North Africa	Near East	No Opinion*
Europeans	10	33	22	35 (502)
North Africans	11	33	25	31 (722)
Near Easterners	7	37	27	29 (278)

*The relatively high percentage of "No Opinion" may likewise be attributed, at least partially, to the ideological norms mitigating against expressions of ethnic prejudice.

Source: J. Shuval, "Emerging Patterns of Ethnic Strain in Israel," *Social Forces* (40, 1962):p. 329.

TABLE 43
HOSTILITY EXPRESSED TOWARDS
NORTH AFRICANS IN 1950, 1953, AND 1959

Year of Study	Question	Percentage Replying "North Africans"
1950	"Which ethnic group in this community do you especially dislike?"	5 (1880)
1953	"What is the country of origin of the neighbors you like least in this community?"	19 (806)
1959	"On the basis of your experience while living here, which ethnic group would you least prefer as neighbors?"	34 (1502)

Source: J. Shuval, "Emerging Patterns of Ethnic Strain in Israel," *Social Forces* (40, 1962): p. 329.

In the first stage of the research, Peres examined the social distance between the various ethnic groups. A rating scale based on Bogardus' social distance scale was used. It measured willingness to maintain both informal and formal social relations, such as those concerning neighborhood, partnership in work, friendship, and marriage. Youths of European origin were asked about their willingness to socialize with others of non-European origin, while their Eastern counterparts were asked about their willingness to establish social relations with Arabs. This study like Shuval's revealed that the relations between the two ethnic groups were not reciprocal insofar as the willingness to social-ize was concerned. The Easterners regarded the Westerners as their reference group, whereas the Westerners were somewhat reserved about relations with Easterners. Of the youths of European extraction, more than 50 percent said that they would not marry Orientals, 35 percent disclosed that they would not choose to be friends with them and 40 percent indicated that they would not care to be their neighbors. In contrast, only 17 percent of the Easterners were negative about marriage with Europeans, 18 percent did not desire their friendship, and 12 percent preferred not to be their neighbors. As shown in Table 44, the dominant tendency among both European and Oriental youth was the wish to marry members of their own group: 79 percent of the European and 75 percent of the Oriental youth wished to marry within their own ethnic group ("certainly willing" or "willing"). However, among the Western group only 37 percent were ready without reservations to take a spouse from the Eastern community, as compared to 79 percent of Eastern youth who were ready to take a spouse of European extraction.

In less intimate situations such as friendship, discrepancy in the relations between the two ethnic groups was also evident. Among the European youth, only 56 percent expressed willingness for friendship with Eastern youth, while the latter wished in greater proportions to have friends among European youth.

Peres also dealt with perceptions of social integration. A modified version of the Bogardus social distance scale was employed. Eastern youth were asked whether they felt that members of the European ethnic group were willing to marry members of the Oriental ethnic group and whether they were willing to be their friends and neighbors. The choices were: 1) all European Jews are so willing; 2) most of the European Jews are willing; 3) only a minority of the European Jews are willing; 4) all European Jews are unwilling. While most answers were moderate, replies show that the Easterners perceive a fairly high degree of nonacceptance. In fact, there was a discrepancy between perception and reality; Eastern youth felt more rejected than they actually were (Table 45.)

TABLE 44
WILLINGNESS TO MARRY (PERCENTAGES)

	Total	No Material	Certainly Willing	Willing	Willing but Prefer a Member of My Group	Willing only with a Member of My Group	Median
European Jews with European Jews from a Different Country	143	2	37	42	16	3	1.80
Eastern Jews with Eastern Jews from a Different Country	195	4	26	49	16	5	1.98
European Jews with Eastern Jews	143	1	13	24	38	20	2.84
Eastern Jews with European Jews	195	4	29	50	15	2	1.92
Research Population with Non-Jewish Americans	337	3	2	9	23	64	3.75
Research Population with Druzes	337	3	0	4	14	79	3.90
Research Population with Arabs	337	2	0	2	9	87	3.94

Source: J. Peres, *Ethnic Identity and Inter-Ethnic Relations.* (Unpublished Ph.D. disseration, Hebrew University, 1968), p. 74.

TABLE 45
FEELING OF ACCEPTABILITY OF ORIENTAL JEWS BY EUROPEAN JEWS
(PERCENTAGES)

	Total	No Material	All Eur. Jews are Willing	Most Eur. Jews are Willing	Few Eur. Jews are Willing	All Eur. Jews are not Willing	Median
Children:							
Marriage	192	1	1	40	56	2	2.66
Friendship	192	1	3	34	61	1	2.71
Neighborhood	192	2	2	31	66	4	2.77
Parents:							
Marriage	20	0	6	25	75	0	2.83
Friendship	20	0	10	40	50	0	2.50
Neighborhood	20	0	10	45	45	0	2.38

Source: J. Peres, *Ethnic Identity and Inter-Ethnic Relations.* (Unpublished Ph.D. dissertation, Hebrew University, 1968), p. 113.

Additional data on attitudes and values in the field of interethnic relations were provided in the research conducted by Leah Adar and Chaim Adler.[5] This study was carried out on a population of 533 boys and girls from several elementary schools. Most of the children were of immigrant families from Islamic countries. The control group consisted of 220 native-borns, for the most part of Western origin.

Attitudes towards other groups were examined by three questions:

1. Which is better—that people from various ethnic groups live together in the same neighborhood or live separately in different neighborhoods?
2. Which is better—that children play with those of their own ethnic group or with those from other groups?
3. Which is better—that the young ones marry members of their own ethnic group or those from other groups?

The answers, as shown in Table 46, revealed that both ethnic groups desired to live together and to play together. However, Western children indicated greater preference for interethnic contact in the areas of residence and play, while Eastern children displayed more willingness to intermarry.

TABLE 46
PERCENTAGE DISTRIBUTION OF THOSE APPROVING OF INTERETHNIC COOPERATION

Field of Cooperation	RESEARCH GROUP		CONTROL GROUP
	Orientals	Westerners	
"To Live Together"	72.6	80.8	79.9
"To Play Together"	73.1	84.8	83.0
"To Intermarry"	69.2	55.1	51.4
Average Score	2.2	2.2	2.1

Source: L. Adar and C. Adler, *Education for Values in Schools for Immigrant Children.* (Jerusalem: School of Education of the Hebrew University, 1965): p.100.

VISITING PATTERNS

In another paper Shuval asked whether social class and ethnicity affected visiting patterns. Her data were gathered in 1953 and came from the same subjects described in her earlier paper on intergroup tensions.[6]

Both "predisposition to personal contact" and "actual neighboring behavior" were studied. Predisposition to personal contact was measured by responses to four questions: whether the respondent liked to visit his neighbors in the community; whether he liked his neighbors to visit him; whether he injoyed chatting with his neighbors when strolling in the community; and whether he injoyed getting to know new neighbors in the community.

The results showed that the higher social groups manifested a greater predisposition to personal contact than the lower groups. Thus 60 percent of the highest social class indicated a positive predisposition to contact as opposed to 47 percent of the lowest class. The differences were significant beyond the .05 level of significance.

In examining the effects of ethnicity, the author analyzed the data first according to each ethnic group separately and then in large categories consisting of Europeans and non-Europeans. The results of this analysis are presented in Table 47. Definite differences existed. The Persians, Yemenites and Turks were characterized by high predisposition to interpersonal contact, whereas Poles and Hungarians showed a low predisposition. Considered in broad categories, the non-Europeans displayed a higher predisposition to interpersonal contact than did the Europeans.

Another set of questions elicited actual visiting patterns. The social class findings resembled the earlier results, viz. that higher class was associated with actual neighborliness. There were differences according to ethnic origin. The Turkish, Moroccan and Iraqi groups displayed a particularly low level of neighboring. While visiting patterns seemed to vary more among the Eastern ethnic communities than among the Western ethnic communities, when the groups were classified as "European" and "non-European," the overall difference vanished. The cross-classification of ethnicity and social class disclosed that both these factors influenced neighboring behavior (Table 48).

For all social class and ethnic groups the actual neighboring behavior was considerably less than the predisposition to interpersonal contact, and this gap was greater among the non-Europeans. This is explained by the author as a result of the different valuations placed by non-Europeans on visiting. For them, casual visiting was less common due to the social obligation of reciprocity demanded by their culture.

TABLE 47

PREDISPOSITION OF ETHNIC GROUPS TO INTERPERSONAL CONTACT

Country of Origin	Percentage with a Positive Predisposition	Percentage with a Negative Predisposition	Total
Rumania	48	52	100 (134)
Poland	32	68	100 (72)
Hungary	38	62	100 (37)
Czechoslovakia	59	41	100 (17)
Other European Countries	63	37	100 (35)
All European	45	55	100 (295)
Morocco	60	40	100 (193)
Tunisia	59	41	100 (27)
Algiers	60	40	100 (20)
Tripolitania	46	54	100 (13)
Egypt	65	35	100 (40)
Iraq	24	76	100 (25)
Turkey	71	29	100 (14)
Yemen	72	28	100 (36)
Persia	83	17	100 (12)
Other Countries	36	64	100 (45)
All Non-Europeans	57	43	100 (425)
Total	52	48	100 (720)

$X^2 = 51.47$

D.F. = 14 (The composite categories "All Europeans" and "All Non-Europeans are not included.)

$P < .001$.

Source: Y. Shuval, "Class and Ethnic Correlates of Causal Neighboring," *American Sociological Review* (21, 1956): p. 456.

Shuval also demonstrated that the North Africans' satisfaction with their neighbors was related to the homogeneity of the "micro-neighborhood," whether the neighborhood was a) completely homogeneous, i.e., both contiguous neighbors were from the same specific country of origin as the respondent; b) homogeneous, i.e., both contiguous neighbors were from countries with cultural backgrounds relatively similar to that of the respondent; i.e., Iraq, Yemen, etc., but were not European; or c) completely heterogeneous, both were of European origin. The results showed that as the neighborhood became more heterogeneous, the North Africans' evaluation of their neighbors increased. In other words, a North African preferred that his neighbor not be another North African.

TABLE 48
NEIGHBORING BEHAVIOR AS RELATED TO CLASS POSITION AND ETHNIC ORIGIN

Class Position	PERCENTAGE POSITIVE OF ACTUAL NEIGHBORING BEHAVIOR	
	Europeans	Non-Europeans
High	47 (117)	65 (59)
Middle	38 (103)	44 (133)
Low	36 (71)	30 (235)
Total	42 (291)	39 (427)

X^2 on the group positive = 19.9
D.F. = 2.
P < .001.
Source: J. Shuval, "Class and Ethnic Correlates of Causal Neighboring," *American Sociological Review* (21, 1956): p. 457.

ATTITUDES TOWARDS ARABS

Peres found that the tendency to reject the Arab minority was stronger among Eastern youth than among Western youth.[7] Adar and Adler also studied the attitudes of immigrants' children towards the Arabs. They averred that one reason for Easterners' greater rejection of the Arabs was their desire to be disassociated from a group who likewise are accorded low status. Another reason given was that rejection of the Arabs enabled Easterners to identify with the majority group. The third reason was historical—they suffered in Arab lands.[8]

The replies given by the Eastern children of the research group were compared to those given by the children of the control group. The former were found to be more extreme in rejecting social relations with the Arabs (Table 49). Although the replies indicated different attitudes on the part of the research and control groups, they did not show a desire to deny the Arabs their rights.

TABLE 49
PERCENTAGE DISTRIBUTION OF DESIRED COOPERATION BETWEEN JEWS AND ARABS

Alternative Answers	Research Group Eastern Children	Control Group Western Children
One should live together and study together	9.5	23.9
Friendship is desirable	77.0	71.4
There is no need to become friendly	5.8	0.5
They should be expelled from Israel	7.6	4.1

Source: L. Adar and C. Adler, *Education for Values in Schools for Immigrant Children.* (Jerusalem: School of Education of the Hebrew University, 1965), p. 107.

SELF-IMAGE AND REJECTION

Peres, in the study discussed above, examined differences in the esteem accorded to various ethnic groups.[9] He explored the extent to which those at the bottom of the hierarchy agreed with the low esteem in which they were held and with the criteria by which their status was judged. The subjects were asked which of the following statements seemed closest to reality:

1a) Most people in Israel esteem Oriental Jews much more highly than they do European Jews.

b) Most people in Israel esteem Oriental Jews a little more highly than they do European Jews.

c) Most people in Israel esteem Oriental Jews and European Jews equally.

d) Most people in Israel esteem European Jews a little more highly than they do Oriental Jews.

e) Most people in Israel esteem European Jews much more highly than they do Oriental Jews.

2a) Most people in Israel esteem the members of my ethnic group very highly.

b) Most people in Israel esteem the members of my ethnic group.

c) Most people in Israel do not highly esteem the members of my ethnic group.

d) Most people in Israel do not esteem the members of my ethnic group.

There is a notable gap between the answers given by European and Oriental Jews to the above questions. The majority of those interviewed, Europeans and Orientals alike, felt that the Europeans are more highly esteemed than the Orientals.

The semantic-differential method was utilized to examine further the esteem of the various ethnic groups. The interviewees were requested to characterize the following: Arabs, European Jews, Moroccan Jews, Yemenite Jews, Oriental Jews, Israeli Jews, My Own Group, My Ideal Image.

The hierarchy that emerged for Western youth was: 1) Self-image; 2) A member of my own group; 3) A European Jew; 4) A typical Israeli; 5) A Yemenite Jew; 6) An Oriental Jew; 7) A Moroccan Jew; 8) An Arab. For those of Eastern origin, the order was: 1) Self-image; 2) A typical Israeli; 3) A member of my own group; 4) A European Jew; 5) An Oriental Jew; 6) A Yemenite Jew; 7) A Moroccan Jew; 8) An Arab.

There is an affinity between the rankings of the Eastern and Western youth. Both ranked their own self-image as first and both preferred the Yemenites to the Moroccans, who were the least-liked Jewish group. Still, what stands out is that Eastern youth ranked Eastern Jews lower than they ranked European Jews. This indicates the existence of self-hatred, where the minority group accepts the negative stereotypes imputed to it by the majority group.

The following comments made during the interview are revealing:

Concerning the esteem for European Jews: "They have a higher standard of living, are more advanced, and are liberal in their thinking."

Concerning the esteem for Yemenite Jews above other Eastern groups: "They are full of the joy of life; most of them are fond of work; they are simple and nice people."

Concerning the low esteem for Moroccan Jews: "They are
indecent people; there is an expression 'Moroccan-knife' which
is true; I know several such Moroccans."

Adar and Adler explored the characteristics attributed by children
of Oriental origin to the veteran Israeli (which means in effect "Western")
as well as the characteristics attributed to the immigrant (which means
in effect "Eastern").[10] They also studied the attitudes of children of
Western origin towards the veteran (i.e., someone of their own group)
and towards the immigrant (i.e., someone of the Oriental group). Thirty-
four traits were listed, seventeen positive and seventeen negative, and
the children were asked to designate those which characterize the
immigrant and those which characterize the veteran in the country.
Table 50 shows that veterans had more approval than immigrants.
This preference for veterans over immigrants was found for Western
and Eastern children.

TABLE 50
DISTRIBUTION OF AVERAGE POSITIVE AND
NEGATIVE CHARACTERISTICS ATTRIBUTED
TO "IMMIGRANTS" AND "VETERANS"

| | RESEARCH GROUP | | CONTROL GROUP | |
	Image of Immigrants	Image of Veterans	Image of Immigrants	Image of Veterans
Positive Characteristics	71.6	84.7	75.2	81.8
Negative Characteristics	28.4	15.3	24.8	18.2
Total	13.22	14.53	9.00	11.09

Source: L. Adar and C. Adler, "Education for Values in Schools for Immigrant
Children." (Jerusalem: School of Education of the Hebrew University), p. 114.

A negative image of the immigrants was evinced by children of
Western origin, claiming that the former were socially backward. The
same negative image was felt by children of Oriental extraction. In
certain Eastern ethnic groups this negative image reached vast proportions. For instance, in a class of thirty-one pupils of Asian-African
origin, 186 positive characteristics and 201 negative ones were imputed
to immigrants, in contrast to 419 positive characteristics and sixty-two
negative ones attributed to the veterans. This is an extreme example,
no doubt; yet, the same tendency was found, although to a lesser degree,

in every elementary school where the majority of pupils consisted of
children of Oriental origin.

The main differences between the image of the veterans and that
of the immigrants were that the immigrants were thought of as being
religious and loyal to their families (among immigrants the latter took
the second and the third places, while among veterans, the tenth and
fourteenth places). They were also characterized as having no education
and as being indifferent to matters concerning the state and its welfare.
The veterans, on the other hand, were thought of as being more educated,
having a stronger attachment to the country, and being more politically
active. This portrayal of each group was to a certain degree realistic.

Self-rejection among North African immigrants was studied by
Shuval,[11] who hypothesized that the prejudice directed against North
Africans would be transformed into self-hatred.

The data were those which she collected in her 1959 study of four
immigrant development centers. Of the 1,511 men and women interviewed, 719 were immigrants from North Africa. Residents were asked
from which ethnic group they would least like to have people as
neighbors and from which ethnic group they would most prefer to
have neighbors. The results are shown in Table 51.

These data show that the North Africans were most frequently
cited by all the groups as least desired. What is of special interest
is that the North Africans themselves did not want to be neighbors
of other North Africans. Since they could have rejected Near Easterners
instead of their own ethnic group, the self-rejection was particularly
poignant. Moreover, the North Africans did not exhibit much hostility
to European residents. The Near Easterners, who were also rejected,
showed less self-rejection than did the North Africans.

In an open-ended question, the respondents were also asked the
reasons for their choices. Table 52 presents the negative stereotypes
classified according to the three major ethnic groups. All three ethnic
groups characterized the North Africans as "aggressive." Additional
traits mentioned were "dirty," "uncultured," and " no common
language." The most prominent finding of this table is that the North
Africans applied the same stereotypes to themselves as did the non-
North Africans.

Shuval also examined the effects of self-rejection on sex, the length
of time the immigrant had been in Israel, the level of education
attained, the occupation of the chief breadwinner in the family, and

the extent of religious observance. Only the age of the respondent was found to be significantly associated with self-rejection, the younger immigrant showing greater feelings in that regard.

TABLE 51
REJECTION OF VARIOUS ETHNIC GROUPS AS NEIGHBORS BY THREE MAJOR ETHNIC GROUPS IN THE COMMUNITIES

Ethnic origin of respondent	PERCENTAGE INDICATING THAT THEY WOULD NOT LIKE TO HAVE MEMBERS OF THE FOLLOWING ETHNIC GROUPS AS NEIGHBORS*				
	Europeans	North Africans	Near Easterners	No Opinion**	No. of Cases
European	10	32	22	36	(542)
North African	12	33	24	31	(722)
Near Eastern	7	38	25	30	(238)

*In the interview respondents were asked for the specific country from which they preferred not to have neighbors. For purposes of analysis these replies were divided into three general ethnic groups.

**The large group's refusal to answer can be explained in terms of the strong equalitarian norm in Israeli society which militates against the over-rejection of any specific ethnic group. Interviewers were instructed to probe as much as possible, in order to encourage responses despite this norm.

Source: J. Shuval, "Self-Rejection Among North-African Immigrants to Israel," *The Israel Annals of Psychiatry and Related Disciplines* (4, 1966):p. 103.

CONCLUSION

The evidence is clear—prejudice towards Easterners does exist, not only among the older generation, but among the native born as well. The Moroccans, the most troublesome Eastern ethnic group in terms of crime, have been particularly singled out. Moreover, while there is no definite proof, it appears that prejudice is increasing; at least it is not abating.

Jews have historically been the minority group on the receiving end of prejudiced treatment. It is a bitter irony that with the creation of the Jewish state, a minority group has been formed from within the people itself.

TABLE 52
NEGATIVE STEREOTYPE OF NORTH AFRICANS AS PERCEIVED BY ETHNIC GROUPS

Percentage indicating the following traits as reasons for rejecting North Africans as neighbors	ETHNIC GROUP OF RESPONDENTS		
	Europeans	Near Easterners	North Africans
	(204)*	(122)*	(268)*
Dirty	12	18	10
Too religious	1	1	—
Disloyal to country	—	—	—
Proud, superior	2	—	3
Uncultured	15	5	11
No common language	11	1	3
Bothersome children	9	8	10
Aggressive	31	42	33
Undesirable personal traits	7	14	20
Different customs	5	2	1
"Primitive"	3	2	1
Other	2	5	8
No Answer	2	1	—

*Some respondents gave more than one trait and these were recorded. Likewise a few respondents did not indicate any reason for their dislike of North Africans. The totals in this table represent the total number of traits mentioned and percentages are calculated on these totals. The latter therefore do not always correspond to the number of persons who indicated dislike of North Africans.

Source: J. Shuval, "Self-Rejection Among North African Immigrants to Israel," *The Israel Annals of Psychiatry and Related Diciplines* (4, 1966): p. 105.

NOTES

1. A general discussion of intergroup relations in Israel is found in Alex Weingrod, *Group Relations in a New Society.* (New York: Praeger, 1965); P. S. Cohen, "Ethnic Hostility in Israel," *New Society* (February 28, 1963); P. S. Cohen, "Ethnic Group Differences in Israel," *Race* (9, 1968): pp. 303-310.

2. Judith T. Shuval, "Patterns of Inter-group Tension and Affinity," *International Social Science Bulletin* (8, 1956): pp. 72-123.

3. Judith T. Shuval, "Emerging Patterns of Ethnic Strain in Israel," *Social Forces* (40, 1962): pp. 322-330. See also, "The Role of Class in Structuring Intergroup Hostility," *Human Relations* (10, 1957): pp. 61-75.

4. Yohanan Peres, *Ethnic Identity and Inter-Ethnic Relations.* (unpublished Ph.D. dissertation, Hebrew University, 1968).

5. Leah Adar and Chaim Adler, "Education for Values in Schools for Immigrant Children" (Jerusalem: School of Education of the Hebrew University, 1965).

6. Judith T. Shuval, "Class and Ethnic Correlates of Causal Neighboring," *American Sociological Review* (21, 1956): pp. 453-458. See also Judith Shuval, "The Micro Neighborhood: An Approach to Ecological Patterns of Ethnic Groups," *Social Problems* (9, 1961): pp. 272-280.

7. Peres, *op. cit.*

8. *Idem.*

9. *Idem.*

10. Adar and Adler, *op. cit.*

11. Judith T. Shuval, "Self-Rejection Among North African Immigrants to Israel," *The Israel Annals of Psychiatry and Related Disciplines* (4, 1966): pp. 101-110. See also her article on the effect of the micro-neighborhood, "The Micro-Neighborhood: An Approach to Ecological Patterns of Ethnic Groups," *op. cit.*

SECTION II

5

Family

The family has not been intensively studied from an interactionist frame of reference. There is virtually no research on such topics as power relationships, dating and courtship, child-rearing practices and social class, attitudes of children toward their aged parents, successful marriages, mate selection and propinquity, the woman's role, or the three generation family.

The kibbutz family, undoubtedly the most studied family unit in Israel, is presented in another chapter. Much of the research deals with the family as it affects absorption. We first present the research on intergenerational tension. These studies (done in the 1950s, which rather dates them) deal not only with the "generation gap" but in a larger sense with the successful or unsuccessful integration of second generation youth of Eastern descent. The second section deals with typologies. Two attempts have been made to classify families; one, in the early 1950s, focuses on the immigrant family as a factor in integration. The other, a product of the late 1960s, is based on applied anthropological data and covers the range of Israeli families.

The third section entitled "The Eastern and Western Family" is surprisingly impoverished. Whereas one would have expected many studies on this area in an attempt to explain the reported differences to which we have become accustomed, we find only *one* empirical study. Perhaps the most significant contributions have been two papers by three social psychologists, which deal with consequences

145

of differential socialization practices of Easterners born abroad, Easterners born in Israel, and those of Western extraction. This section is followed by a description of the ultraorthodox family.

The position of women in Israeli society is the subject of the following section. Here two women sociologists show three major trends underlying the woman's position. The last section deals with demographic change in the ages of marriage, the rate of inter-ethnic marriage, child planning and abortion. Again the major factor that distinguished the population is country of origin.

INTERGENERATIONAL TENSION

The clash of norms and psychological tensions between immigrants and their children is a familiar theme; the children suffer the conflict between the traditional culture of their parents and the modern values of the new country. In such a setting the "generation gap" is not an empty phrase.

From the very beginning the adjustment of the Asian-African family was more difficult than that of the European family. Culture conflict existed only for the Oriental groups, for Israeli society was Western-oriented, characterized by small families and equality of women. Of further importance is the concentration of Eastern families in the lower class, where the largest number of social problems are located.

Reports of intergenerational tension are found in various works published in the early fifties. Dina Feitelson reported in her study of the change of educational models in the Kurdish Jewish community:

From the moment that the child enters the kindergarten he is placed within two value systems. The children learn to distinguish one way of behaving at home and in the neighborhood, and another way of behaving at school. They outwardly accept the value system of the teacher. They are ashamed of their parents, the large number of children in the family unit, their traditional dress. The children leave school and imitate superficially what they conceive to be Israeli behavior. The parents react to this situation by saying: "In Israel they take the children away from us."[1]

When a youth establishes himself in his work after a stay in a kibbutz
or army service, he does not return to the family and does not support
his parents.

Peretz Cohen painted a similar picture in his study of Rosh Ha'Ayin,
another immigrant town. Cohen wrote:

> The undermining of the authority of the father and the consoli-
> dation of the position of the woman have brought forth a re-
> action of indifference on the part of many fathers to their
> children's future. There have been many instances where youths
> wish to leave their homes which they regard as being bad for
> them. According to their accounts they dislike their parents
> and wish to live among better individuals. There is a tendency
> to show hatred towards their parents.[2]

Fanny Beer, a teacher in a ma'abara, reported her impressions on
the father-son relationship in immigrant families of Eastern extraction.
In an article entitled "Clash of Values Among Immigrant Children,"
she stated that the young generation saw in the teachers and the values
which they imparted an ideal of progress and success. The knowledge
they gained at school gave them a sense of superiority over their parents.
The immigrant child thus experienced the conflict of who was right,
the parents or the teacher.[3]

The parents felt that the esteem and love of their children had been
stolen from them. Their frustration was displayed by non-cooperation
and aggression towards the absorbing institutions. Disappointment
with their children's education expressed itself in such statements as:
"In the Diaspora (countries outside of Israel) the children were not
disrespectful to their fathers and mothers."

Still, it is one thing to say that the children are confused and even
doubt the wisdom of their parents and it is another to conclude that
this leads to estrangement and loss of love. Thus, although similar
examples of the above can be cited, the majority of investigators did
not find serious signs of family disintegration among second-generation
immigrants.

Dov Weintraub and Miriam Shapiro[4] in their study of the traditional
family in the process of change, and Elihu Katz and Avraham Zlozcower[5]
in their study on the continuity of ethnic community patterns, concluded that change in the family and even the lowering of the authority

of its head was not accompanied by a serious weakening of the solidarity between the generations. Hagit Rieger, too, in her study on Yemenite youth showed that side by side with the increased independence on the part of the youth, tradition was valued and parents were esteemed.[6]

In 1949 and 1950, Hagit Rieger maintained continuous contact for about ten months with a community consisting largely of Yemenites. Her study dealt with a population which had suffered as a result of moving to Israel. Before arriving in Israel many of the families had lived for several years in a transit camp in Aden. During this time, the men were faced with the necessity of adapting themselves to a world previously unknown to them. Signs of change in the traditional system of customs and practices were already seen in the camp. Many youths had begun to be less religious; they had cut off their sidelocks and were less inclined to observe the religious commandments. The movement from Aden to Israel accelerated the process of disintegration of the traditional culture. In sending the immigrants to a number of villages, many large families were broken up. The physical conditions in the new surroundings were bad and contact with the absorbing society was limited. Within the village under study, the Yemenites attempted to appear as a cohesive unity, but the fact remained that the inhabitants came from different localities in Yemen with varying traditions and customs. Thus, despite the community's outwardly unified appearance, there was a great deal of tension and friction among the various family units. The traditional leaders were in part replaced by the more active young men.

The absorption of the youths into the modern educational and social framework did not occur at the expense of filial attachment; the stability of the family unit was preserved. Thus the majority of parents evinced an interest in the work, schooling and social life of their children. In turn, most of the youth were happy with the interest displayed in them by their parents, and only a small number preferred that their parents should not become involved in their outside activities. By and large, girls showed a stronger family attachment than did boys.

Considering the low status of the parents and their difficulties in adapting to the new occupational and social demands, one might have expected the children to experience some shame. This was not found, although the majority felt that they were superior to their

fathers with regard to political orientation, social life and, the ability
to make their way in Israel.

There existed a demand for more independence on the part of the
youth, but it was not acute. Most of the disagreements between parents and children concerned religion. The second most frequent topic
of disagreement was connected with money. A small number quarrelled
with their parents on the subject of education.

The youth appeared to combine restrained respect for tradition with
a tendency towards modernity. They were ready to modify or deviate
from the traditional pattern of marriage, yet they did not wish to destroy
all the old customs. Thus, while advocating a freer relationship between
the sexes, they still felt that one should discuss the impending marriage
with one's parents and determine the conditions before speaking to the
parents of the designated spouse. After marriage they preferred to live
in their own home, close to their parents.

A change was noted in attitude toward the type of woman desired
for marriage. The young man wanted an intelligent girl from a good
family. He esteemed beauty and domestic ability but did not rate highly
the traditional bearing of many children. The desirable age for marriage
was twenty years for the man and nineteen years for the woman—much
higher than the marriageable age in Yemen. A large portion of the young
men wanted their prospective wives to be as educated as they were.
For the girls, the traditional type of husband was still desired.

This intermediate attitude—a drawing apart, but not breaking away—
was manifested in the area of religion, which no longer played an important role in the lives of many youths. Nevertheless, they continued
to observe the commandments that were family-centered, visiting the
synagogue together with their fathers and on the surface obeying the
religious precepts. A minority was strict in its religious observance
while an even smaller minority had totally stopped participating in
religious life. As usual, the girls tended more towards religious observance than did the boys.

The work of Dov Weintraub and Miriam Shapiro was conducted
in an immigrant settlement consisting of seventy families from Kurdistan.[7] There they lived in hamlets where the unit of organization was
the extended family and the economic and political authority was
concentrated in the hands of the head of the family. The position
of the woman was weak.

A questionnaire was distributed to youths aged 16-24 as well as to heads of families who were first generation immigrants. A section of the questionnaire addressed itself to the youths' acceptance of the traditional orientations of their parents.

Communication among members of the family was measured by asking: "Do you generally consult with members of your family about personal matters? And if so, with whom especially?" Most were accustomed to consult with at least one of their elders. Mobility versus family ties was examined by asking: "If work were offered to you in the vicinity of your family's home or elsewhere with higher pay, which would you prefer?" Of the twenty interviewed, fifteen wished to live near the family, even when this involved a lower salary.

In order to study the similarity of attitudes between parents and their children, a comparison was made of the answers given by the father and his son. In eleven instances there was a definite correlation between the outlook of the parents and that of the children; both father and son agreed that the parents should decide or that children must choose from suggestions by the parents. Only in two instances were contrary opinions expressed.

Further questions, presented to sixteen families, concerned the eating of kosher food, smoking and travelling on the Sabbath, and daily prayer in the synagogue. Fathers and sons agreed concerning kosher food and smoking on the Sabbath but less so on the other two matters.

The family in the settlement maintained its solidarity due to the permissive stance of the parents with regard to their children's new attitudes. The sons distinguished between the positions of their fathers as heads of families and their status in other areas of society, while the fathers closed their eyes to their sons' deviations from tradition.

One may suppose that the degree of intergenerational tension is influenced in no small measure by the form of social organization and the character of the settlement in which the family lives. In a homogeneous village (such as the ones cited above) not closely connected with an urban center, change may cause relatively mild disorganization. In order to examine whether the lack of serious intergenerational conflict did not result from the special conditions of the settlement, an urban neighborhood study is cited.[8] It was

assumed that the neighborhood's proximity to an urban center
(Jerusalem) would sharpen the conflict between traditional and
modern family values and raise the level of aspirations, thereby
giving rise to feelings of frustration and alienation towards the family.
The majority of the residents were immigrants from Eastern communities. Fifty percent had immigrated from Morocco, the rest from
twelve other countries. Overcrowding was prevalent; about
25 percent were supported by the Welfare Department. The level
of education was low and there was a concentration in the lower
levels of occupation.

One hundred boys and girls aged 14-18 were interviewed about
their attitudes toward family and community. It was found that a
third of the youth had frequent contact with their families while
the remaining two-thirds did not. Nevertheless, 70 percent ate their
main meal together with their families. Concerning relations with
parents, 40 percent claimed that they were very good, 34 percent
that they were good, and 14 percent that they were average. Only
3 percent indicated that serious tension existed. The majority of
the youth supported their families or contributed their earnings to
the family budget. The youth who both studied and worked displayed
a high degree of family attachment.

The degree of parental supervision was also examined. This was
found to vary with the situation. In schooling and work the parents
exercised the highest degree of supervision; 85 percent of the parents
interested themselves in their children's schoolwork. Similarly,
about 70 percent of the parents were strict with regard to the hour
at which the children had to return home at night. The parents
were more lax with regard to the supervision of their children's
leisure time activities.

The results, then, showed that the family was changing in its
traditional attitude concerning parental strictness and supervision.
Still, it had not foregone many of its traditional functions and
serious intergenerational conflict was minimal. The youth's
attachment to his peer group was not accompanied by manifestations
of antagonism to his family.

The only study to employ a control group, that is, the inclusion
of European youth, was that of Katz and Zloczower.[9] They studied
Yemenites living in the neighborhood of Sha'arayim, near Rehovot

(an ethnic group which possesses stable and singular ethnic patterns).
This community is relatively long-settled; the majority of the elder
generation migrated to Israel before 1920. Nevertheless, despite
their long residence they have not mixed outside their own ethnic
group.

Two characteristics make this study unique. First, the subjects
of the study were of a group of second generation Eastern immigrants
born and raised in Israel. They learned in a neighborhood school where
there were no pupils of European extraction. Despite their *sabra* birth,
and a fair amount of physical contact with members of their own age
group of European extraction, their social life was mainly confined
to their own ethnic community. Second, the study compared children of Yemenite immigrants with the children of European immigrants.

The investigators assumed that the Yemenites of the second generation would reject parental authority to a greater extent than would
second generation children of European extraction. The findings in
Table 53 (Row 1) show that Western children rejected (60 percent
boys, 33 percent girls) parental authority more than did Yemenite
children (17 percent boys, 23 percent girls). The relationship between
sex and ethnicity was revealing. European boys (60 percent) were
more prone to reject parental authority than were European girls (33
percent) while among the Yemenites a reverse pattern was found; a
slightly larger percentage of girls (23 percent) than boys (17 percent)
rejected parental authority. The Western boys differed from all the
other groups, being clearly more rebellious than either Western girls
or Yemenite boys or girls.

Education was also related to acceptance of parental authority
but operated differently for each ethnic group. For the Western youth,
acceptance of parental authority increased with level of education,
while for the Yemenites the more educated were less prone to accept
authority. Among the Europeans, non-married men and women rejected parental authority (69 percent) more than did married men
(32 percent). An opposite trend was again found among the Yemenites; the non-married (74 percent) rejected parental authority to a
lesser extent than did the married (27 percent).

The youth were also asked to express their agreement or disagreement with the following three additional statements measuring
traditional parental authority: (1) a grown-up child should be allowed
to go out in the evening only when accompanied by a member of

the family; (2) friendship between grown-up boys and girls only leads to trouble; (3) a married woman's friends should consist only of those of her husband and their wives. On each question the responses of the Yemenites were considerably more traditional than were those of the Europeans.

TABLE 53
ATTITUDE TO PARENTS ACCORDING TO ETHNICITY AND SEX

	BOYS		GIRLS	
	West.	Yem.	West.	Yem.
Non-acceptance of Parental Authority	60%	17%	33%	23%
Serious Quarrelling with Parents	21%	13%	4%	10%
Non-Agreement with the Statement "Parents always know better."	72%	48%	60%	56%
(N)	(11)	(21)	(20)	(23)

Source: E. Katz and A. Zloczower, "Continuity of Ethnic Patterns in the Second Generation," *Megamot* (9, 1958): p. 193 (in Hebrew).

While this study found a measured change among the second generation, it did not show estrangement from the parents. No less important was the unanticipated finding that rejection of parental authority was greater among the second generation of European descent.

TYPES OF FAMILIES

We present two typologies, one by Shmuel Eisenstadt, the other by Phyllis Palgi. Eisenstadt's classification of family type was based on the immigrants' predisposition to change, and was constructed on the basis of a large interview study conducted in 1949-1950.[10] Two criteria were employed: *participation* within the social system and *identification* with its values and symbols.

Isolated Apathetic Family

This type is characterized by "the swift breaking down of the solidarity and action-potential of the small primary groups, as a result of the unrealizability of their rigid ritualistic aspirations and values." It is generally negative towards the new social structure and its social values, including the false hopes that had motivated them to come to Israel. This negative identification is more or less indiscriminately directed against all the aspects of the social structure, with little attempt to differentiate its workings and principles. Complaints, easily stirred into open aggression, are usually out of proportion to the concrete problems. There is a very uncertain orientation to the general values of the social system, coupled with no belief in the possibility of effecting any change.

One hundred and forty-five such families were reported, the vast majority of which came from the traditional sectors of the Jewish communities that suffered from status anxiety. Usually, they immigrated as family units rather than as parts of large cohesive groups.

Isolated Stable Family

Its basic characteristics are continuity, stability, and a manifest readiness to adjust. There is generally positive identification with the country; an ability to differentiate between the country, the Jewish people in general, and the Government on the one hand, and the officials and "bosses" on the other, against whom most of the complaints are directed. Its main interest is confined to its immediate social field—family life and economic and social security. Most complaints are rationally made on the basis of concrete instances and are usually confined to these instances. They may, however, be aimed at the evils of bureaucracy and the lack of interest shown by the old inhabitants towards the new immigrants. However, the possibility of organizing and effecting any changes is not considered.

One hundred and seventy-eight such families were identified. Most of them were negatively predisposed to change but did not manifest a high degree of status anxiety.

Isolated Active Family

The family is stable, an active participator in the new country, but isolated from other families. While it is essentially positive, it is also critical of the new society. Only twenty families of this type were found; of these, many were ex-elite European families.

Cohesive Ethnic Group

This type of family continued its traditional ways of life while displaying a willingness to change its basic value system. It demonstrates positive, initial identification with the Jewish nation and with the state, as well as some meaningful differentiation between its various aspects (except for the usual differentiation between the people, the Government, and the actual officials they meet.)

Since the very strong orientation to the general values of the social structure are couched mainly in its traditional-religious values and symbols, it is critical of the lack of religiosity within the absorbing community. Two hundred and forty-seven families, all from Asia-Africa, were so identified.

The Self-Transforming Cohesive Ethnic Group

This type of family shows a very high positive disposition to change. Very strong identification with the country is found along with mutual identification and group cohesiveness.

Very strong and stable relations are maintained with fellow immigrants. They are characterized by: (a) strong *elites,* some of them patterned according to the old social structure, but mostly arisen through the process of immigration (Zionist and political leaders and intellectuals, organizers etc.), and very intensive relations between the *elites* and the immigrants; (b) high degree of family solidarity; (c) very slight insistence on their specific cultural patterns, and a consequently large extent of activity according to the patterns of the new country but with a strong organization on ethnic lines within the new framework; (d) intensive extension of social participation to different spheres—study, language, occupational education, civic, cultural, and political activities; (e) very strong orientation to the general formal values and symbols of the social structure, which, owing to the basic similarity of cultural and sociopolitical settings, is of a mainly institutional character; (f) very pronounced differentiation between different aspects of the social structure. One hundred and eighty-nine families, mostly from the Balkans, were so identified.

Phyllis Palgi distinguished various types of families.[11] Her classification is based on country of origin, periods of migration, and adjustment to Israel. The classification presented in Table 54 is based largely on her work, but includes additional categories gleaned from other studies.

TABLE 54
FAMILY TYPES

Country of Origin	Period of Arrival	Patterns of Kinship-Relationship	Characteristics
Europe	1882-1942	Nuclear family, one generation, small families.	Rejection of traditional patterns, equality, division of labor not based on sex.
Europe	1948-	Nuclear family, second generation.	Strong intergenerational relationships; social activity within the family.
European Survivors of World War II	1948-1953	Nuclear family.	Adults relatively old.
Asia-Africa	1948-	Extended family, large families. Patriarchy. Mutual dependence among family members.	Tradition directed; division of labor according to sex; low age at marriage; spouse chosen by parents, marriage to relative preferred.
Morocco-village	1952	Extended family, large family, group settlement.	Change from authoritarianism to greater equality between the sexes; greater toleration of the children and attempt to minimize intergenerational conflict.
Morocco-city	1952	Nuclear family, large families.	Extended family already disrupted while in Morocco. Difficulty adjusting to the low social status.
Yeminite long residence in Israel	1904-1908	Extended family, tendency to residential clustering, strong intergenerational relationships.	Gradual transition towards equality, minimizing of intergenerational conflict, tending to continue traditional patterns.
Yemenite, immigrants	1949	Extended and large families.	Questioning of authority of head of household, wife may work, occasional quarrelling between husband and wife.
Kurdistan, immigrants	1950	Authoritarian father, preference for sons, division of labor on the basis of sex.	Decline in economic status, intergenerational conflict, tendency of children to be estranged from the parents.

Source: Based in part on an article by P. Palgi: "The Adaptability and Vulnerability of Types in the Changing Israeli Society," in A. Jarus et al. (eds.), *Children and Families in Israel: Some Mental Health Perspectives.* (Jerusalem: Henrietta Szold, 1970), pp. 97-135.

East-West Family

Unfortunately, there is only one study which empirically examined family patterns of Easterners and Westerners. This is the work of Rivkah Bar-Yosef.[12] Her samples consisted of two groups. One from Rehavia, a middle-class area, was comprised predominantly of Jews of Western descent who were mostly white-collar workers. The other was from Nahalat, a lower-class area comprised largely of Jews of Eastern descent, where the majority of the heads of households were blue-collar workers. As would be expected, there were marked differences in the level of education between the two communities. Furthermore, Rehavia was characterized by smaller families, and by a larger percentage of women working outside the home.

The author was particularly concerned with ascertaining whether the couples shared common roles, whether or not family roles were ascribed, and what was the pattern of authority. Some differences between the two groups were found, but what is striking is their similarity. On questions concerning housekeeping (e.g., cooking, cleaning, decoration), clear-cut sex roles were found for both groups. Likewise, in the area of socialization (e.g., daily care of the child, responsibility for his education), both groups held the woman to be the main agent. However, the father was considered the punisher in the middle-Eastern, lower-class group, while the mother or both the mother and father were the punishers in the other group. In Nahalat (the lower-class area) 50 percent of the mothers made decisions concerning the school, whereas in Rehavia joint decisions were made in 90 percent of the families. The most frequent pattern for both neighborhoods was joint husband and wife participation in leisure time activities, although such participation was somewhat lower among the Eastern group. The author summarizes her findings in Table 55. As shown, there are differences; Nahalat is more traditional than Rehavia; in Nahalat behavior is quite specific for a given sex. However, we feel that the table, in dichotomizing the responses, overemphasizes the differences between the two groups. The more refined analysis in the text points to a high degree of similarity between the neighborhoods. Nevertheless, whatever the magnitude of the differences in these two communities, since they not only differed according to ethnicity but also with regard to occupational status and educational level, it is unclear whether the observed differences reflect the impact of social class or ethnicity.

TABLE 55
SCORES FOR TWO AREAS OF FAMILY FUNCTIONING

	Nahalat	Rehavia
Division of Labor		
Common to both sexes	29	47
Specific to one sex	71	53
	100%	100%
Criteria for Division of Labor		
Ascribed by sex	77	62
Not ascribed by sex	23	38
	100%	100%

Source: Adapted from R. Bar-Yosef, "Role Differentiation in the Urban Family in Israel, in R. Bar-Yosef and I. Shelach (eds.), *The Family in Israel.* (Jerusalem: Akadamon, 1970), p. 178.

It would be fallacious to conclude on the basis of this one study that the differences in family patterns between Jews of Eastern and Western descent are minimal. The study was limited to eighty-five families in the Jerusalem area and, perhaps more importantly, we do not know which of the Eastern ethnic groups were represented. Furthermore, the results are confined to the particular measures and methods employed.

There are two psychological studies, which while concerned with extending a finding on birth-order to Israeli society, are perhaps the most pertinent empirical studies of differential socialization practices. These are the research of Yehudah Amir, Shlomo Sharon and Yacov Kovarsky.[13] Their first investigation was based on Schachter's finding in the United States that under the conditions of high anxiety, first-born children were more anxious and affiliative than later-born children.

Among the real-life situations that Schachter brought to support his laboratory findings was that of the success of fighter-pilots. Assuming that anxiety would have a deleterious effect on the pilot's performance, it was hypothesized that those pilots who were first-born would perform less well than those pilots who were fortunate not to be the eldest child in the family. Using data collected by another researcher, Schachter showed that this was indeed the case; first-born pilots brought down significantly fewer enemy planes than did later-born pilots. Amir, Sharan and Kovarsky suggested an alternative explanation, namely that the poorer performance of first-born pilots resulted from their avoidance of direct engagement with the enemy. They suggested that more first-born than later-born would avoid situations which are potentially anxiety arousing. This general hypothesis was tested by the frequency with which soldiers in the Israeli Defense Forces volunteered for officer training, for the situation of the combat officer was seen as one which arouses considerable anxiety.

After pointing out that family size affects the relationship between anxiety and affiliation, the authors compared the extended family structure of Eastern families to the nuclear structure of Western families. They pictured the extended family as one in which the mother is not terribly anxious about her child-rearing competence and therefore such anxieties are not communicated to her first-born child. In this family setting, the mother receives help from other women such as grandmothers, aunts, and sisters-in-law. The prominence of the first-born is a tradition stemming from Biblical times and an integral part of religious tradition so typical of Eastern families. Thus, the position of the first-born in the Oriental family carries more status than the position of the first-born in the Western family. The authors point out that recent anthropological and sociological studies confirm that this tradition remains in force today.

On the basis of the above discussion, the following hypotheses were advanced:

1) First-born males of Eastern (extended) families who were born abroad will appear as candidates for officer training more frequently than will later-born males from these families.
2) First-born males from Eastern families (nuclear) born in Israel will not differ significantly from later-born offspring from these families in the frequency with which they appear as candidates for officer training.
3) First-born males of Western (nuclear) families will appear as candidates for officer training less frequently than will later-born males from these families.

The population consisted of two samples: a) 2,523 males, constituting a representative sample of candidates for officer training for the period of 1964-1966, and b) 2,388 males, constituting a

representative sample for the years 1961-1963. Analysis of the two
samples confirmed the first two hypotheses but not the third.

   Additional analyses were undertaken in an attempt to determine
the possible source of the surprising reversal of the third hypothesis.
Accordingly, the Western group, similar to the Eastern group, was
divided into native and foreign-born, though this distinction did not
imply two different kinds of family structure (nuclear and extended)
as it did for the Middle Eastern group. A justification for this division
was the fact that many of the foreign-born Western candidates were
reared in unusual circumstances, having been born towards the end
of or shortly following World War II. The conditions attending their
early life were thus different from those of the men of Western ethnic
origin born in Israel. The third hypothesis was confirmed, but only
for Israeli-born Western males.

   Thus the unsubstantiated part of hypothesis 3, that the first-
born males of Western origin born abroad would appear for officer
training with greater than expected frequency, ran counter to the
authors' (and Schachter's) hypothesis. The authors offered two explanations: a) that foreign-born Western candidates were born during,
or immediately after, World War II, and their parents, as a result of
their own deprivation, might have instilled into them an unusually
high level of aspiration; and b) that many survivors of the holocaust
had lost their children, so that the first-born in the sample were not
the first children reared by their mothers.

   In another study by the same authors, based on data from the
officer training school of the Israeli Defense Forces, the following
question was asked: "Are first-born sons more effective than later-
born sons in task performance, and what is the influence of ethnic
group membership on the relationship?" The population studied
consisted of a representative sample of 1,045 men who had successfully completed the three-day entrance examination during the period
of 1965-1967. For the group as a whole, the first-born performed
significantly more effectively than did the later-born.

   The data were broken down into the following four groups: (1)
foreign-born of Western origin; (2) Israeli-born of Western origin;
(3) foreign-born of Eastern origin; (4) Israeli-born of Eastern origin.
The results of this analysis showed that the first-born from abroad
of both Western and Eastern origin (groups 1 and 3) succeeded more

frequently than later-born males born abroad. However, there were no consistent findings for first-born Israeli males. Those of Western origin performed significantly less successfully than did their later-born counterparts, whereas there were no significant birth-order differences for the Israeli-born of Eastern origin.[14]

Ultraorthodox Families

A study of the family patterns of ultraorthodox women was undertaken by Esther Goshen-Gottestein, who studied the courtship patterns and attitudes to marriage and pregnancy of twenty such women living in the Geula district of Jerusalem.[15] Seventeen of them had been born in Israel and all except one were of European descent. These women were fairly well educated; two-thirds had received between nine and twelve years' schooling. At the time of the interview, conducted in 1957 and 1958, their average age was twenty-two years.

Some of the characteristics of their subculture were uncovered. The group is entirely dedicated to the perpetuation of Jewish religious law. Religious observance penetrates all aspects of daily life. It is a man's culture; the woman's status is definitely secondary. Reared in a closed culture, the girls and women neither read novels nor attend the movies. There is complete segregation of the sexes; boys and girls, even in the early grades, do not attend the same classes.

Parents choose the marriage partner, usually with the aid of a marriage broker. Personal happiness, romance, self-fulfillment and the husband as a social companion are all foreign conceptions. All the women maintain a kosher household, observe the Sabbath (do not write, work or travel on this day), take a ritual bath after menstruation, cover their hair after marriage, and for the sake of modesty wear clothing that completely covers their bodies.

Their husbands are for the most part student-scholars who do not work but enjoy high prestige. Families live on grants or are maintained by the women. The interviews revealed the following:

Courtship: Eighteen of the women reported that they had met their husbands via a marriage broker. Two-thirds of the women hardly knew their prospective husbands at the time of engagement. There was relatively little contact during the engagement period. The primary reason for marriage was "cultural expectations," as expressed in such remarks as: "It is natural to marry," or: "We are commanded to do so." None of the women mentioned love or sex as a reason for marriage.

One-fourth of the women did not answer the question concerning the qualities of an ideal husband. The most frequently cited characteristic was "intellectual," that the husband should be a rabbinical student or at least a person who could "learn" (the reference was to Talmudical study only). Other traits concerned the right kind of personality, such as "understanding," "virtuous," "considerate." None said that they wanted to be loved.

Marriage: Sexual adaptation: The key terms were "sexual duty" and "commandments," not pleasure and enjoyment, which were regarded as incompatible with religious behavior. None of the women reported that they had experienced orgasm.

Social life: There was virtually no going out together, except for Saturday walks. The husbands were unacquainted with their wives' friends and vice versa. Not surprisingly, there was little communication between husband and wife.

Role of the mother: The large majority were closely attached to their mothers, and visited them often.

Family planning: There was no discussion of family planning. Seventeen of the women said that they would never use contraceptive methods. They wanted large families.

Pregnancy: Eleven of the twenty women became pregnant during the first three months of the marriage and all were pregnant by the end of two years of marriage. Pregnancy, as would be expected, was enthusiastically welcomed. There were little or no pre-delivery preparations for the baby, owing to (the author thinks) the belief that such preparations would negatively affect pregnancy and the baby. Unexpectedly, only five women reported that they preferred a son. Perhaps the women were reticent about their preference, because of their superstitious fears about pregnancy.

These women apparently internalized completely the norms of their subculture. They completely accepted their secondary status in a man's society, and likewise did not resent the lack of communication with their husbands.

POSITION OF WOMEN

Rivkah Bar-Yosef and Ilana Einhorn Shelach, two female socio-

logists, have described the position of women in Israel.[16] They
analyzed the women's situation according to three criteria: 1)
where women are considered similar to men and both sexes receive
equal treatment; 2) where the qualitative differences between the
sexes are taken into account and both sexes receive equal treatment;
and 3) where men and women receive unequal treatment.

Similar and Equal

"The State of Israel will maintain equal social and political
rights for all citizens, irrespective of religion, race and sex." This
basic universalistic principle led to the introduction of laws in the
institutional sphere. Women, like men, may vote at the age of eighteen
and be elected to office at the age of twenty-one. Military service is
compulsory for both sexes.

Women have equal status in respect to all property rights and legal
activities. In matters of salary, seniority and severance pay they have
the same rights as men. Alimony is paid by the earning partner to
the nonearning partner irrespective of sex. The husband and wife
are held to be equally responsible with regard to the guardianship
of their children, their education and maintenance.

Dissimilar and Equal

On the grounds that women are more vulnerable than men, much
of the welfare legislation is protective, giving them preferential treatment. Thus, married and pregnant women, as well as mothers, are
exempt from army service. An employer must hold a job open for a
woman who is away on childbirth leave and he cannot dismiss a pregnant woman. The woman's retirement age is sixty as compared to
sixty-five for the men.

Dissimilar and Unequal

Religious laws are in force in the area of family law. Whereas secular
legislation is universalistic and egalitarian, religious legislation is parti-
cularistic and nonegalitarian. This inequality is seen most poignantly
in the case of remarriage, where there are at least three problem areas.
The first is what is called the levirate proscription, viz., that if a married
man dies childless, his brother must marry the widow or free her. If the

brother refuses to marry her, the woman is not allowed to remarry until
the prescribed ritual is performed. In Europe this custom was not followed,
but was practiced to an extent by Jewish communities in Moslem countries. In Israel, secular law attempts to force the male to release the
widow. Since in the last analysis the release must be given by the deceased
husband's brother and not the court, the giving of the release is at times
exploited for economic gain; the widow is forced to pay the brother in
order that he perform the ceremony that enables her to remarry.

The second aspect concerns legalization of adulterous relationships.
A woman proven guilty of adultery is forbidden both to her husband
and to the adulterer. There are cases where the woman preceded her
husband to Israel and while outside Israel the husband had obtained
a civil divorce. The woman is still considered married, even though the
husband is regarded as divorced. If she in the meantime has a child by
someone else, it is proof of her adultery and she cannot marry the
father of the child. Similar restrictions are not binding for the husband
maintaining an illicit relationship.

The third concerns a situation where the husband's whereabouts
are unknown, an event which often happens in wartime. In such a
case the woman cannot obtain a divorce, for the courts are reluctant
to grant the woman a divorce without definite proof of the husband's
death. There is no such difficulty for the male.

The difficulty of remarriage in the case of women has given rise
to three forms of quasi-institutionalized practices. The first is performed
within the religious system, but outside the formal religious requirements.
Religious ritual is followed, except that the marriage ceremony is ex-
ecuted by a layman and not a rabbi. The parties contend that the
marriage ceremony was in accordance with traditional Jewish law,
where a rabbi is not needed to officiate. In a test case brought before
the secular courts, an ambiguous decision was given concerning the
legal status of such marriages.

The second is a civil marriage contracted outside the country.
Cyprus is the preferred place, because of its proximity to Israel and
its minimum requirement of a fortnight's residence. While the legal
validity of such marriages remains in doubt, at least for administrative purposes the marriages are officially recorded. The third is a
de facto solution without concern for the *de jure* situation—common
law marriage. While this kind of marriage is not legally valid, the
economic rights of the wife are recognized by the law.

JEWISH-ARAB MARRIAGES

Little appears to be known on the subject of Jewish-Arab marriages, as indicated by the estimate of their number, which varies between three hundred and one thousand. One reason for this large variation in the estimate has to do with the fact that a number of these appeared to be civil law unions, a category whose status is not clearly defined. While both Eastern and Western Jews in Israel are decidedly against intermarriage, marriage to an Arab is regarded as a much more serious defection than marriage to a Christian. Eastern Jews show more enmity towards such marriages, but then, the Jews of Europe had no dealings with Arabs. Arabs, on the other hand, are receptive to such marriages, as for them there is no shameful loss of daughters to non-Muslims. Furthermore, Islam permits marriages between non-Arab women and Arab men, and Jewish women who marry Arab men usually accept the Arab way of life.

As part of a community study, Eric Cohen reported thirteen Jewish-Arab marriages.[17] Examination of the cases showed that in all instances the marriage was between an Arab man and a Jewish woman. Four types of marriages were seen. Arranged according to legitimacy, they were:

Conversion of Arab spouses to Judaism—1 case
Civil law marriage—1 case
Conversion of Jewish spouses to Islam—3 cases
Common-law unions—6 cases
(Plus 2 additional cases in the immediate past, which ended in divorce before the research began)

In virtually every instance the Jewish women had been marginal in Israeli society; they were either prostitutes, mentally retarded, or had left home at an early age. In every instance except one they had been completely rejected by their families upon marrying. Most if not all of the women had problems of personality, identity, and security before their marriage. To the extent that they were part of any community, it was the Arab, not the Jewish one.

Most of the Arab husbands were likewise marginal members of their community, some being pimps or fortune tellers. As a group they were somewhat less marginal than their spouses; several of them worked in conventional occupations (carpenter, fisherman and public employee).

One positive function of such marriages might have been to serve as a bridge between Jews and Arabs. Due to the marginality of both the men and the women, their underground connections and the common-law unions, this function could hardly be fulfilled.

CHANGES IN THE PATTERN OF MARRIAGE AND FAMILY PLANNING

Table 56 presents the average age of marriage for grooms and brides according to region of birth and time of immigration to Israel. These figures show that Easterners marry earlier than Westerners, although this difference is diminishing, especially for the brides. This is attributable to the fact that the age of marriage declined for Western brides while remaining more or less constant for Eastern ones. The age of marriage for the Israeli-born brides was lower than that of the Eastern and European-born.

Marriages between people of different geocultural origins are clearly an important index of integration. The data show a consistent but not marked trend to contract ethnically mixed marriages. Inter-group marriages rose from about 9 percent in 1952 to nearly 15 percent in 1960. In these mixed marriages the majority of the cases involved a European groom and an Oriental bride. This pattern of marriage between a majority group male and minority group female is in contrast to the more widespread intermarriage pattern of a majority group woman and minority group man found in other countries.

These figures, however, do not completely reflect the number of ethnic group marriages, for they omit interethnic differences among the varying Eastern communities. Between 1952 and 1957, 44 percent of the marriages occurred between persons from different countries of birth. In these years, 53 percent of Israeli-born brides married foreign-born grooms and 37 percent of Israeli-born grooms married foreign-born brides.

Table 57 presents an attraction index according to country of birth. This is an index of inter-group marriages, that is, the extent to which people of the same ethnic group marry within that ethnic group. The higher the index, the greater the tendency to marry with-

TABLE 56
AVERAGE AND MEDIAN AGE OF BRIDES AND GROOMS ACCORDING TO COUNTRY OF ORIGIN AND PERIOD OF MIGRATION

Year	ISRAEL BORN	BORN IN ASIA-AFRICA			BORN IN EUROPE			Total
		Before 1955	Migrated After 1955	Total	Before 1955	Migrated After 1955	Total	
BRIDES								
AVERAGE AGE								
1960/62	24.8	25.7	25.4	28.7	28.7	29.7	29.0	26.4
1963	25.1	25.9	25.5	25.9	28.6	28.5	28.6	26.4
1964	24.9	26.0	25.4	26.0	28.6	28.2	28.5	26.2
1965	24.8	25.9	25.2	25.7	28.2	28.0	28.1	26.0
1966	24.7	25.9	25.0	25.6	27.1	27.5	27.3	25.7
GROOMS								
AVERAGE AGE								
1960/62	21.7	21.1	21.5	21.3	23.6	24.9	24.1	22.0
1963	21.6	21.1	21.6	21.3	22.5	24.1	23.2	21.9
1964	21.5	21.2	21.8	21.5	21.8	23.7	22.8	21.8
1965	21.6	21.3	21.6	21.4	20.9	23.2	22.0	21.6
1966	21.5	21.2	21.6	21.4	20.8	22.5	21.6	21.5

Source: *Statistical Abstracts No. 19*, Central Bureau of Statistics. (Jerusalem, 1968): p. 65.

in the group. The table shows that inter-group marriages are high among people born in Iraq, Yemen, Morocco, Algeria and Tunisia. For European countries, the rate of inter-group marriages is lower, an expected statistic since the different countries in Europe cannot be regarded as being composed of distinct ethnic groups.

TABLE 57
ATTRACTION INDEXES ACCORDING TO COUNTRY OF BIRTH OF BRIDE AND GROOM, 1962

Yemen and Aden	0.82	Greece	0.37
Morocco, Tunisia and Algeria	0.74	Israeli: Asian-African Origin	0.36
Iraq	0.70	Egypt	0.36
Libya	0.61	Argentina	0.34
Iran	0.60	Syria and Lebanon	0.29
Rumania	0.58	Hungary	0.28
Israeli: European origin	0.56	Germany	0.26
Total	0.52	Soviet Union	0.18
Poland	0.48	Yugoslavia	0.18
Turkey	0.45	Czechoslovakia	0.16
Bulgaria	0.37	United States	0.12

Source: *Jewish Marriages in Israel,* Publication Series No. 194.
(Central Bureau of Statistics, 1965):p. 123.

Rationalization of Child Bearing

Several studies conducted by Matras and his colleagues on fertility and on what he calls "rationalization of child bearing" present interesting data on both family change and integration.[18] They found that there is a trend to control child bearing among families of Eastern origin, which have the highest fertility rate, as well as among religious families of European descent. Matras feels that these trends signify an important aspect of integration of the various origin groups.

The fertility rate of women born in Asia and Africa is considerably higher than that of women born in Europe or Israel. Thus in 1960 60 percent of the births were by mothers born in Asia and Africa, and 22 percent by mothers born in Europe. Gabriel (cited by Matras) found that the fertility rate of women of Eastern origin appears to decline with length of residence in the country. Thus in 1951 and 1954 fertility rates of women of Eastern origin who migrated before the establishment of the state were 5.71 and 4.22, respectively. For these same years, the fertility rates of women of Eastern origin who immigrated in 1948 or later were 6.50 and 5.96. Matras' own study, conducted in 1958, is based on data collected from twenty-three hospitals in Israel. The study included all women giving birth in the hospitals during a sixty-day period in Tel Aviv, a forty-day period in Jerusalem, and a twelve-day period in hospitals elsewhere. The following findings emerged from the author's analysis.

There was a marked difference in geocultural origin and reported past practice of contraception. More than twice as many women born in Israel (61 percent) and in Europe (64 percent) reported contraceptive practice than did women born in Asia-Africa (25 percent). While social class had little influence on the fertility patterns of Israeli-born women, it had a large impact on the number of births and family planning for women born in Asia and Africa. These differences were particularly manifest between women with no formal education (illiterate in any language) and those with some education.

Particular attention was given to the change found among Eastern females and the religious women of Western origin—a change from no birth control to conscious planning. In fact, a large number of the women who practiced contraception were children of mothers who did *not* practice contraception.

The interviews were also aimed at eliciting the reasons for not practicing contraception. Three reasons were forthcoming. The first was of a religious nature. The majority of religious couples objected to the use of contraceptive methods; large families were considered both desirable and normal. Moreover, the religious community, by its own charities and welfare services (which supplemented the many basic services generally available throughout Israel), provided assistance to these families.

The second reason was a temporary or permanent indifference or inability to abstract the concept of "a desirable number of children." This refers to a group of women who did not believe that they had any power to control the number of children. For these women abstractions such as "number of children," or "size of family," were not meaningful. The women in this group were for the most part illiterate Oriental women who did not speak or understand Hebrew, were near the end of their fertility cycle, and lived in isolated areas. High fertility was a source of status for these women, and a proof of the health and virility of their husbands.

The third reason was that there existed an ambiguity and vagueness regarding contraception. This applied to a group of women who were midway through their fertile life and were interested in slowing down the pace of pregnancies. While formally orthodox, they differed from their Western orthodox sisters in that their religious knowledge and commitment seemed to be superficial. They were therefore less likely to avoid the use of contraceptive methods for religious reasons.

Other reasons elicited by the investigator for not using birth control methods included the strangeness of the concept of birth control (there were few "role models"; mothers, relatives and most friends did not use them); and real or imagined objections on the part of the husbands. Discussions of sex relations and family planning were never held between a woman and her husband.

One group of women, designated as the "early intervention group," consisted of women who reported using contraceptive devices after the second birth. In contrast to the religious and partly religious women in this group, these nonobservant women were more likely to begin the practice of contraception earlier in marriage, to use "artificial" methods (and use them consistently), and to resort to induced abortion in case of failure.[19]

The abortion rate and the rate of premature deliveries as affected by ethnicity has been studied by Z. Faulshouk and S. Halevi.[20] The authors' clinical impression was that European women had a higher rate of abortions and premature deliveries than did Eastern women. To determine the accuracy of their observation, they surveyed 3,095 women registered in several hospitals, 834 European, 1,298 Eastern (excluding Yemenites), 235 Yemenites, 506 Arabs, 222 Druzes. The results strongly confirmed their impressions. Women born in Europe had the lowest number of full-term births (55.2 percent compared to 78.5 percent for Eastern women and 88.9 percent for Yemenite women) and the highest rate of artificial abortions (23.3 percent compared to 7.3 percent for Eastern women and 1.5 percent for Yemenite women). Moreover, European women had the lowest average number of children (3.76, compared to 4.56 for Eastern and 4.77 for Yemenite women).

European women also had the highest rates for premature deliveries
and early and late abortions.

The higher rates of miscarriages and premature deliveries among
European women do not derive from the higher rate of artificial
abortions, nor do they stem from the larger number of pregnancies
or the increased number of first cousin marriages found among Eastern
women. The authors are at a loss to explain how the ethnic factor
operates here, although they suggest that dietary habits may somehow
be partly responsible, as the membranes of the afterbirths of the
European women contain considerably more fat than do the membranes
of the afterbirths of the Eastern and Yemenite women.

CONCLUSION

Had we incorporated the research on the kibbutz family and
discussed some of the anthropological studies mentioned in the
chapter on immigration and absorption, one might then feel that
more research had been undertaken in this area of sociology. As it
is, several topics have received special study. One is that of intergenerational conflict which at the time the researches were undertaken
was a subject of societal concern. The assumption underlying these
investigations seemed to be that children of Eastern parents would
be under greater family stress than children of Western parents.
Surprisingly, the results indicated little conflict. However, these
studies were limited to a particular period of time, the early 1950s.
Little research on intergenerational conflict has been undertaken
since. Such conflict might emerge after the youth has been living in
the country for a longer period of time. For this reason it is to be
regretted that such research has been terminated. The author, for
example, has met a number of female college students of Eastern
descent whose parents objected to their attending college. In the
cases of the author's acquaintances, the girls won, although often
with compromises such as attending a college closer to home or not
living in a dormitory.

In general, however, it is difficult to understand the lack of
studies examining family functioning in Eastern and Western families.
Since so much of the research has been concerned with demonstrating

consequences (differential school performance, crime rates, income), it would be expected that family dynamics would be studied. We are unaware of such studies being planned by sociologists. In 1970, however, a group of social psychologists (all except one from the Department of Psychology) met on this particular issue and decided to seek support for such a study. The proposed budget was $100,000, a high sum in Israeli terms.

Similarly, one would think Eisenstadt's typology of families would have stimulated further research, particularly his concern for the relationship between kind of family and successful integration. Perhaps Eisenstadt's interest changed, and with it the direction of his students' research.

In some ways the most interesting findings are the data which show movement over time—the demographic materials, changes in the age of marriage, increase in interethnic marriages, and readiness to plan the size of one's family.

NOTES

1. Dina Feitelson, "Some Changes in the Educational Patterns of the Kurdish Community in Israel," *Megamot* (6, 1955): pp. 275-298 (in Hebrew). See also D. Feitelson, "Education of Pre-School Children in Kurdistan Communities," *Megamot* (5, 1954): pp. 95-109 (in Hebrew).

2. Peretz Cohen, "Community and Stability in an Immigrant Town," in M. Lissak, B. Mizrachi and O. Ben-David (eds.), *Immigrants in Israel*. (Jerusalem: Academon, 1969), pp. 217-233 (in Hebrew).

3. Fanny Bier, "Value Conflicts in Immigrant Children—Reflections of a Ma'abara Teacher," *Megamot* (5, 1954): pp. 386-391 (in Hebrew).

4. Dov Weintraub and Miriam Shapiro, "The Traditional Family in Israel in the Process of Change-Crisis and Continuation," in Rivkah Bar-Yosef and Ilana Shelach (eds.), *The Family in Israel*. (Jerusalem: Academon, 1969), pp. 215-228.

5. Elihu Katz and Avraham Zloczower, "Ethnic Continuity in the

Second Generation: A Report on Yemenites and Ashkenazim (European Jews) in a Small Israeli Town," *Megamot* (9, 1958): pp. 187-200 (in Hebrew).

6. Hagit Rieger, "Some Aspects of the Acculturation of Yemenite Youth Immigrants," in C. Frankenstein (ed.), *Between Past and Future.* (Jerusalem: Szold Foundation, 1953), pp. 82-109. A similar version appears in Hebrew under the title, "Problems of Adjustment of Yemenite Children in Israel," *Megamot* (3, 1952): pp. 259-291.

7. Weintraub and Shapiro, *op. cit.*

8. C. Adler, *et al.,* "Youth in the Morasha Neighborhood in Jerusalem" (Office of the Prime Minister, 1965) (mimeographed in Hebrew).

9. Katz and Zloczower, *op. cit.*

10. S. N. Eisenstadt, *The Absorption of Immigrants.* (London: Routledge and Kegan, Ltd., 1954), pp. 143-168, and S. N. Eisenstadt, "The Process of Absorption of New Immigrants in Israel," and Institutionalization of Immigrant Behavior," *Human Relations* (5, 1952), pp. 223-246 and 373-395.

11. Phyllis Palgi, "The Adaptability and Vulnerability of Types in the Changing Israeli Society," in A. Jarus, J. Marcus, J. Oren, C. Rapaport (eds.), *Children and Families in Israel: Some Mental Health Perspectives.* (Jerusalem: Szold Foundation), pp. 97-135. A version of this article appears in Hebrew in Rivkah Bar-Yosef and Ilana Shelach (eds.), *The Family in Israel, op. cit.,* pp. 115-123.

12. Rivkah Bar-Yosef, "Role Differentiation in the Urban Family in Israel," in Rivkah Bar-Josef and Ilana Shelach (eds.), *The Family in Israel, op. cit.,* pp. 167-182.

13. Yehuda Amir, Shlomo Sharan and Yacov Kovarsky, "Birth Order, Family Structure and Avoidance Behavior," *Journal of Personality and Social Psychology* (10, 1968): pp. 271-278.

14. Shlomo Sharan, Yehuda Amir and Yacov Kovarsky, "Birth Order and Level of Task Performance: A Cross Cultural Comparison," *Journal of Social Psychology* (78, 1969): pp. 157-163.

15. Esther R. Goshen-Gottestein, "Courtship, Marriage and Pregnancy in Geula'," *The Israel Annals of Psychiatry and Related Disciplines,* (4, 1966): pp. 43-46. Also, Esther R. Goshen-Gottestein, *Marriage and First Pregnancy – Cultural Influence on Attitudes of Israeli Women.* (London: Tavistock, 1966).

16. Rivkah Bar-Yosef and Ilana Shelach, "The Position of Women in Israel," in S. N. Eisenstadt, R. Bar-Yosef, R. Cahana, I. Shelach (eds.), *Stratification in Israel.* (Jerusalem: Academon, 1968), pp. 414-454.

17. Eric Cohen, "Mixed Marriages in an Israeli Town," *Jewish Journal of Sociology* (11, 1969): pp. 41-50.

18. Judah Matras, *Social Change in Israel.* (Chicago: Aldine, 1965), pp. 171-195; Judah Matras, "The Social Strategy of Family Formation: Some Variations in Time and Space," *Demography* (2, 1965). J. Matras "Religious Observance and Family Formation in Israel: Some Intergenerational Changes," *American Journal of Sociology* (69, 1964): pp. 465-475.

19. Roberto Bachi and Judah Matras, "Contraception and Induced Abortion among Jewish Maternity Cases in Israel," *Milbank Memorial Fund Quarterly* (40, 1962): pp. 207-229; J. Matras and Hanah Auerbach, "On Rationalization of Family Formation in Israel," *Milbank Memorial Fund Quarterly* (42, 1964).

20. Z. Faulshouk and S. Halevi, "The Ethnic Factor in Abortions and Premature Deliveries," *Harephuah* (68, 1965): pp. 291-294 (in Hebrew).

6

Criminology

CRIME RATES AND COUNTRY OF ORIGIN

The migration of Asian-African Jews from their native lands was bound up with a clash of cultures[1] encompassing a loss of respect for the norms and authorities valid in their country of origin. Their educational level, vocational training, and adaptability to a modern economic system failed to meet the demands of the economic life in Israel. Although, for many, almost two decades have elapsed since their immigration to Israel, their economic situation has not greatly improved. The poverty centers in the big cities, a potential breeding ground for crime and delinquency, are predominantly comprised of an Oriental ethnic population.

Resettlement into a new country does not only affect the immigrant but may have an adverse effect on the second generation as well. Adopting the larger society's high level of ambition, the second generation may consider their families obstacles to their advancement. Conflict with parents, coupled with a lack of family unity caused by the weakening of traditional reference and the family's own difficulty in adjusting may lead to affiliation with criminal subcultures. Sociological literature has pointed out that a combination of poverty, culture conflict, lack of family unity, low socioeconomic status, and minority group status constitute a basis for deviant social behavior. The Eastern population in Israel is subject to nearly all these conditions.

Table 58 shows crime rates according to geographic origin in 1957 and 1958. These years were chosen because they reflect a rela-

175

tively static situation following the period of mass migration from
Moslem countries. Table 58 shows marked variations in the crime
rates of immigrants from different continents; most striking is the
low crime rate of Jews born in Israel.

TABLE 58
CRIME RATES ACCORDING TO CONTINENT OF BIRTH IN 1957 AND 1958

	1957			1958		
	First Offenders	Recidivists	Total	First Offenders	Recidivists	Total
Israel	6.1	6.7	12.8	9.1	6.6	15.7
Asia	19.3	9.2	28.5	18.1	9.8	27.9
Africa	19.1	10.0	29.1	19.6	10.3	29.9
Europe	17.6	8.1	25.7	16.5	7.4	23.9
Unknown	1.8	2.1	3.9	1.5	1.1	2.6

Source: Criminal Statistics, 1949-1962. (Institute of Criminology, Jerusalem,
1965), p. 138.

A comparison of the crime rates for 1957 and 1958 shows a rise
in the Israeli-born group, with a contrasting decline for the
European-born.

Table 59 presents rates of juvenile delinquency according to
country of origin for the same years. While over a period of one
year there was no general rise in the rate of delinquency, sharp differences among the various countries of origin were noted. The highest rate of juvenile delinquency was found among those of African
extraction, the lowest among those of European origin.

Even before 1948, many of the Moslem countries were moving
from a feudalistic traditional society to a modern one, with a consequent manifestation of anomie and deviant behavior. Nevertheless,
the post-1948 immigration was more problematical to the Jewish
immigrant, following as it did persecutions and sanctions against
the Jewish communities in Moslem countries, the disintegration of
traditional family relationships, and the sudden culture conflict.
Data pertaining to the period of immigration to Israel are presented

in Table 60. These data show a higher concentration of delinquents of all ethnic extractions among those who immigrated to Israel after the foundation of the state. This is so even for the Israeli-born; the rate of delinquency for those whose parents had immigrated before 1947 was lower than for those whose parents immigrated after 1947.

TABLE 59
JUVENILE DELINQUENCY ACCORDING TO
COUNTRY OF ORIGIN FOR 1957 AND 1958

	1957			1958		
	First Offenders	Recidivists	Total	First Offenders	Recidivists	Total
Israel	22.2	6.7	28.9	20.1	8.2	28.3
Asia	28.7	4.6	33.3	23.4	6.2	29.6
Africa	24.7	3.8	28.5	25.5	5.9	31.4
Europe	6.6	1.3	7.9	8.2	1.3	9.5
Unknown	0.6	0.8	1.4	0.8	0.4	1.2

Source: Criminal Statistics, 1949-1962. (Institute of Criminology, Jerusalem, 1965), p. 138.

TABLE 60
DELINQUENCY ACCORDING TO ETHNIC ORIGIN
AND PERIOD OF IMMIGRATION

	1957	1958
Total, Israeli-born	12.8	15.7
Total, Asian-African born	52.3	60.2
Immigrated before 1947	5.4	6.6
Immigrated after 1947	46.9	53.6
Total, European-born	24.4	24.8
Immigrated before 1947	8.9	9.0
Immigrated after 1947	15.5	15.8

Source: Criminal Statistics, 1949-1962. (Institute of Criminology, Jerusalem, 1965), pp. 134-135, 182-185.

Data indicating a relationship between the socioeconomic status of the parents and the delinquency rates are supplied by a study conducted by the Ministry of Welfare. This research deals with juvenile delinquents under the supervision of Youth Protection Authority in the year 1966. The group comprised 500 youths convicted and sent to institutions. The figures of Table 61 show clearly

TABLE 61
RATES OF DELINQUENCY OF INMATES OF YOUTH INSTITUTIONS ACCORDING TO FATHER'S OCCUPATION

Occupation of Father	No. of Delinquents
Clerks and Salesmen	11
Small-Business Owners	38
Transportation Workers	11
Manual Workers	32
Service Workers	35
Non-Skilled Workers	235
No Permanent Work	46
Don't Know	62
Total	500

Source: "Survey of Government-run Homes under the Auspices of the Protection Authority." (Jerusalem, Ministry of Welfare, 1966).

that the rates of delinquency rise as the occupational status of the father declines. The majority of fathers (47 percent) were non-skilled workers. Another indication of the relationship between social class and delinquency appears in Table 62, which cites the educational level of the incarcerated youth, cross-classified according to their country of origin. Not surprisingly, the youth were poorly educated. However, the majority turned out to be Israeli-born. To ascertain whether these native-born youth were of Eastern or Western extraction, we turn to Table 63 where the data are classified according to the father's country of origin and educational level. From this table we learn that the majority of Israeli-born youth were of North African descent and that the educational level of the parents of convicted juvenile delinquents was unusually low. In fact, the

TABLE 62
EDUCATIONAL LEVEL OF INSTITUTIONALIZED YOUTH
ACCORDING TO COUNTRY OF BIRTH

Educational Level	Israeli-born	Eastern Europe	Southern Europe	Western Europe	North Africa	Middle East	Far East	South Africa
1-4 years	130	3	—	1	58	4	1	—
5-6 years	106	1	1	2	35	1	1	—
7-8 years	24	1	—	1	12	6	—	—
High School	6	—	—	3	—	—	—	—
Religious School	—	—	—	—	2	—	—	—
Other	—	—	—	—	—	—	—	—

Source: "Survey of Government-run Homes Under the Auspices of the Youth Protection Authority." (Jerusalem, Ministry of Welfare, 1966).

TABLE 63
EDUCATIONAL LEVEL OF INCARCERATED YOUTH ACCORDING TO FATHER'S COUNTRY OF ORIGIN

Educational Level	Israeli-born	Eastern Europe	Southern Europe	Western Europe	North Africa	Middle East	Far East	South Africa
1-4 years	8	13	1	2	122	52	1	—
5-6 years	5	7	4	—	71	56	1	—
7-8 years	2	2	—	—	21	18	—	—
High School	1	1	—	—	4	3	—	—
Yeshiva	—	—	—	—	2	—	—	—
Other	—	—	—	—	1	—	—	—

Source: "Survey of Government-run Homes Under the Auspices of the Youth Protection Authority." (Jerusalem, Ministry of Welfare, 1966).

majority of the fathers had not completed their elementary schooling, while the proportion of fathers who had attended secondary school was negligible.

The facts presented above testify to the significantly higher delinquency rate of immigrants from Asia and Africa. Yet as we have already emphasized, these two continents include many ethnic groups with different cultures. As we have seen earlier, some of these ethnic groups were more successful in adjusting to Israeli society. In order to gain a clearer understanding of these ethnic differences, we present the crime rates according to the specific country of origin (Table 64). The most notable fact in Table 64 is the very high crime rate found amongst Jews who migrated from Morocco, who constitute about one-third of the total of the non-Israeli-born criminal population.

TABLE 64
CRIME RATES ACCORDING TO COUNTRY OF ORIGIN

Country of Origin	Rate
Total Born Outside of Israel	9.6
Morocco	33.4
Algeria, Tunisia, Libya	18.5
Asia	15.0
Turkey, Syria, Lebanon, Egypt	10.6
Greece, Bulgaria	5.7
Hungary, Rumania	5.3
Remaining Countries in Asia-Africa	3.9

Source: Criminal Statistics, 1949-1962. (Institute of Criminology, Jerusalem, 1965).

An explanation of the unusually high crime rate of Moroccan immigrants is supplied by the numerous studies which deal with this ethnic community. These studies emphasize the especially low social status of the Moroccan Jews who serve as a target for hostility and prejudice.[2] In her study on patterns of ethnic tension in Israel, Judith Shuval pointed out that Moroccans were ranked lowest of all ethnic groups and were a particularly disliked group. An important fact is that the proportion of people expressing hostility towards Moroccans had increased with time. In 1950 only 5 percent of the

respondents mentioned that they disliked Moroccans; the rate of
rejection of this group reached 39 percent in 1959.[3] The high concentration of Moroccans in many development towns, coupled with
their occupational concentration on the lower levels of the social
scale, made them conspicuous as a low status group, a convenient
target for hostility.

In addition to the ethnic group hostility and the subsequent negative self-image internalized by its members, the specific historical
conditions that set Moroccan Jewry apart from other African and
Asian immigrants aggravated the situation of this ethnic group. The
Moroccan Jews were already undergoing a transitional phase at the
time of their immigration. Having abandoned their conservative
character, they were in the middle of a process of integration into
the wider social system. This very process of modernization
led to ambitions for a higher standard of living, but within North
African society no chance existed for their realization. They had
thus emigrated with high hopes of attaining a higher social and economic status in Israel. Confronted by the difficulties of absorption,
they soon found themselves with low occupational status and with
a low standard of living. With a sense of frustration, bitterness, and
anger, they resigned themselves to these conditions, and gave vent
to their feelings by resorting to crime. Data pertaining to the types
of criminal activity most common in different ethnic groups illustrate
this tendency. The North African group was responsible for a considerable proportion of offenses of all kinds, but its role in crimes
against property (robbery, stealing and housebreaking) was especially great.

STIGMA THEORY, PROSTITUTION, AND NARCOTICS

Shlomo Shoham offers an interesting explanation for the high
rate of prostitution among girls of North African extraction. He
bases his explanation on the theory of stigma which he has advanced
in several articles[4] and a book.[5]

Stigma is defined as a "derogatory attribute imputed to the
social image of an individual or groups, and used as a tool of social
control." The concern is not with the stigmatization imposed by
the court but with the stigma imputed to the individual by society

prior to this and the resulting self-definition of the individual. The author points to three focal points of criminology: the cause of the process by which a person commits his first offense or a child makes his first steps towards delinquency; the problems of recidivism and the process which leads a first offender to be persistent, professional, and, ultimately, a hardened incorrigible criminal; and the phenomenon of crime on the social level, i.e., the fluctuation of crime rates in a given time, the genesis and volume of special types of crime and their interrelationships between crime, delinquency and social change. Shoham's concern is with preconviction stigma, that is, the second of the above three stages.

A causal model of social stigma is presented. The model has two focuses. The first refers to factors linked to social stigma; reference is to an individual or a group being stigmatized. The second relates to the actual process in which society brands the object.

A CAUSAL MODEL OF SOCIAL STIGMA

The Predisposition Configuration
of the Stigmatized Deviant Behavior

1. Autustic
2. Self-destructive
3. Escapist
4. "Bohemian"
5. Accidental
6. Acquisitive
   I. Occasional
   II. Semi-Professional
   III. Professional
7. Rebellious
   I. Chaotic
   II. Ideational

Value Deviation

1. Rejection of socially accepted
life goals (personal anomie)
2. Immorality and amorality

The Dynamic Process of
Stigmatization Psychogenic
Motives

1. An Outlet of Aggression
2. Projection of Guilt
3. Displacement of Resentment
4. The stigmatized as "scapegoat"

Socio-psychological Pressures

5. The stigmatized as a symbolic
source of danger
6. Relative powerlessness
7. Exposure to the source of stigma
8. "Somebody to look down upon"
9. "Explaining away" alters
achievement

Social Level

Social Stigma as an Act of Power

Source: S. Shoham and G. Rahav, "Social Stigma and Prostitution," *International Annals of Criminology* (6, 1967): p.485.

The last category of the model, the social level, deserves elaboration. "The stigma of deviance is gained in a way similar to the stigma of a criminal. It is not necessarily linked with ethics, metaphysics or justice but with an act of power directed against an individual or a group who are too conspicuously different, and their existence or behavior is detrimental to the power-backed stigmatizing agencies."[6] Thus the designation of the person who is to receive "the mark of Cain" is a matter of whom the power element wishes to brand. The deviant or the criminal is that person (or persons, group, or groups) who is so designated by those in power. Clearly the criteria for branding are various and dynamic depending on the given society and the people who rule. However a person or group is stigmatized, the effect is strong, reinforcing and most difficult to overcome. Deviant behavior is then both a predisposition to and result of stigmatization.

Following is a model of the stigma theory applied by Shoham and Rahav to account for the prostitution of girls of North African extraction.

A MODEL OF STIGMA PROCESS APPLIED TO ETIOLOGY OF NORTH AFRICAN PROSTITUTES FROM AUTHORITARIAN FAMILIES IN ISRAEL

Transmission of the Stigma by the family (mostly the father) and other relevant others.	The Girl
1. Scapegoating as an outlet of aggression and projection of guilt through extra punitiveness.	1. She would be significantly conspicuous, behaviorally, physically, or by any other trait which would set her apart, as far as her social visibility is concerned.
2. Authoritarian family, coupled with authoritarian personality of stigmatizer.	2. She would be intolerant of ambiguity.
3. Change in social position of the parent and/or personal incapacitation.	3. Objective perception of the girl's powerlessness by stigmatizing adult.
4. Transmission of stigma with the stigmatizer's deprivational change of social position or personal incapacitation.	4. Tendency to conform.

5. North African Jewish families prescribing for girls the internalization of an ego-identity within the nuclear family, irrespective of its being non-stigmatizing or stigmatizing.	5. A high tendency for other-directedness.
6. Distortion of age and sex roles in the attitude of the stigmatizing father towards his daughter.	6. The girl would be in a subjective state of mind of powerlessness.
7. Scapegoating would be directed by the stigmatizing father towards his daughter as a consequence of his tension with his wife.	7. She would be subject to an attitudinal definition of conspicuity as related symbolically to the cause of tension.

Source: S. Shoham and G. Rahav, "Social Stigma and Prostitution," *International Annals of Criminology* (6, 1967): p. 494.

A number of factors operate in the transmission of stigma from the perspective of the girl. Since she is different from other Moroccan girls (she may be uglier or prettier, darker or lighter, more stupid or smarter, first born or later born, or physically deformed), members of the family treat her differently. The girl is powerless to defend herself against the process of stigmatization due to her youth and subordinate status in the authoritarian family. Having minimal contact outside the family, the significant contacts are the family members. She soon accepts as her self-concept the definition of others that she is depraved. Lacking inward strength, she becomes other-directed, strongly conformist, and highly intolerant of ambiguity.

The dynamic process of stigmatization operates mainly during the preadolescent and adolescent period, while the girl is still (to use Erik Erikson's term) in the "ego-diffusion" stage. In developing her ego-identity she is confronted with previous negative self-definitions where she sees herself as evil, polluted, inadequate, or as a source of trouble. Her reaction is either *intrapunitive* in which she views herself as having caused her own failure, or *extrapunitive* in which she blames her family. In either case, she attempts to live up to the behavior which she thinks her parents expect of her and which she feels will be acceptable to them. After having been rejected by her parents for sexual promiscuity, which she engaged in to live up to her derogatory image, she may in turn reject them.

Leaving home when her first boy friend abandons her, she looks for work and a new boy friend in another town. Often she will meet a pimp who at first spends money on her and treats her well, unlike the behavior to which she has been accustomed. Soon, in the hands of the procurer, she either willingly or unwillingly accepts his demands, or she may meet other prostitutes who introduce her to the profession. Another reason for the girl's proclivity to prostitution is her inability to find preferred work. With little education, either academic or vocational, she is psychologically unprepared for competitive work.

In order to examine aspects of the above theory, the authors located and interviewed seventy prostitutes in the Tel Aviv area. To ascertain whether this nonrandom sample was representative, comparison was made with sixty-four randomly selected prostitutes and pimps from the central register of the police general headquarters. No significant demographic differences were found between the two groups. The ethnic distribution is given in Table 65.

TABLE 65
ORIGIN OF PROSTITUTES

Country	Percentage	Percentage of Foreign Born	Percentage of Foreign Born in Israel's Population
North Africa	42.6	52.7	13.0
Asia	11.8	14.6	22.0
Balkans, Turkey	11.8	14.6	4.1
East Europe	10.3	12.7	44.2
West Europe	4,4	5.5	4.5
Israel	19.1	—	—

Source: S. Shoham and G. Rahav, "Social Stigma and Prostitution," *International Annals of Criminology* (6, 1967): p. 506.

The salient finding is the preponderance of girls of North African and to a lesser extent Asian extraction. Girls of North African origin constituted 42.6 percent of prostitutes in the study, while girls of European origin constituted 14.7 percent. The majority of prostitutes of North African extraction were less than ten years old when they entered the country.

The interview findings were consistent with the above theory of stigmatization, particularly in regard to low status and incapacity of the parents. The father was described as authoritarian and rigid (55 percent), and was an unskilled laborer or petty peddler (50 percent). A large percentage of fathers were drug addicts or alcoholics (30 percent); the mother was kind and permissive. One or both parents had been physically ill (60 percent) (based on a low percentage of cases). A large percentage of the girls came from broken homes (39 percent) or had suffered inadequate family relationships in other ways (49 percent). Sixty percent of the girls claimed continuous conflict with the parents. Fifty-seven percent left home before the age of fifteen, and 49 percent started work before the age of fourteen. The girls themselves came from large families; 16 percent were illiterate, 34 percent had only a fourth grade education, and 54 percent had no vocational training. Most of the girls with training had received it at institutions for wayward girls.

All this was consistent with the stigma theory, which sees the girl as forming an "evil" ego identity at a preadolescent age, having conflicts with her parents, and leaving or being expelled from home at an early age. In the majority of cases the girls were sexually promiscuous before having left or having been expelled from home. This later finding is particularly relevant to stigma theory as applied to prostitution, which claims that sexual promiscuity occurred before the girl leaves home.

Certain types of offenses common to a designated ethnic group are an integral and legitimate part of local custom in the native land and receive the stamp of illegality only in the new country. Under the pressures of adjustment, the tendency to indulge in these customs in Israel may be even stronger than before. Drug consumption, particularly the smoking of hashish, is common and acceptable in Arab countries. Due to varied cultural values, we may then anticipate a considerable difference in rates of crime according to country of origin.

Of the 582 arrested in 1966 for sale and use of drugs, 430 were Jews. The number of drug users is clearly increasing. The main sources of hashish, the most prevalent drug, are the Bedouin tribes, who receive the drug from Jordan, Syria, and Lebanon, and often smuggle it by tying it to sheep's bellies. There are four main drug centers: Tel Aviv (particularly Jaffa) which is Israel's crime center, the port

city of Haifa, Beer-Sheva (located in the area where most of the
drugs enter the country and which has a large proportion of new
immigrants), and Arab villages. Four types of drug users have been
noted: Arabs and Jews of Oriental descent who smoke hashish at
family celebrations and do not consider it illegal; bohemians and
beatniks; "fun" groups, who use the drug to increase their sensual
ecstasy; and delinquents. There are only two studies on drug addiction in Israel, which is not surprising in view of the fact that until
the Six Day War it was a minor problem.

Narcotic offenders were divided by T. Drapkin and S. Landau
into three groups according to involvement in other offenses.[7]
Table 66 shows that an overwhelmingly high percentage of narcotic

TABLE 66
CATEGORY OF NARCOTIC OFFENDERS ACCORDING
TO COUNTRY OF BIRTH

| Country of Origin | DELINQUENCY GROUP | | | |
	A*	B**	C***	Total
Israel	28.0	32.1	35.8	34.3
Middle East	42.0	17.9	22.1	24.9
North Africa	18.0	46.5	35.0	33.4
Far East	4.0	3.6	0.4	1.2
Europe	8.0	—	5.8	5.6
Unknown	—	—	0.8	0.6

*Narcotic offenders not involved in any other type of criminal activity.
**Criminals involved in other offenses, whose first offense was in the field
   of narcotics.
***Criminals involved in other offenses whose first offense was not connected
   with narcotics.
Source: T. Drapkin and S. Landau, "Drug Offenders in Israel," *British Journal
of Criminology* (6, 1966): p. 381.

offenders were immigrants from countries where drug consumption
prevailed. Furthermore, most of the Israeli-born offenders were of
Oriental extraction. The fact that a large proportion of narcotic
offenders of Middle-Eastern origin (almost half of the offenders in
this group) were not involved in any other type of criminal activity
is highly instructive, for we may assume that these people would

never have been labelled criminals had it not been for their traditional habit of consumption. In the North-African group we find a high rate (46.5 percent) of offenders whose first contact with criminal culture was made through narcotics. The representation of immigrants of European origin among narcotic offenders was negligible.

A study exploring the socioeconomic backgrounds of narcotic offenders showed that the majority were nonskilled or semiskilled workers and that there were an insignificant number of professionals. However, this social class finding was linked with ethnicity, as the majority of offenders were of Oriental extraction.[8]

An examination of other types of crime in which drug offenders were involved indicated that the second most common offense was stealing. This type of offense obviously had its root in problems specific to drug addicts, i.e., obtaining money to feed their habit.

Two students of Professor Shoham, Irit Friedman and Ilana Peer, studied drug addiction among pimps and prostitutes.[9] They addressed themselves to the testing of four hypotheses:

1. Delinquency precedes addiction.
2. Addiction is acquired through learning.
3. Drug addiction is a norm in the criminal subculture.
4. The use of drugs influences sexuality.

Unfortunately the sample consisted of only twenty-one prostitutes and pimps, but the small number is understandable in view of the difficulty of finding interviewees. The few names given to the researchers by the police proved to be of no value, so the investigators obtained names from other prostitutes, pimps, and their acquaintances. Many of the interviewees at first suspected that the interviewers were policewomen. Greater difficulty was experienced in interviewing the prostitutes than the pimps. (The best time to interview prostitutes is between 12 and 3 p.m. as they sleep in the morning and start working in the late afternoon.) Of the twenty-one, only five were of Western origin; all had arrived in Israel between 1948 and 1958. Their level of education was low. In only three cases were both parents of the prostitutes living together.

All four hypotheses were confirmed:

1) Entry into the criminal subculture preceded addiction. In the words of a prostitute: "A girl starts smoking only after somebody has already got her to be a prostitute; then when her man uses it, she gets used to the smell, he gives her some, and then she is hooked."

2) Prostitutes and pimps are introduced to drugs by veteran users. This occurred in all cases except one. As one prostitute remarked: "You never start smoking by yourself; it always comes from other people. My first boy friend gave it to me when I started going with him."

3) The use of the drug is a binding norm among members of the subculture. One girl's remark illustrates the phenomenon: "With drugs there is no difference, primitive or educated—all prostitutes smoke hash."

4) The use of drugs increased one's sexuality. Many of the prostitutes pointed out that they took the drug before going out to work. As one girl said: "You just take it to forget all the dirt; you don't enjoy it with the client in any case, and you don't go to the end. We only pretend. A prostitute doesn't look for satisfaction from the client and doesn't get it either."

Among other aspects, the study also investigated ways in which the drug is taken. The following five methods were found:

1) Smoking it in a cigarette: "You take apart a Chesterfield or a Dubek. The other brands are no good. You put in a bit of hashish and mix it up till it's like a Turkish cigarette. You pass it around and everyone takes a drag."

2) Smoking it in a bottle: "You break a bottle and put hash in the neck and 'sniff smoke'."

3) "You put a lit cigarette on the fire and the hash smoke comes up. You take a filter and inhale the smoke. It's stronger because it is cleaner."

4) Like a narghile pipe: "You put hashish in a pipe and inhale the smoke from it."

5) "You cook it up with coffee without sugar. Some people spread it on brown bread, like butter."

ECOLOGICAL INFLUENCES

In the literature of criminology the ecological factor carries much weight.[10] Slum neighborhoods such as Kfar Shalem, the Hatikvah Quarter, and the Yemenite Quarter in Tel Aviv are reputed centers of criminal activity; the overwhelming proportion of the population is of Asian-African extraction. This fact provides a link in explaining the finding that crime rates and types of crime vary according to ethnic group.

A. Nadad's study of Kfar Shalem describes the organization and methods of criminal activity in an urban slum.[11] The nucleus of criminal activity in the slum was centered around a relatively small number of hardened criminals who exerted a great influence on the neighborhood. Of particular importance was the recruitment of potential accomplices. The crowded housing conditions and the close-knit web of relations in the neighborhood facilitated frequent contact with the young people of the quarter. The youth of Kfar Shalem had failed to achieve the prerequisites necessary for upward mobility. They had a very high elementary school dropout rate. Seventy percent of these youths had received no vocational training whatsoever. Unemployed and unemployable youths, as well as youngsters working for low wages might easily be influenced by the charisma of a criminal gang leader. Crimes were often perpetuated by a partnership of a professional criminal with a youth with no criminal record. In fact, the family itself sometimes served as a breeding place for criminal activity; brothers with criminal experience recruited inexperienced kin as accomplices.

Furthermore, the geographical situation of Kfar Shalem, located as it was in the vicinity of other slums (e.g., the Hatikvah Quarter), facilitated meetings between the youth of different neighborhoods and made it easy for local youth to join up with professional criminals. These meetings occurred in the accepted amusement centers of this particular urban stratum, such as certain cafes, card clubs and brothels.

The types of crime most common to the inhabitants of Kfar Shalem were those connected with narcotics, gambling and prostitution. Criminal activity in Kfar Shalem can be viewed as an aspect of the generally low standard of the neighborhood, and a program designed to reduce the criminal activity would have to consider a general rehabilitation of the slums.

Another study dealing with ecology as a factor conducive to crime was made by Shlomo Shoham, Nahum Shoham, and Aba-El-Razak in 1966.[12] All the participants in this study were juvenile cases dealt with by the police from 1948 to 1963.

The main findings of this study were as follows:

1) The rate of juvenile delinquency increased, the higher the degree of urbanization in a community, and the greater the cultural discrepancy among the various ethnic groups within it.

2) The highest rate of delinquency was linked to second generation juveniles of immigrant parentage, who arrived with their parents immediately after the establishment of the state of Israel, or were born shortly after their parents' immigration.

3) The bigger the cultural gap between the immigrants and the receiving community and the stronger the barriers against upper vertical mobility of the immigrants, the higher were the rates of delinquency. This was especially apparent in Yemenite neighborhoods.

4) The lowest delinquency rates occurred in homogeneous agricultural settlements with a strong, internalized normative system, which served as a buffer against crime and delinquency.

5) Immigrant groups that had settled in agricultural areas and possessed a high internal cohesion were hardly exposed at all to culture conflict, and their delinquency rates were negligible.

6) The rates of delinquency among immigrants were significantly higher than among nonimmigrants. Exceptionally high rates were observed in the residual of social cases in evacuated immigrant transit camps.

7) The ranking of the variables in relation to the strength of their link with delinquency seemed to be in the following increasing order: homogeneity, ethnicity, length of stay in the country, and degree of urbanization.

8) Higher rates of delinquency were positively linked to higher rates of recidivism.

9) The starting age of immigrant delinquents was significantly lower than that of nonimmigrants. The latter's delinquency was considered more conventional and was linked to the various phases of faulty socialization before, during, and after adolescence.

The types of offenses committed by immigrant youths were significantly less severe than those committed by nonimmigrants. The

former indicated general neglect and lack of family control, whereas
the latter indicated a more profound syndrome of maladjustment.

MIDDLE-CLASS DELINQUENCY

The aim of the study undertaken by Shlomo Shoham and Meir
Hovav was to investigate the nature and extent of middle-class delinquency.[13] The research population consisted of the total number
of delinquents aged fourteen to sixteen who were listed in the register of the Juvenile Probation Service in the three major cities in
Israel (Tel Aviv, Haifa and Jerusalem) in 1960. The total number
was 1,213 boys and 137 girls. Four criteria were employed to define middle-class membership: parent's occupation, income (as
determined by the probation officer), education, and quality of
the residential area. The education of the juvenile (i.e., whether he
was studying at secondary school or still in elementary school) was
an additional criterion. Two hundred and fifty-two boys were designated as *B'nei Tovim* (middle-class children), i.e., 29 percent of
the delinquent population. The control group consisted of 260
boys selected at random from a list of juvenile offenders who came
from the same towns, were of the same age, did not attend high
school, and whose families were of lower socioeconomic status.

Most of the middle-class delinquents were born in Israel (70
percent), while the majority of the control group were born outside
Israel (58 percent). Sixty-two percent of the parents of the B'nei
Tovim were born in Europe, while in the control group 63 percent
immigrated from Asia and Africa. Thus the middle-class delinquents
were from affluent families who had emigrated from Europe and
were residents of long standing in Israel. The educational level of
the middle-class delinquents was almost identical with the distribution of urban secondary education for the country as a whole,
showing that for them education was not related to delinquency.

Table 67 indicates that the control group consisting of
lower-class delinquents was subject to poorer primary socialization
than were the middle-class delinquents. (The information of Table
67, however, is based on the judgment of probation officers.) Thus
lower-class youth were more truant, had changed school more often,
had poorer school records and were more disturbed than the middle-

TABLE 67
EVIDENCE OF POOR SOCIALIZATION AND PERSONALITY DISTURBANCE AMONG B'NEI TOVIM AND LOWER CLASS DELINQUENTS (PERCENTAGES)

	B'nei Tovim	Control Group
Inadequate adjustment in kindergarten	6	14
Truancy	2	10
More than three changes of elementary school (not because of change of residence)	7	12
Poor school record	2	24
Personality defects and disturbances	4	20

Source: S. Shoham and M. Hovav, "Social Factors, Aspects of Treatment and Patterns of Criminal Career Among the *B'nei Tovim*," *Human Relations* (19, 1966): p. 50.

class delinquents. They also had a more difficult time adjusting while in kindergarten. Moreover, as shown in Table 68, parents of the control group showed a considerably higher rate of emotional instability and a greater possessive attitude towards their children than did parents of the B'nei Tovim. The middle-class delinquents, however, showed a higher incidence of broken families as a result of divorce and separation. They also came from smaller families. They were also more negativistic and defiant (19 percent *vs.* 7 percent). This is consistent with the position of Cloward and Ohlin, who maintain that the lower-class American delinquents negate middle-class values and therefore do not suffer from guilt feelings.[14] The middle-class delinquent, Shoham argues, feels guilty for infringing upon societal values, which by their nature are middle-class. The present finding that family inadequacy is more closely related to delinquency in the lower class than in the middle class is an important contribution.

Table 69 shows that the delinquency of the B'nei Tovim is less of a professional and subcultural phenomenon and, perhaps most important, is transitory. The number of previous offenses was fewer among B'nei Tovim and they were less likely to commit further offenses. An examination of the disposition of cases by the Probation Service revealed that 50 percent of the files of B'nei Tovim, in contrast to 26 percent of the control group, were closed without additional action

TABLE 68

EMOTIONAL INSTABILITY AND PASSIVITY TOWARDS CHILDREN AMONG B'NEI TOVIM AND CONTROL GROUP PARENTS

| | B'NEI TOVIM | | | CONTROL GROUP | | |
	Father	Mother	Total	Father	Mother	Total
	%	%	%	%	%	%
Instability	1	9	10	10	10	20
Passivity	10	4	14	18	15	33
Total	11	13	24	28	25	53

Source: S. Shoham and M. Hovav, "Social Factors, Aspects of Treatment and Patterns of Criminal Behavior Among the *B'nei Tovim,*" *Human Relations* (19, 1966):p. 50.

being taken. These findings on differential treatments of delinquents of a higher social class are similar to those of many American studies.[15] For recidivists, however, social class was unrelated to disposition of the offenses.

PERSONALITY AND VALUES OF DELINQUENTS: CROSS-CULTURAL STUDIES

We present two studies in which the authors were interested in determining whether the values and personality of Israeli delinquents differed from nondelinquents. The first study by Shlomo Shoham, Ruth Erez, and Walter C. Reckless, was concerned with value orientation and awareness of differential opportunities.[16] Studies conducted in the United States essentially support the Cloward and Ohlin notion that delinquents perceive fewer opportunities for advancement than do nondelinquents.[17] There is also support for Albert Cohen's theory that delinquents are less prone to accept middle-class values than are nondelinquents.

The two scales, "value orientation" and "awareness of limited access to legitimate opportunities," were translated into Hebrew and administered to twenty-five boys residing in an institute for juvenile delinquents. Nondelinquents from the ninth grade served as a control group.

TABLE 69
PERCENTAGE DISTRIBUTION OF CASES OF FIRST OFFENDERS AND RECIDIVISTS

Segment of the Research Population	File Closed	Discharged	Bound Over	Fined	Probation	Institutionalized	Suspended Sentence
B'NEI TOVIM							
First Offenders	50	15	21	1	3	0	0
Recidivists	18	15	37	6	15	6	3
Total	45	15	23	10	5	1	1
CONTROL GROUP							
First Offenders	26	26	24	15	6	1	2
Recidivists	16	7	19	19	18	17	4
Total	22	20	22	16	10	7	3

Source: S. Shoham and M. Hovav, "B'nei Tovim—Middle and Upper-Class Delinquency in Israel," *Sociology and Social Research* (48, 1964): p. 465.

On the value orientation scale, which measures adherence to middle-class values (for example: "The law is always against the ordinary guy"; "The only thing I ought to be responsible for is myself"; "It's mostly luck if one succeeds or fails") the differences were highly significant for eleven of the thirteen items comprising the scale and almost significant for the remaining two statements.

Internal analysis showed that in contrast to the nondelinquents, few delinquents gave a "don't know" response to any of the thirteen questions comprising the scale. The authors interpreted this as indicating the delinquent's intolerance of ambiguity, which they interpreted as an intervening variable between conflict situations and delinquency. Accordingly, the rigid personalities of the youths are then seen as stemming from their inability to reconcile contradictory norms imposed upon them by conflict situations in which they find themselves.

The second scale measured perceived opportunities and was characterized by such statements as: "I probably won't be able to do the kind of work that I want to do, because I won't have enough education"; "The world is usually good to guys like me"; and "My family can't give me the opportunity that most kids have." Here again the differences were statistically significant, but less so than in the previous scale.

To sum up, the highly significant differences between the delinquent and nondelinquent groups on the value orientation scale support the view that relatively speaking the former group does not accept middle-class values. Since social classes are much less defined in Israel than they are in the United States, these findings are most intriguing.

In the second study, Shlomo Shoham and Leon Shaskolsky were interested in comparing personality and other characteristics between delinquents and nondelinquents, particularly to see if the presumed differences were in accord with American findings.[18] To this end they administered a schedule to one hundred nondelinquents, all of whom were between sixteen and seventeen years of age. The group of delinquents consisted of consecutive referrals to the intake department of the Tel Aviv juvenile court. The comparison group consisted of 100 nondelinquent boys matched for age and attending the same schools as the delinquents. However, for three particularly relevant variables, ethnicity, length of residence in Israel, and occupation of the father, the authors were not always successful in finding a good match to the delinquents. Consequently, the delinquents differed from the nondelinquents; they tended to be recent immigrants of Eastern origin whose parents had lower occupational status.

Both groups were given a questionnaire composed of eight scales, previously used in America. These scales were: Rothstein Self-Concept Inventory; Psychopathic Deviate (PD) Scale of the Minnesota Multiphasic Personality Inventory, which has been very effective in distinguishing between delinquents and nondelinquents; Moral Judgement Scale, which measures judgments or rightness and wrongness about various kinds of behavior; Normlessness; Powerlessness; Despair; Family Cohesiveness; and Family Consensus. The schedule also contained questions on the background of the interviewee.

Particularly because the delinquent and the nondelinquent groups were not successfully matched, one would expect to find pronounced differences on many if not all of the scales. The results showed no significant differences on seven of the eight scales, although the trends were in the predicted direction. The scale Normlessness yielded the only significant finding, but the result was opposite to what had been anticipated; nondelinquents indicated more normlessness than the delinquents.

The authors offered the following explanation. The Jew in the Diaspora was concerned with his ethnic identity, particularly the third generation which wished to affirm it. In Israel the immigrant child (including the delinquent), be he second or third generation, is interested in conforming to the normative system of the wider Israeli society and will thus copy its attitudes and behavior.

The results of both studies taken together are perplexing; for while one found highly significant differences, the other found virtually no differences at all. It would seem that delinquents and nondelinquents differ only in regard to middle-class values and perception of opportunities, but not with regard to personality, self-image and family relationships. A study by Leonard Weller, Israel Glanz and Iris Klein adds some information on the relationship of personality to delinquency. In their research, an omnibus personality test, the California Psychological Inventory, was administered to two kinds of criminals, property and violent offenders, and first-time offenders

and recidivists.[19] Particular attention was paid to the Socialization
Scale, which had proved particularly useful in distinguishing a criminal from a noncriminal population, and a Feels Different from Others
Scale, a new scale constructed from the CPI items by Eliezar Karni
of Tel Aviv University. The results showed that recidivists who were
property offenders resembled recidivists who were violent offenders.
However, first-time offenders significantly differed from redicivists
on the Socialization and Feels Different from Others scales, as well
as on three additional personality measures.

THE JUDGE AND THE SENTENCING POLICY

The following set of papers is concerned with the influence of the
judge, the kind of sentence, and penal institution. In the first research,
Shoham questioned the extent to which sentencing policies are influenced by the attitude of the trial judge.[20] The data were taken from
convictions in 1,105 cases heard in 1956.

Punishments were scaled according to the following degree of
severity: binding over to keep the peace; probation; suspended sentence; suspended sentence and fine; imprisonment up to one year;
imprisonment from one to three years; and imprisonment from three
years upwards.

Since Israeli judges state the grounds for their judgments, it was
possible to analyze their attitudes toward punishment. Six sentencing
grounds were distinguished: those which a) emphasized the retributive
purpose of punishment, b) emphasized the deterrent purpose of punishment, c) incorporated elements of both retribution and deterrence,
d) were of a reformative nature, e) were of a preventive nature, and
f) incorporated elements of both reformation and prevention.

A strong relationship was found between the grounds for sentencing
and the severity of punishment.

Assuming that a judge would not be strongly influenced by his personal feelings, and given a large sample size, a similarity in the sentences
imposed by different judges would be expected. To this end the sentences of eight district court judges were examined.

Table 70 gives the means for crimes against property and for crimes
against the person, and also the general means; the latter refer to other
sentences not included in the sample. There were large differences

among the judges. With regard to general severity there was a difference of 41 percent between the most lenient judge (Judge D, 30 percent) and the most severe judge (Judge N, 71 percent). When the type of offense was examined, a contrast was observed. The judge who was most severe when trying offenses in general was the most lenient when trying offenses against the person (Judge N). The order of severity in offenses against property was quite different from the order of severity in offenses against the person. For example, Judge D gave the most severe sentences in cases of property offenses, whereas in cases against the person his sentences were next to the most lenient.

TABLE 70
SEVERITY OF GENERAL SENTENCES COMPARED WITH
SENTENCES FOR OFFENSES AGAINST PERSON
AND PROPERTY

Judge	OFFENSES (Percentages)		
	Against Person	Against Property	General
R	49	48	50
S	50	52	49
L	90	55	62
J	46	33	40
D	15	72	30
N	10	59	71
G	46	55	46
A	88	48	62
Others	49	42	44

Source: S. Shoham, "Sentencing Policy in Criminal Courts in Israel,"
Journal of Criminal Law, Criminology and Police Science (50, 1959): p. 333.

The different methods of punishment employed by the various judges were also examined. As shown in Table 71, pronounced differences were found; the attitude of the judge influenced both the severity and the actual choice of the punishment.

EFFECTIVENESS OF SUSPENDED SENTENCES

In another paper Shlomo Shoham and Moshe Sandberg examined

the effectiveness of suspended sentences in Israel,[21] which are similar to those of other countries. It is assumed that such sentences, unaccompanied by disruption of everyday life and the stigma of imprisonment, would be highly effective deterrents. The offender is to be imprisoned for a certain period if he offends again, or fails to observe certain conditions within a specified time. The authors' hypothesis was that suspended sentences would be more effective for first offenders than for recidivists.

TABLE 71
RELATIVE FREQUENCY OF VARIOUS METHODS OF PUNISHMENT USED BY JUDGES IN SAMPLE (IN PERCENTAGES)

Judge	Suspended Sentence and Fine	Up to 1 Yr.	From 1-3 Yrs.	3 Yrs. and up	Bound Over	Pro-bation	Suspended Sentence
R	57	26	7	0	0	6	10
S	34	31	6	0	2	3	24
L	11	35	18	0	0	4	32
J	35	20	7	0	0	0	38
D	4	26	20	0	0	10	40
N	16	42	10	0	10	0	22
G	43	18	6	7	0	0	26
A	29	32	16	3	0	2	18
Others	30	22	9	3	0	6	30

Source: S. Shoham, "Sentencing Policy of Criminal Courts in Israel," *Journal of Criminal Law, Criminology and Police Science* (50, 1959):p. 335.

A 50 percent sample was drawn (accounting for 3,321 cases) of all offenders who had been given suspended sentences during 1955 and 1966. The success (no offense committed during the designated period) or failure of each case was ascertained. The control group consisted of offenders who received sentences other than suspended imprisonment. The research and control groups were similar in age, sex, and previous criminal history.

No differences were found in the success rates of the two groups. However, suspended sentences were more effective in the case of those who had committed property offenses than in the case of those who had committed offenses against a person. Neither place of birth, ethnic origin, sex, occupation, or length of stay in the country were related to success. Age and previous number of offenses were, however, related: the younger offenders were more likely to be failures, and for those with previous sentences the "good risks" were the ones who had received lighter sentences. Thus while the kind of punishment that the criminal had received did not affect the likelihood of his committing another offense, his age and the number of previous offenses did.

FOLLOW-UP STUDY OF DELINQUENTS

A large scale follow-up study of juvenile delinquents who had been in penal institutions in Israel was undertaken by Shlomo Shoham, Yaron Kaufman, and Michal Menaker.[22] The sample consisted of all the inmates released in 1966 from a prison for young adults. The control group comprised army recruits, who as far as possible were matched with the research population according to occupation, ethnicity, and socioeconomic status. The research had three objectives: the correlation of factors associated with recidivism, the institutional impact on the offender (whether the inmate was "positively" or "negatively" institutionalized), and his behavior after he had left the institution, particularly the effect of the stigmatization process and the consequent limitation of occupational possibilities. The results of the first stage only were presented.

The following factors were related to success (i.e., failure to commit subsequent offenses):

1) *Length of time spent with own family.* The longer the inmate stayed with his own family, the greater were his chances of success ($r = .90$).
2) *Control by the father* ($r = .42$) and *the boy's reaction towards this control* ($r = .52$), as measured by his acceptance, surrender, rebellion or ambivalence. The scales were adapted from the Gluecks' prediction table.
3) *Age at the delinquency onset.* The younger the delinquent was at the time he committed his first offense, the smaller were the chances of success ($r = .89$). This result, which is consistent with studies in the United States and the last mentioned research, probably indicates that the younger a boy is when he starts his criminal career, the more hardened he becomes.
4) *Severity of first penalty.* The severer the first penalty, the less

likely were the chances of success (r = .89). This finding, which indicates that severe punishment is connected with recidivism, may mean that either the boy received a severe first sentence because of a long history of delinquency that went unpunished or he felt the social stigma very keenly.

5) *Education.* The less the education, the greater was the recidivism (r = .87). This finding is likewise consistent with that of previous studies in the United States.

6) *Stability of work.* Instability of occupation was associated with "failure" (r = .82).

7) *Second-generation immigrants.* The son of immigrant parents was likely to be a failure (biserial correlation = .82). The culture conflict hypothesis can account, at least in part, for this finding. Studies in the United States have also shown that second-generation boys of immigrant parentage displayed high delinquency rates.

8) *Criminality in the family.* Youths whose family members were criminals were more likely to be failures (biserial correlation = .70).

9) *Change of schools.* Frequent change of schools was correlated with recidivism (r = .82).

10) *Length of imprisonment following "determining offense."* The longer the term of imprisonment, the greater were the chances that the youth would commit further criminal acts (r = .70). This factor, like "severity of punishment for the first offense" showed the weakness of imprisonment as a deterrent to future criminality. The longer the youth was in prison, the more he became enmeshed within the criminal group.

11) *Membership in a youth movement.* The longer the boy's membership in a youth movement, the higher were his chances of success (r = .67). Youth movements in Israel stress positive values, such as the virtue of work.

12) *Property offenses.* Property offenders were more likely to be recidivistic, nonproperty offenders less so (biserial correlation = .49). Crimes against property were presumably characteristic of professional delinquency, whereas acts of violence and offenses against the public order tended to be of a one-time nature.

13) *Crime committed in a group.* Boys who committed crimes in concert with others were apt to be somewhat more recidivistic than boys who were individual offenders (r = .30).

CONCLUSION

The crime rate in Israel is increasing. Still, many of the offenses are not serious, being mostly against property. It is Jews of Oriental descent, particularly recent immigrants, who are responsible for the major portion of delinquent acts.[23] As the previous chapters have shown, Jews of Eastern descent, including those born in the country, are not making it. Their educational performance, their income, and their occupations, fall behind their Western counterparts. As Jews of Eastern descent are increasingly becoming more discontent because of their inability to succeed, we foresee no decline in the crime rate of this group. Among the Asian-African groups it is the Jews who migrated from Morocco who have the highest crime rate. Their high rate of delinquency can be attributed to their failure to achieve a higher standard of living while living in Morocco. They had hoped that in Israel they would be able to achieve middle class status. Confronted with difficulties of absorption, they still find themselves occupying a low status and thus experience a high degree of relative deprivation. Their frustration and their consequent bitterness often result in criminal activities.

The importance of the army as a deterrent to crime should not be overlooked. At a critical age when a youth could be starting a criminal career, he joins the army, where he can prove himself. It is an excellent way of relieving himself of his surplus energy and aggressive impulses in a positive manner. The army also operates an educational program to which many a youth may not have been attracted while moving in a civilian milieu. Moreover, during their stay in the army, youths are trained to become responsible citizens. Many soldiers have faced battle and have seen their friends die. What effect this has on a potentially delinquent career is not known, but it may have a restraining influence.

Much of the delinquency is centered in the slums of the big cities and confined mostly to the youth of Asian-African extraction. To date there is little evidence of different kinds of organized gang behavior (see epilogue). It is safe to walk at night in virtually any neighborhood of Tel Aviv, Jerusalem or Haifa, the metropolitan areas of Israel. Nevertheless, the ecological-ethnicity-social class overlap, coupled with the fact that there are now second- and even third-generation slum residents, may give rise to gang behavior and to the development of a lower-class subculture.

The chapter on social class and mobility discussed the increased desire for a higher standard of living. Middle-class delinquency will no doubt grow as a result of this and other factors. The use of drugs is also on the increase, and this will work its way more and more into the middle class. One reason for this is simply the easy availability of drugs. Apart from the fact that they are being brought into the country by American students, drugs, since the Six Day War, can be obtained without difficulty in such cities as Jerusalem and Beer-Sheva, or purchased from Bedouins in the desert. It is too early to forecast whether the use of drugs will become a symbol of discontent in Israel, but it is not unlikely that it will find its way into upper-middle class circles. The extent to which drugs will become a serious problem would seem to be linked to the security situation. If there will be fighting, such as the "war of attrition" waged by the Egyptians after the Six Day War, internal dissension will be minimized and the country will not be able to afford the luxury of experimentation in narcotics by its youth. Should the prolonged cease-fire continue, the use of drugs may become more general.

As for criminological research, there is no reason to believe that there will be a change in the quality of the studies which cover such a wide range of topics. If anything, as the Institutes and Departments of Criminology develop, the additional staff joining the faculties will increase the productivity. In sociology, as in all other disciplines, there is an increasing number of Israelis who have obtained their doctorates abroad and are now returning to their homeland. Several of these will, no doubt, be numbered among the new generation of criminologists.

EPILOGUE

From 1971 to 1972 we have witnessed a drastic change in criminality in Israel. The crime rate has increased considerably, and perhaps more importantly, the nature of the crime has changed. The crimes are no longer undertaken by a lone bandit. They are more organized, more daring, and more professional. Banks are robbed more frequently, and a group of thieves, pretending to be moving men, may come and empty out an apartment when families are on vacation. Just recently, when a local bank manager checked with the main office to determine if a client had coverage for his check, he received an affirmative reply, not from the manager, but from an accomplice who had intercepted the call. This kind of crime is not new to Americans, but it is in Israeli society. Furthermore, there is no question that organized crime has appeared, not in the sense that the police or politicians are bought, but in the delimitation of gang territory. Interestingly, as in the case of the FBI's denial for many years of the existence of the Mafia, the Israeli police deny the existence of organized crime. Moreover, drug use, while hardly reaching American proportions, has spread more rapidly than anyone had anticipated, so that it is now a serious concern in Israeli society.

As far as we are aware, there has been no research on the new kind of crime to date. We do not know to what extent it is an American import or an indigenous development. It is easy to assume that it is related to the relative quiet at the borders during the last two years, but there have been other periods of relative quiet without a significant increase in criminality.

This change in the nature of crime has been too recent to have an impact on criminological research. But it is an additional sad note that no sociologist or criminologist in the country, including myself, who wrote this chapter before the upsurge in crime, predicted these changes.

NOTES

1. Shlomo Shoham, "The Culture Conflict Hypothesis and the Criminality of Immigrants in Israel," *Journal of Criminal Law, Criminology and Police Science* (53, 1952): pp. 202-214.

2. Judith T. Shuval, "Patterns of Inter-group Tension and Affinity," *International Social Science Bulletin* (8, 1956): pp. 75-123; Judith T. Shuval, "Emerging Patterns of Ethnic Strain in Israel," *Social Forces* (40, 1962): pp. 323-330; J. T. Shuval, "Self-Rejection among North African Immigrants to Israel," *Israel Annals of Psychiatry and Related Disciplines* (4, 1966): pp. 101-110.

3. Judith T. Shuval, "Emerging Patterns of Ethnic Strain in Israel," *op. cit.*

4. Shlomo Shoham and Giora Rahav, "Social Stigma and Prostitution," *International Annals of Criminology* (6, 1967): pp. 479-513; Shlomo Shoham and Giora Rahav, "Social Stigma and Prostitution," *British Journal of Criminology* (15, 1968): pp. 402-412; Shlomo Shoham, "Social Stigma and the Criminal Group," *The Irish Jurist* (7, 1968): pp. 1-23; Shlomo Shoham, "Psychopathology as Social Stigma: A Myth Revisited," *Journal of Corrective Psychology* (13, 1967): pp. 21-41.

5. Shlomo Shoham, *The Mark of Cain, The Stigma Theory of Crime and Deviation.* (Chicago: University of Chicago Press), 1968.

6. Shlomo Shoham and Giora Rahav, "Social Stigma and Prostitution," *International Annals of Criminology* (6, 1967): p. 486.

7. T. Drapkin and S. Landau, "Drug Offenders in Israel," *British Journal of Criminology* (6, 1966): pp. 376-390.

8. I. Berman, "Drug Abuse Among Israeli Youth in 1967: A Survey" (Jerusalem: Ministry of Social Welfare, 1969) (in Hebrew).

9. Irit Friedman and Ilana Peer, "Drug Addiction Among Pimps and Prostitutes," *International Journal of Addictions* (3, 1968): pp. 271-300.

10. In America in such works by C. Shaw and R. McKay, *Juvenile Delinquency and Urban Areas.* (Chicago: University of Chicago Press, 1942); in England by Terrence Morris, *The Criminal Area.* (London: Routledge and Kegan Paul, 1957).

11. Abraham Nadad, "The Village of Shalem—Image of a Poor Neighborhood," *Megamot* (7, 1956): pp. 5-40 (in Hebrew).

12. Shlomo Shoham, Nahum Shoham and Aba-El-Razak, "Immigration, Ethnicity and Ecology as Related to Juvenile Delinquency in Israel," *The British Journal of Criminology* (5, 1966): pp. 391-409.

13. Shlomo Shoham and Meir Hovav, "B'nei Tovim—Middle and Upper Class Delinquency in Israel," *Sociology and Social Research* (48, 1964): pp. 454-468; Shlomo Shoham and Meir Hovav, "Social Factors, Aspects of Treatment, and Patterns of Criminal Career Among the B'nei Tovim," *Human Relations* (19, 1966): pp. 47-56.

14. Richard A. Cloward and Lloyd H. Ohlin, *Delinquency and Opportunity*. (New York: The Free Press of Glenko, 1960).

15. For example, A. L. Porterfield, "Delinquency and its Outcome in Court and College," *American Journal of Sociology* (49, 1948): pp. 199-208.

16. Shlomo Shoham, Ruth Erez and Walter C. Reckless, "Value Orientation and Awareness of Differential Opportunity of Delinquent and Non-Delinquent Boys in Israel," *British Journal of Criminology* (5, 1965): pp. 325-332.

17. J. R. Landis, S. Dinitz and W. C. Reckless, "Implementing Two Theories of Delinquency: Value Orientation and Awareness of Limited Opportunity," *Sociology and Social Research* (47, 1963): pp. 408-416.

18. Shlomo Shoham and Leon Shasklosky, "An Analysis of Delinquents and Nondelinquents in Israel: A Cross-Cultural Perspective," *Sociology and Social Research* (53, 1969): pp. 333-343.

19. Leonard Weller, Israel Glanz and Iris Klein, "Personality Characteristics of First-Time Offenders and Recidivists, Property Offenders and Violent Offenders," in Shlomo Shoham (ed.), *Israel Studies in Criminology*. (Vol. II) (Jerusalem: Jerusalem Academic Press, 1973), pp. 113-125.

20. Shlomo Shoham, "Sentencing Policy of Criminal Courts in Israel," *Journal of Criminal Law, Criminology and Police Science* (50, 1959): pp. 327-337.

21. Shlomo Shoham and Moshe Sandberg, "Suspended Sentences in Israel: An Evaluation of the Preventive Efficacy of Prospective Imprisonment," *Crime and Delinquency* (50, 1964): pp. 74-83.

22. Shlomo Shoham, Yaron Kaufman and Michal Menaker, "The Tel-Mond Follow-up Research Project," *Houston Law Review* (5, 1967): pp. 36-62.

23. See Shlomo Shoham, "The Culture Conflict Hypothesis and the Criminality of Immigrants in Israel," *Journal of Criminal Law, Criminology and Police Science* (53, 1953): pp. 202-214.

7

Religion

If the difference between Jews of Eastern and Western descent can be regarded as Israel's foremost problem, then the religious conflict may be considered its second. For the country is divided into the religious and the nonreligious camp, and while the religious group is a minority (albeit a sizeable one), its influence far surpasses its number.

In Israel practically the only religious form is that of orthodoxy, which requires observances such as abstaining from travelling and writing on the Sabbath. Conservative Judaism and Reform Judaism are largely absent from the Israeli scene, although of late both groups have been attempting to establish additional congregations. The major difficulty facing Conservative and Reform Jews in gaining a foothold in Israel is their lack of political power. The Government has granted the Rabbinate jurisdiction over matters of marriage and divorce, and the Rabbinate is Orthodox.

The religious–nonreligious distinction affects the everyday life of the country. For while the majority of the population (although it is not clear how much of a majority) is nonreligious, the religious parties have successfully secured the legislation of a number of laws displeasing to the nonreligious. This is because the largest political party, Mapai, having never received a majority of the votes, preferred the major religious party as a member of the coalition. The price paid by Mapai was the acceptance of many of the demands of the religious party, a far larger proportion than would be justified by its number

of seats in the Knesset. Thus the religious party was responsible for
the banning of public transport on the Jewish Sabbath. Sunday is a
regular work-day and, since only a minority of the population owns
a car, this law directly affects the lives of many citizens.
The school system itself reflects the religious cleavage in the country.
The state supports two parallel school systems, religious and secular,
in both elementary and secondary schools. In addition, there are religious schools of the ultraorthodox which are not financed by the state
The exemption of religious girls (if they so choose) from the army
is a particularly sore issue, for at the age of eighteen girls, like boys,
are drafted. Many religious families, particularly those of Oriental
communities, feared the adverse influence on their daughters, and
clearly such exemptions have been justified. However, the fact is
that a number of girls have used their presumed "religiosity" as an
excuse for exemption. Moreover, when a recent suggestion was made
to establish a voluntary work group for religious girls, not within the
context of the army, elements within the orthodox community strongly
opposed it. No wonder, then, that when the Tel Aviv Municipality
decided to portion off a small part of the beach for orthodox bathers
(orthodox men and women do not bathe together) a number of nonorthodox protested the infringement of their rights.

The situation is, of course, not so terribly polarized. For the
majority of religious people do serve in the army, and the religious
youth movement, Bnei Akiva, is the most active youth movement in
the establishment of settlements on the borders, and is regarded by
many to be the best youth movement in Israel. Furthermore, some of
the most anti-establishment leaders are found within the religious party.

This all too brief summary serves as a background to the present
chapter on research in religion. Three kinds of research are to be
noted. The first is concerned with assessing the percentage of the
population who are religious and the factors associated with changes
in religious observance. The second consists of studies determining
the extent to which the religious factor is influential in shaping
attitudes, values, and behavior. While we count seven studies dealing
with this topic, the number of studies is surprisingly small in view
of the importance of the religious factor. The third is of a different
type; it examines changing funeral practices during the Talmudic
period.

RELIGIOUS OBSERVANCE

We now turn to the question raised earlier, that of religious observance. In an opinion poll conducted in 1963 by the Israeli Institute of Applied Social Research (headed by Professor Louis Gutman) some 30 percent of the respondents claimed that they observed all or most of the religious precepts, 46 percent reported that they observed "traditions to some extent," while 24 percent declared themselves to be completely secular.[1] In addition to this, we cite a survey of maternity cases, conducted in 1959-1960, in which women were questioned about their religious observance.[2] A woman was classified "observant" if she observed the ritual bath tradition, an observance associated with abstinence of marital sexual behavior for one week after menstruation. "Partially observant" refers to those women who observed some traditions such as adherence to the dietary laws but did not observe the ritual bath regulation. The data are presented in Table 72.

The results resemble those of Antonovsky. For the entire sample, 46.3 percent reported being observant and another 26.2 percent as being partially observant. The table also shows marked differences with regard to ethnicity and length of residence in the country. Women from Asia and Africa were overwhelmingly observant (66.9 percent) while Israeli and European-born women were considerably less observant (16.6 percent and 17.4 percent, respectively). A comparison between veteran residents and new immigrants showed a higher percentage of observant women among the latter group (19.4 percent compared to 56.2 percent).

Matras also described intergenerational changes in religious observance.[3] The data, based on informants' reports of their own and their mothers' religious observances, disclosed that approximately 40 percent of the women were less religiously observant than their mothers, while the remaining 60 percent did not change. The greatest amount of change took place for the group of women whose mothers were observant; the daughters of these observant mothers did not completely break from religion, for they were inclined to be partially observant. Furthermore, when the mother was "partially observant" the daughter was not likely to become less religious. If their mothers had been observant, daughters of European or Israeli mothers were

TABLE 72
RELIGIOUS OBSERVANCE OF JEWISH MATERNITY CASES IN ISRAEL, 1959-1960, BY CONTINENT OF BIRTH, ORDER OF PRESENT BIRTHS, AND PERIOD OF IMMIGRATION (PERCENTAGE DISTRIBUTION)

Place of Birth, Birth Order, and Period of Immigration	Total	EXTENT OF RELIGIOUS OBSERVANCE			N
		Non observant	Partially Observant	Observant	
All Periods of Immigration:					
All Maternity Cases	100.0	27.5	26.2	46.3	2973
First Births	100.0	41.0	32.0	27.0	822
Born in Israel-Total	100.0	49.2	34.2	16.6	648
First Births	100.0	56.6	30.7	12.7	255
Second Births	100.0	48.1	40.9	11.0	199
Born in Europe-America-Total	100.0	49.2	33.4	17.4	749
First Births	100.0	57.4	34.6	8.0	224
Second Births	100.0	53.7	35.0	11.3	275
Born in Asia, Africa-Total	100.0	12.2	20.9	66.9	1576
First Births	100.0	20.0	31.2	48.8	343
Second Births	100.0	16.5	22.3	61.2	314
Veteran Residents-Total	100.0	48.3	32.3	19.4	1019
Born in Israel	100.0	49.2	34.2	16.6	648
Born in Europe, America	100.0	48.8	29.7	21.5	220
Born in Asia, Africa	100.0	31.8	29.8	38.4	151
New Immigrants-Total	100.0	20.0	23.8	56.2	1954
Born in Europe, America	100.0	49.2	35.0	15.8	529
Born in Asia, Africa	100.0	10.8	20.3	68.9	1425

Source: R. Bachi and J. Matras, "Fertility and Contraception" Summary Tables of Findings of Surveys of Jewish Maternity Cases in Israel. (Jerusalem: Hebrew University Press, mimeographed in Hebrew and English, 1961), Table 5, page 6, and Table A, pp. 43-44.

more likely to remain observant than were daughters of Oriental mothers.

For the European women, length of residence in Israel did not affect the degree in intergenerational change in religious observance. However, longer length of residence did affect the religious observance of Oriental women.

The impact of education on religious observance was dependent on one's country of origin. For the Oriental women, higher education meant less religious observance. Therefore, of the Eastern women in the sample, one-third of those with no education, almost 60 percent of those with an eighth grade education or less, and two-thirds of those with at least some high school education were less religious than their observant mothers. For European women the relationship was reversed: the more educated the woman, the more likely it was that she would remain observant.

These data indicate that it is among the Eastern groups that religious behavior is declining. The longer the residence in the country, and the more educated the woman, the greater the chances that she will become less religious. It is not clear why length of residence in Israel and level of education among European women should be relatively unimportant in affecting religious change.

INFLUENCE ON BEHAVIOR AND ATTITUDES

We turn now to the question of how religiosity affects behavior and attitudes. Investigators have examined its influence on fertility rates, political attitudes, authoritarianism, nursing behavior, occupational interests, and general attitudes.

The greater fertility of the Eastern family is clearly associated with greater religious observance. Matras and Auerbach show that the desired number of children and the practice of contraception were influenced by religious observance; the less religious the couple the greater the likelihood that they had considered family planning.[4] In the Jerusalem sample, 72 percent of the nonobservant women, 40 percent of the partially observant women and 8 percent of the observant women reported previous contraceptive practice. Similarly, 59 percent of the nonobservant women, 37 percent of the partially observant women and 5 percent of the observant women reported having considered family planning. Since a large proportion of women practicing contraception are daughters of mothers who did not practice contraception, it might have been expected that the partially observant or nonobservant daughter of a partially observant mother would more readily resort to contraceptive devices than would such a daughter whose mother had been religious. This was studied and found not to be the case.

Leah Adar and Chaim Adler sampled over five hundred children from various kinds of communities that included children going to the state religious schools and state secular schools.[5] The authors expected that the values of religious students would be closer to the values of a traditional culture than would be the values of students attending secular schools. Pupils of religious schools, it was argued, would be less prone to accept universalistic, democratic values, the appreciation of the intrinsic value of work, and equality between the sexes. They also anticipated that religious children would be less tolerant of other religious and ethnic groups.

As expected, the children of religious schools registered higher scores on a religiosity scale composed of nine questions. In one of these questions the pupils were asked to make one of the following four choices: a) every Jew in Israel should be religious; b) it is desirable that every citizen in Israel, even the nonreligious, should observe the Sabbath and attend synagogue; c) Israeli citizens could be religious or nonreligious according to their desire; and d) it is not necessary that Israeli citizens be religious.

Table 73 lists the results.

Religious students of Eastern origin were the most amenable to the idea of religious imposition, 30 percent choosing the first possibility listed in the table. What could be regarded as anti-religious sentiment ("it's not necessary that Israeli citizens be religious") was not found among nonreligious students.

In an ethnocentric scale, measuring attitudes to other people, the scores shown in Table 74 were found. In all cases, the students in religious schools proved to be more ethnocentric. In one specific case, the statement was offered that "The Jewish people are more important than other people." Approximately 75 percent of the students attending religious schools answered affirmatively, in contrast to 25 percent

TABLE 73
PERCENTAGE DISTRIBUTION OF ANSWERS TO QUESTION ON DESIRED DEGREE OF RELIGIOSITY

The Question, the Answer, and the Choice	RESEARCH GROUP				CONTROL GROUP	
	Eastern		Western			
	Religious	Secular	Religious	Secular	Religious	Secular
Which of the following statements do you agree with?						
1. Every Jew in Israel should be religious.	29.6	2.7	19.6	1.2	22.6	1.4
2. It is desirable that every citizen in Israel, even the nonreligious, should observe the Sabbath and attend synagogue.	45.2	22.3	37.0	16.9	60.6	14.5
3. Israeli citizens could be religious or nonreligious according to their desire.	23.0	73.2	43.5	76.6	16.8	82.6
4. It is not necessary that Israeli citizens be religious.	2.2	1.8	—	5.2	—	1.4

Source: L. Adar and C. Adler, *Education for Values in Schools for Immigrant Children in Israel.* (Jerusalem: The School of Education of the Hebrew University, 1965), p. 134.

of the students attending secular schools. However, no significant differences concerning attitudes towards Arabs were found.

Attitudes towards citizenship were also examined (such as preferences for a democracy and rights of the citizens). The results are found in Table 75. They show that religious students have less citizenship orientation than their nonreligious counterparts.

TABLE 74
ETHNOCENTRICISM AND RELIGIOUS SCHOOL ATTENDANCE

	Religious School	Secular School
Research Group - Students of Eastern Origin	2.31	1.68
Research Group - Students of Western Origin	2.00	1.05
Control Group - Students of Western Origin	1.50	0.80

Source: L. Adar and C. Adler, *Education for Values in Schools for Immigrant Children in Israel.*(Jerusalem: The School of Education of the Hebrew University, 1965), p. 135.

TABLE 75
ATTITUDES TOWARDS CITIZENSHIP AND
RELIGIOUS SCHOOL ATTENDANCE

	Religious School	Secular School	Sig. Dif.
Research Group - Eastern Descent	3.27	3.64	p = .001
Research Group - Western Descent	3.94	4.42	p = .01
Control Group - Western Descent	4.37	4.84	p = .05

Source: L. Adar and C. Adler. *Education for Values in Schools for Immigrant Children in Israel.* (Jerusalem: The School of Education of the Hebrew University, 1965), p. 136.

Three questions were asked concerning ethnic relationships. They concerned the willingness to live in the same neighborhood, nonobjection to children playing together, and readiness to marry outside one's ethnic group.

The results show significant differences (in the research group only) on the first two questions, but not on the question concerning marriage.

In these two questions, students of religious schools showed greater social distance than children of nonreligious schools.

Another question examined the reasons for pursuing education. Children of Eastern descent, regardless of whether they attended a religious or secular school, showed the same attitude to education. However, the kind of school one attended had an effect on children of Western descent. Pupils of religious schools valued education more than did children of nonreligious schools. This finding is, of course, consistent with the importance attached by orthodox circles to learning although it is not clear why such differences were not found among Eastern children. With regard to values concerning work, only among the Western children of the research group was a significant difference obtained. Those Western children who attended a religious school valued work for its own sake more often than did Western children who attended nonreligious schools. The latter tended to regard work as a necessary evil. In the other two comparisons (Eastern children of the research group and the Western children of the control group), the differences were in the same direction but not statistically significant.

To sum up, significant differences were generally found between religious and nonreligious students in the areas concerning religious values and in areas not concerned with religious values. Yet these differences were greater in the research group, composed of those of lower socioeconomic status, than in the control group. Thus, almost half of the comparisons performed on the religious and nonreligious pupils of the research group proved statistically significant, with most of the nonsignificant comparisons being in the predicted direction. Only one-third of the comparisons on the religious and nonreligious pupils of the control group yielded statistical significance, with less than a third of the nonsignificant comparisons being in the expected direction.

In the research group, the comparison among children of Eastern origin did not show more marked results than did the comparison among children of Western origin. This leads us to suspect that the observed differences in religious values were due to religious values common to both Eastern and Western immigrants and were not intrinsic to the Eastern group itself. In this interpretation of the data, we differ with the authors, Adar and Adler, who attribute the differences to ethnic values.

Judith Shuval inquired into the occupational interests of a sample of 1,266 students in the last two years of high school.[6] Her hypothesis that religious girls would be more interested in nursing than would non-religious girls was partly supported. The very religious girls were the most interested in nursing, but there were no significant differences between the nonreligious and partially observant girls. When ethnicity was cross-classified with religiosity and family tension, there was found a very high interest in nursing among religious immigrant girls who had been experiencing strain in their family relationships. The interpretation offered is that the nursing role, because it is consistent with traditional family patterns, offers a legitimate avenue of escape for the girl who does not wish to sever relationship with her family.

Shuval found the more religious girls to be interested in teaching, another feminine profession. Twenty-five percent of the nonreligious girls, 32 percent of the partially religious girls, and 37 percent of the very religious girls professed an interest in teaching.

Leonard Weller and Ephraim Tabory raised the question whether religious nurses relate to patients differently than do nonreligious nurses.[7] Specifically, it was predicted that nurses who were not religious sould be more likely to manifest a "scientific-technical orientation," by which is meant the perception of the patient as a "case" to be cured, coupled with an understanding that the nurses' tasks are to assist the doctor. On the other hand, nurses who were religious were expected to manifest an "affective orientation," by which is meant a desire to "be with" the patient, to consider him as a "whole" person, and to assume responsibility and act independently.

One hundred and fourteen students from two hospitals served as subjects. One of them is a religious hospital, recruiting mostly religious nurses. The other is a secular hospital. The student nurses filled out a questionnaire on their religiosity and their orientation towards nursing. On the basis of their responses the nurses were categorized as to whether they were religious, traditional or secular. After unsuccessful attempts to construct a unidimensional scale of patient orientation (scientific-technical—affective) each question was analyzed separately.

The following items were presented: 1) Whenever possible it's fun to sit down with patients and just pass the time; 2) nurses should discourage patients from discussing their personal problems

with them; 3) as far as is reasonable, nurses and doctors should treat
patients as their equals; 4) in certain matters the authority of the
nurses should be greater than that of the doctor; 5) one of the problems
confronting nurses who become too friendly with their patients is
that the latter don't know where to draw the line; and 6) the main thing
to be demanded of nurses is a thorough knowledge of general medicine.

Four of the six items were statistically significant and consistent
with the hypothesis that religious nurses would be more person-
oriented than nonreligious ones. One statement was not statistically
significant, but in the predicted direction. In only one item, the last,
was there virtually no difference between the religious and nonreligious nurses. No trend, however, was found for the middle group,
the traditionally observant. Depending on the specific question, the
patient orientation of the traditionally observant either resembled
the religious nurses, resembled the nonreligious nurses, fell in-between
the two groups, or bore no resemblence to either the religious or
nonreligious nurses.

There are several reasons for expecting that religious people would
be more authoritarian. First, being orthodox may imply a general
submissiveness. Second, religious people might be less tolerant of
other groups, which is itself related to authoritarianism. It may also
be, that religious families, in their desire to train their children to
be religious, resort to punishment more often than do nonreligious
families. Then again, it is just as reasonable to expect a high degree
of association between authoritarianism and religiosity as it is between authoritarianism and political ideology, a much studied relationship.

Leonard Weller and several of his assistants felt that such would be
the case.[8] Two independent samples were used. The first consisted
of 176 high school students, who were given a translated version of
a modified F Scale. On the basis of their reported religious behavior
the students were classified as religious, traditional, or secular. They
also answered whether they considered themselves as being religious,
traditional, or nonobservant. On both the objective and subjective
measures of religiosity, the more religious were significantly more
authoritarian (p. $<.001$).

In another sample, this time with 125 college students between
the ages of twenty-one and twenty-nine, the differences were again

highly significant; the religious were more authoritarian than the traditional or nonreligious. In the amount of authoritarianism, the traditional students were closer to religious students than they were to secular students. Thus among the college students the mean authoritarian score for the religious students was 5.02 as compared to 1.08 for the traditional students and -6.79 for the secular students. (The higher the score, the greater the authoritarianism.)

In the sample of college students, the respondents were further divided into four groups: a) both student and father religious; b) son more religious than father; c) son less religious than father; and d) both son and father not religious. It was hypothesized that authoritarianism would be highest in group a, next to highest in group b, next to lowest in group c, and least in group d. The results confirmed the hypothesis at or better than the .001 level of confidence. The means for the respective groups were 9.06, 6.83, -4.29 and -8.07.

Yehoshua Rim and Z. E. Kurzweil thought that religious Jews would be more likely to risk a material loss than would secular Jews.[9] To test this hypothesis, a group of seven individuals was given a problem, along with instructions to arrive at a unanimous recommendation. Each recommendation involved a different degree of suggested risk. After the discussion and the group decision (as a rule unanimous), the subject stated his individual opinion, which often differed from the one he expressed in the group. One hundred and fifty subjects from diverse backgrounds participated in the study. Significant differences on risk taking between orthodox and nonorthodox Jews were not found.

CHANGE IN JEWISH MOURNING RITES

Nissan Rubin examined the sociological significance of Jewish mourning rites in the Land of Israel during the Mishnaic and Talmudic periods.[10] He had two basic concerns—to study the evolvement of Jewish funeral rites, as they were influenced by societal change, and to investigate the psychological and sociological functions of these rites. To this end Rubin first searched the Bible and the Talmud for any reference to funeral rites and attitudes towards the dead.

For Whom One Must Mourn

The relatives for whom one was required to mourn were most numerous in the latter part of the second century when mourning was undertaken for the entire extended family. During the third century mourning gradually became confined to one's nuclear family—a change attributed to the changing socioeconomic conditions in Israel. When the economy was based on agriculture (as in the second century), the extended family lived together and all its members participated in mourning for any dead relative. As a result of urbanization, the reign of terror against the farmers by the Roman regime, and the continuous division of the farmer's estate (required by the laws of inheritance), the nuclear family grew in importance and mourning rites changed.

Stages of Mourning

The stages of mourning are three:

1) "Seven days" (shivah), including the day of death, during which the mourner may not observe many of the religious commandments.
2) "Thirty days" (shloshim), during which only certain restrictions on the mourner remain in force.
3) "Twelve months," during which few restrictions are placed on the mourner. This period applies only to mourning for one's parents.

These three stages are seen as giving social support to the mourner. They also approximate Geoffrey Gorer's three phases of mourning: shock (a few days after death); intensive mourning (with much introspection and isolation for six to twelve weeks); psychological and physical recuperation.[11]

Mourning laws are less stringent for widows than widowers. The widow is permitted to remarry after three months, while a widower has generally to wait twelve months before remarrying. These laws were established in an agricultural society where it was difficult for an unmarried woman to support herself and her children. Still, under certain circumstances the man could remarry immediately, as when he had no children (to beget children is a religious commandment) or had no one to care for him.

The Funeral Process

While preparations for the funeral or mourning may not be made prior to death, the funeral must be performed as quickly as possible after the death. The prompt burial lessens the possibility that the funeral will be an ornate affair and emphasizes the equality of all men. Many other equalitarian customs were instituted after the destruction of the Second Temple (70 A. D.) by Rabbi Simeon Ben Gamlial II.

The only words that may be spoken during the funeral are those praising the deceased. A latent function of this practice is to prevent the funeral from becoming mainly a family reunion.

From the second century B. C. until the fourth century A. D. the body of the deceased was interred and apparently, when the flesh rotted, the bones were reburied in an ossuary. The primary purpose of this custom seems to have been economical. Land was scarce, so when the cemeteries were filled bones were removed to make room for new corpses. The desire to bury the corpse in the family grave may have been another reason for this custom, for the ossuary was easier than a heavy coffin to transport a long distance.

Mourning Customs and Their Functions

In terms of Talcott Parsons' theory, one fear is that the mourner will desist from "output," causing a loss to society.[12] For this reason (as well as to ensure the psychological well-being of the mourner) obligations and prohibitions, aimed at directing and controlling the mourner's social behavior, are imposed on him. In addition, nonmourners are required to behave according to norms which demonstrate their solidarity with the mourner, giving him psychological support.

According to Parsons, the mechanism governing the potential deviate are composed of four stages: *permissiveness* toward the deviate (mourner) concerning the free expression of his emotions; *support* for and *solidarity* with the deviate; *denial of reciprocity,* by means of which the society refuses to completely identify with the deviant's expectation; and *manipulation of rewards* whereby the mourner recognizes that his "deviation," "permitted" by the society, is of temporary duration. In Jewish mourning rites "permissiveness" and "support" are temporary phenomena allowed during the seven days and to an extent during the thirty days period. After that time the mourner must once again participate in the social system.

Obligations and Prohibitions

Obligations and prohibitions relating to the mourner's body, his possessions, and his immediate social environment are presented in the following table:

TABLE 76
OBLIGATIONS AND PROHIBITIONS PERTAINING TO MOURNER

Action	Obligation	Prohibition
Body		1. Showering and bathing 2. Intercourse 3. Shaving and haircut*
Possessions	1. Rending of garment 2. Covering of the head 3. Removal of the shoulder sleeve 4. Turning the bed over	1. Wearing shoes 2. Laundering 3. Ironed Clothes*
Possessions	1. Rending of garment	1. Learning Torah
Social Environment		1. Learning Torah 2. Greeting Others 3. Parties* 4. Work 5. Trade* 6. Marriage*

*Forbidden for thirty days; all the rest forbidden for the seven day period only.
Source: Nissan Rubin. "Changes of Funeral Practices in the Period of the Talmud."'(Unpublished M.A. thesis, Hebrew University, 1971).

The table shows that the bereaved is forbidden to mutilate his body; nor is he permitted to initiate or participate in social activities. He is, however, allowed to tear his clothes and "act out" towards his possession (e.g., by turning over his bed). The society on its part initiates social activities towards the mourner (e.g., condolence visits, eulogy, and the mourner's meal).

The table also points to the fact that in each area (body, possessions, and social environment) at least one of the prohibitions in force during the seven day period extends to the thirty days (e.g., not shaving, wearing ironed clothes, or going to parties). The rending of garments and other behaviors identify the mourner, enabling society to respond to him accordingly.

Judaism limits egocentrism (which occurs among mourners in most societies) by forcing the bereaved to become dependent on friends and relatives. The eulogy, condolence visits, and mourner's meal are all aspects of this forced dependence. The eulogy emphasizes the importance of the deceased and, indirectly, of the mourner. On the day of the funeral, the bereaved is not allowed to prepare his own food. Food is brought to him during condolence visits. (After the destruction of the Second Temple it was decreed that funeral societies undertake preparation of the mourner's meal. Ostensibly this rabbinical decree was an attempt to prevent competition between the rich and the poor, since the latter could not afford to bring expensive food to the mourner.)

At the death of one's parents one is forbidden to attend parties for a period of a year. At times marriage may be allowed immediately.

CONCLUSION

Two topics have been dealt with: the extent of and change in religious observance and the effect of religiosity on attitudes and behavior. The determination of who is and is not religious is a difficult methodological problem, depending on whether subjective or objective measures are used and what constitutes the objective indices. There are few surveys on this topic, a circumstance somewhat surprising in view of the importance of the religious factor in Israeli society. It would seem safe to say that at least 25 percent of the population are orthodox. The effect of the degree of religiosity on attitudes and behavior has not been thoroughly studied, although the results are rather consistent. In such areas as family planning, occupational preference (i.e., teaching and nursing), patient orientation, authoritarianism, and general values, the religious and nonreligious differ. Several researches demonstrated that the observed religious differences are not specious influences of social class or ethnicity.

Nevertheless, the "religious factor" would seem to warrant further study; for when one carefully examines the findings, the internal pattern is not as consistent as at first appearance. Thus for Oriental women higher education meant less religious observance, but not so for European women, where the more educated female was more likely to remain observant. Why this is so is not clear. Similarly, Matras and Auerbach demonstrated a strong relationship between religious observance and contraceptive practice; the more religious the woman, the less likely it was that she had considered family planning. This finding was clearly according to expectation. However, the authors also anticipated that a partially observant or nonobservant daughter of a nonobservant mother would more likely use contraceptive devices than such a daughter of a religious mother—a plausible but unconfirmed hypothesis.

Judith Shuval found that religious high school students were more interested in nursing than were nonreligious high school girls, but she did not find statistically significant differences in interest in nursing between the nonreligious and partially religious students. Matras and Auerbach showed marked differences between the partly religious and nonreligious in contraceptive behavior, albeit Weller and Tabory's findings are interesting both for what they did and did not reveal. The general hypothesis was again confirmed; religious nurses showed an affective orientation to their patients, in contrast to nonreligious nurses who displayed a scientific-technical orientation. However, the traditional nurses did not show a middle pattern as predicted; in fact, they revealed no consistent pattern at all.

While there was no ambiguity about the finding that the more religious were more authoritarian, no relationship was found between taking risky decisions and degree of religiosity.

The middle group, called the "traditional" group, would seem to be deserving of more study. We also feel that the studies have been rather simplistic in their breakdown of the population into "religious" and "nonreligious." It would be fruitful to employ more refined criteria of religiosity, as for example that of intrinsically and extrinsically religious. Finally, none of the studies examined the cause of these religious differences. We do not know if they reflect values of two subcultures, the religious and nonreligious, or if they arise out of differential socialization practices. This is the kind of question we may assume will be asked in future research on the religious factor in Israeli society.

NOTES

1. Aaron Antonovsky, "Israeli Political-Social Attitudes," *Amot* (No. 6, 1963): pp. 11-22 (in Hebrew).

2. Judah Matras, "Religious Observance and Family Formation in Israel: Some Intergenerational Changes," *American Journal of Sociology* (69, 1964): pp. 464-475; Judah Matras, *Social Change in Israel.* (Chicago: Aldine, 1965), pp. 199-208; Roberto Bachi and Judah Matras, "Contraception and Induced Abortion among Jewish Maternity Cases in Israel," *Milbank Memorial Fund Quarterly* (40, 1962): pp. 207-229.

3. Judah Matras and C. Auerbach, "On Rationalization of Family Formation in Israel," *Milbank Memorial Fund Quarterly* (40, 1962): pp. 453-480

4. *Idem.*

5. Leah Adar and Chaim Adler, *Education for Values in Schools for Immigrant Children in Israel.* (Jerusalem: The School of Education of the Hebrew University, 1965) (in Hebrew).

6. Judith T. Shuval, "Parental Pressure and Career Commitments," *Megamot* (13, 1964): pp. 33-39 (in Hebrew).

7. Leonard Weller and Ephraim Tabory, "Religiosity of Nurses and Their Orientation to Patients," in H. Hirschberg, Y. Don and L. Weller (eds.) *Memorial to H. M. Shapiro* (Ramat-Gan, Israel: Bar-Ilan University, 1972), pp. 97-110.

8. Leonard Weller *et al.*, "Authoritarianism and Religiosity," Mimeographed, 1971.

9. Yehoshua Rim and Z. E. Kurzweil, "A Note on Attitudes to Risk-Taking of Observant and Non-Observant Jews," *Jewish Journal of Sociology* (7, 1965): pp. 238-245.

10. Nissan Rubin, "Changes of Funeral Practices in the Period of the Talmud." (Unpublished M.A. Thesis, Hebrew University, 1971).

11. Geoffrey Gorer, *Death, Grief, and Mourning.* (Garden-City: Doubleday, 1965), pp. 72, 112-113.

12. Talcott Parsons, "General Theory in Sociology," in R. K. Merton, L. Broom and L. S. Cottrell, Jr. (eds.), *Sociology Today.* (New York: Basic Books, 1959), pp. 3-38; Talcott Parsons, *The Social System.* (Glencoe, Ill.: The Free Press, 1951), chs. 7 and 10.

8

The Kibbutz

The most thoroughly documented section of Israeli society is certainly the kibbutz. It is probably one of the most researched societies of the world. A recently published bibliography recorded 883 publications in English, French, German, Dutch, Spanish, Portuguese, Russian, and Polish on different aspects of kibbutz life.[1] Most of these publications were written by Israeli authors, though a sizeable number were contributed by well-known Western scientists like Bettelheim,[2] Rabin,[3] Spiro,[4] and Schwartz.[5] The motivation (to inquire into kibbutz life) of Western and especially American scientists was different from that of the Israeli scientists: the former were challenged by the peculiarities of kibbutz life which were unique in modern societies and which could be considered as deviations, casting doubt on generally accepted theoretical assumptions and scientific statements, such as the universality of the family, the functionality of inequality in society, and the dire consequences of maternal deprivation. This peculiar motivation gave rise to a "kibbutz complex" in those scientists who wanted to find that the kibbutz has failed. This complex was described, with laudable impartiality but without exhaustive analysis, by Rosenfeld.[6]

The approach of Israeli scientists was of a more applied nature and was intended to analyze the problems of kibbutz society and to help it in solving those problems, or at least to help the kibbutz movement understand them. As a side effect, however, the Israeli sociolo-

gists contributed considerably to the elucidation of important theoretical questions.[7]

The sociological research of Israeli authors on the kibbutz began
only in the mid-fifties. Interestingly, no demand to apply scientific
methods arose during the first four decades of the existence of
kibbutz society. In the first years after the establishment of each
individual kibbutz, no attention was paid by its members to the
emerging social reality in the life of the group. There was an un-
limited confidence that every problem could be solved by the omni-
potent, ideological will of the group: it was enough to know the
"right way" and the right answer to the questions would immediately
be found. All intellectual effort was invested in finding how things
"should be" and no attempt was made to analyze "social" facts.
Later, however, stubborn social facts appeared, which resisted the
usual ways of problem solving, and the policymakers of the kibbutz
came to the conclusion that in order to solve those problems they
had first of all to analyze them and understand them. The development and the differentiation of the kibbutz economy, the emergence
of the multigenerational kibbutz family, the growing heterogeneity
of the social group, and especially the decisive social change in the
surrounding Israeli society, brought with them social facts which
were independent of the creative ideological will and resistant to its
formative power. It was no surprise that when the leaders of one of
the Kibbutz Federations decided to ask for the assistance of the
Hebrew University in planning some social research, they were not
able to formulate the problems to be researched! Consequently, the
first project was necessarily explorative and had a diffuse character;
it included all the institutional spheres of kibbutz society: family
economy, stratification, polity, socialization, and values.

The Hebrew University appointed for this purpose a young
associate professor, Dr. Yonina Gerber-Talmon, who was attracted
to the topic because of her interest in chiliastic movements. She
organized a research team consisting mainly of advanced graduate
students, one of them an active kibbutz member. A sample of twelve
kibbutzim was selected, representing the different kibbutz units in
the Federation according to their size, seniority, social differentiation,
cultural background, and locality. In each kibbutz a random subsample
was taken, and the members in the sample were interviewed according
to a lengthy schedule, using 148 open-ended questions. A detailed

observation schedule covered the observable social facts and was used as a check to the material collected in the interviews.

The material was analyzed manually and several research reports were first prepared as internal publications for the use of the Federation. They were published later as articles in Hebrew and English periodicals. Due to the lack of advanced research technology and of funds, ten years passed before the most important research reports came to be published. Their effect on the kibbutz movement was considerable; they were studied by the management of the Federation and were taught in the ideological and refresher courses. Unfortunately, Professor Talmon could not continue her research acitivities. After 1964 her health declined rapidly and she died in 1966. Her contribution to the sociology of the kibbutz was both quantitatively and qualitatively invaluable. Her articles were collected and published in Hebrew[8] and an English edition is due to appear.

Her assistants continued her work. Two Federations established Institutes for Social Research while the Hebrew University maintained the research seminar of kibbutz sociology. The new research topics were essentially extensions and deepenings of the original exploratory study. Whereas at first only one Federation opened its gates to sociological research, after 1964 all the Federations[9] gradually joined in the scientific work. Through the Research Institutes of the Kibbutz Federations, the sociology of the kibbutz reached all the sociology departments in the Israeli universities.

One survey cannot exhaust the hundreds of research reports hitherto published by Israeli authors. Our selection is intended to cover the following topics:-

1) Family.
2) Second Generation.
3) Work and Organization.
4) Social Participation and Direct Democracy.
5) Values.
6) Kibbutz and Israeli Society.

THE FAMILY

Characteristically, the family was one of the most important foci in the research of the Israeli and the Western sociologists who worked on the kibbutz. The Israelis concentrated their attention on the family because it offered the most important key to the understanding of the social change that the kibbutz had undergone. Talmon saw in the changes within the status of the family in the social structure of the kibbutz the central indicator of social change, for which she coined the term, "the institutionalization of the Bund" (communion) into a fully fledged community. Using the term Bund of the German sociologist Schmalenbach[10] for the emerging revolutionary group that characterized the newly founded individual kibbutz, she found that in this social system the status of the family constituted a problem. (The Bund was characterized by an all-embracing solidarity which bound the founders together by an uncompromising devotion to the values of the group by laying heavy emphasis on value orientation, by paying comparatively less attention to economic and organizational problems, and by stressing cultural homogeneity. The family in such a system created a serious problem, through competing with the all-embracing solidarity.) A couple expected devotion to each other, and this impaired the possibility of devotion to the group. Therefore, the family in such kibbutzim led a quasi-underground life; it was founded informally by merely occupying a common dwelling unit without any wedding ceremony. The couple did not appear as a unit either in the communal dining room or in the General Assembly. They called each other by their first names and referred to each other as "my boy" and "my girl" (Hebrew: *bachur sheli, bachurah sheli*–lit. "my chosen one"). The functions of this family were extremely limited; it was merely a unit of legitimate sexual cohabitation and reproduction. It had no function whatsoever in the different institutional spheres (economic, politic, ritual) and even in the sphere of socialization its function was emphatically secondary. The kibbutz was responsible for the socialization of the children who occupied separate houses of their own.[11]

Interestingly enough, this form of "functionless" family led Spiro to his famous misunderstanding of the family in the kibbutz,[12] in which he declared that there was no marriage or no family in the kibbutz. Talmon found in her research that this severely diluted form of the family was only transitional. Two factors contributed to the gradual rise in the status of the family in the social structure of the kibbutz. In the first place there was the process of differentiation in the economy and in the social structure of the kibbutz. More diverse economic tasks required a complex division of labor which again necessitated organization, thus diminishing spontaneity. Additional groups joined the kibbutz, and this led to compromises in the tight solidarity of the founding group.

Secondly, the arrival of a great number of children enhanced the status of the family, in spite of the fact that the children were educated by trained nurses and not by the parents. A quasi-underground existence was out of the question, when most of the members were married and had children.

The status of the family gradually rose in these circumstances. The establishment of new families became a more formal event, and after the establishment of the state the traditional Jewish wedding rites (*chupah,* the only legal form of marriage for Jews) were incorporated into the wedding ceremony. The terms "husband" and "wife" *(ba'ali, ishti)* were gradually introduced. The family acquired several economic functions, such as the consumption of five o'clock tea in the couple's room and discretion in spending the clothing budget.[13] The couple appeared as a unit in the dining room and in the Assembly and usually spent the annual vacation together outside the kibbutz. They now had more to say in the education of their children. The initial egalitarian division of labor between the sexes changed into discernible, almost sexually polarized, division of labor. Most males worked in agriculture, industry and management, while most females worked in the kitchen, in the laundry, in clothing, and especially in education.

Talmon found that the process of institutionalization worked as a "biogenetic law" in the kibbutz movement and that it was not only the kibbutz movement as a whole that underwent the process of institutionalization but also every new kibbutz, however late it was founded. That was why Talmon could double check her variables of change, through reconstructing the process of development in long-established kibbutzim and through confrontation of kibbutzim in different degrees of institutionalization. She distinguished four types of kibbutz according to their places in the continuum of institutionalization:

1) the Bund type;
2) the Unified Community type;
3) the Community of "Circles" type;
4) the Sectorial Community type.

These types were not in a unilinear continuum, however. The Bund type—which has been described above—developed into one of the three other types, following certain historical events in the life of the particular kibbutz. Thus, if the group succeeded in absorbing the units which joined the kibbutz, the Unified Community appeared. In this type the family was the strongest, since the solidarity of the original group gradually diminished through the efforts of the absorption of the new units. If, however, the kibbutz grew through the fusion of strong units which resisted a complete absorption into the founders' group, the composing units survived as social "Circles" in the kibbutz; that is, as solid subgroups which found a common *modus vivendi,* but nevertheless required devotion from their members. In such a kibbutz the family, though stronger than in the Bund, had nevertheless to take into account the existence of the "Circles." If the different units did not find a *modus vivendi* and lived together in a rather tense situation, we had a Sectorial Community, which was a residual type and was represented in the sample by only one kibbutz.

Talmon found in a series of variables that the familistic approach was strongest in the Unified Communities, weaker in the Community of "Circles" and almost nonexistent in the Bund type. Thus, the ideological patterns concerning fertility were more collectivistic in the Bund type and the Circle type, and more familistic in the Unified Communities. The attitude toward the deviant behavior of eating dinner in the family home instead of in the communal dining hall was most negative in the Bund, less negative in the Circle type, and less negative still in the Unified type. The same order was found in the attitudes toward the controversial question of the housing: should the children sleep in their parents' apartments or in the children's houses? The strongest support for the collective system was found in the Bund types and the strongest support for the familistic system in the Unified and Sectorial Communities. In the Unified Communities, more interviewees thought that second-generation youth had to consider their parents' opinion concerning job selection than did those in the Circle Communities, whereas in the Bund type kibbutzim the interviewees were against such concern.

Summarizing her articles dealing with the changing status of the family in the kibbutz, Talmon warned the kibbutz movement that if no mechanism was found to integrate the familistic tendencies into the social structure of the collective form of life, the family might become a dangerous competitor to the social system. She pointed to certain organizational devices which served the purpose of rendering the family an ally of the kibbutz and not a competitor: e.g., improvement of service and technology in the communal dining room resulted in the return of many families to the communal dinner. Similarly, improved organization and the higher education of the nurses strengthened support for the collective educational institutions and weakened familistic tendencies.

M. Rosner, one of Talmon's assistants, devoted a detailed research project to the problem of division of labor between the sexes.[14] Like most of the socialist movements, the kibbutz movement regarded the emancipation of women as one of its most important social aims. However, while the political socialist movements limited themselves to formal equality between the sexes without changing the basic economic dependence of the woman or the man, the kibbutz disconnected all the ties between economy and family. Women, like men, were individual members of the kibbutz and their economic security was dependent exclusively on their membership, not on the marital status of either the man or the woman. Thus, the economic status of the single woman was not different from that of a married woman, nor was that of a divorcee or a widow. There was a complete, formal equality between the sexes concerning political rights within the kibbutz. Moreover, the system of collective consumption freed the woman completely from housework, at least formally. All the usual work of a housewife—kitchen, laundry, children—was carried out by communal institutions. The small apartment of the married couple did not entail many services, while housework was not at all considerable.

In such circumstances, there was no hindrance to dispensing completely with divisions of labor according to sex. Every job could have been taken theoretically by either sex. Interestingly enough, however, the departure from the traditional division of

labor, according to sex, was a one-way street; women entered
traditionally masculine jobs in considerable number. They found
their way to every agricultural branch, even to road paving and
marsh drying. However, in the few traditionally feminine jobs such
as those of the kitchen, the laundry, needlework, and education
only female workers remained, except for a few males who occasion-
ally did the dishwashing in the kitchen or waited at table in the
communal dining room according to a corvee system. Later, when
more children were born and the communal services were extended
because of the rising standard of living, more and more women were
taken out of the branches of production and transferred to service
branches. During the late forties and the early fifties, a rather polar
division of labor between the sexes emerged. Talmon compared the
percentages of women in agricultural branches and in service branches
in eight kibbutzim of her sample between 1948 and 1955[15] (see
Table 77).

TABLE 77
PERCENTAGE OF FEMALE WORKERS IN AGRICULTURAL, SERVICE, AND INDUSTRIAL BRANCHES IN EIGHT KIBBUTZIM OF ICHUD FEDERATION, 1948-1955

Female Workers in:	1948	1955
Agricultural Branches	11.1	6.3
Service Branches	84.9	89.5
Manufacture and Industry	4.0	4.2
Total	100.0	100.0

Source: Y. Talmon-Garber, "On the Division of Work in the Kibbutz,"
(Jerusalem: Hebrew University, 1956): p. 2 (mimeographed in Hebrew).

During the same period the changes shown in Table 78 were
recorded in the male working power.

The polarization is evident from Tables 77 and 78. It is even more
evident when we point out that the internal division of the service
branches included management tasks in which the males were over-
represented. In 1948, for instance, 7.1 percent of the males worked
in management as against 2.0 percent of the females. The respective
numbers for 1955 are 11.6 and 3.3.

TABLE 78
PERCENTAGE OF MALE WORKERS IN AGRICULTURAL, SERVICE, AND INDUSTRIAL BRANCHES IN EIGHT KIBBUTZIM OF ICHUD FEDERATION, 1948-1955

Male Workers in:	1948	1955
Agricultural Branches	27.6	33.6
Service Branches	42.4	40.2
Manufacture and Industry	30.0	26.2
Total	100.0	100.0

Source: Y. Talmon-Garber," On the Division of Work in the Kibbutz," (Jerusalem, Hebrew University, 1956): p. 2 (mimeographed in Hebrew).

Rosner devoted a special project to the so-called problem of the woman, which was essentially the problem of social change in the status of women and family in the kibbutz. Investigating a sample of 466 women in twelve kibbutzim with a control group of 85 males, Rosner focused his attention on the attitudes toward social ideology and the reality of division of labor between the sexes. Himself a member of a kibbutz, Rosner worked in the left wing Kibbutz Artsi Federation. Politically, this federation was affiliated with the left wing[16] Mapam Party, and was more radical in its ideological conceptions than the other federations. This federation was characterized by an especially radical approach to the question of the emancipation of women. Thus the basic slogan was "let us liberate the women from the yoke of service" (that is: housework). In order to emphasize the equality of the sexes, this federation normally regulated such things as the retention by the woman of her maiden name after marriage, dispensing with wedding rings, avoiding the term "my husband" or "my wife" and using the term "my friend" or "my comrade" instead. Children called their parents by their first names and did not use the words Mom and Dad (*Aba, Ima*).

Rosner found a great lag between ideological desirability and social reality as reflected in the remarks of his interviewees. Thus, whereas the majority of the sample rejected the idea that there were basic differences in attitudes, inclinations, and characteristic traits between the sexes, almost everybody admitted the existence of the polar division of labor. In the sample as a whole, 68.3 percent of all the women worked in traditionally feminine jobs, 4.8 percent in industry, 9.1 percent in agriculture, and 7.1 percent in management and clerical jobs. Since Rosner did not compare the data from earlier years with his findings, he had but one indication of the change; he compared the general women population in old well-established kibbutzim (founded before 1934) with that of the young women in those same kibbutzim. He found that, whereas in the kibbutz as a whole 62.5 percent of the women worked in traditionally feminine jobs (education, kitchen, needlework, nursing), 75.1 percent of the young women worked in those branches. He found also that 54.6 percent of the women had had no public activity at all (membership in committees, chairmanship of committees or branches, or management jobs) during the previous five years, whereas prior to the research 23.5 percent had been members of committees, 17.9 percent had been chairmen, and only 4.0 percent had held management jobs (Rosner did not have comparative data on males, but from other sources we know that women were severely under-represented in public activity).

Rosner, like Talmon, found that polarization of division of labor according to sex was but an aspect of familistic tendencies. Other indications were the aspiration on the part of an absolute majority of the sample to have four or more children, an acceptance of the attitude that five o'clock tea (the only meal consumed at home) had to be prepared by the women, and an acceptance of the attitude that family had a relatively higher importance in the life of a woman than in the life of a man.

Rosner, whose attitude to his research was wholly based on his identification with his movement's values, summarized his article in the following words:

It does not seem possible in the existing situation to avoid the increasing importance of the family unit in the social life of the kibbutz. It is indeed possible to moderate this process by strengthening the integrative factors within the kibbutz as a whole, and within the framework of the social groups which constitute it. It is also possible to restrain the widening functions of the family in the consumer and educational spheres. However, the demographic processes and personal aspirations in this sphere should not be ignored. It is therefore necessary to search for ways

to ensure maximum equality of women in the spheres of work
and social activities on the basis of the growing importance of
the family.[17]

Another aspect of the growing familism in the kibbutz was dealt
with in the research of Joseph Shepher,[18] another former assistant
of Talmon. Shepher worked in the right wing Ichud Federation, which
had requested a comparative study on the subject in order to obtain
directives in the housing systems for children.

The original housing system for children in the kibbutz movement
was familistic; that is, the children spent the night in their parents'
apartment. All the kibbutzim which had been founded before the end
of World War I accepted this system. The wave of immigration after
1918 brought new groups to the kibbutz movement and these new
kibbutzim, influenced by a radical collectivistic ideology, introduced
the collectivistic system. The children lived in special children's houses
from birth until the age of eighteen. Except for a short period of two
to four hours in the afternoon, when they paid a visit to their parents'
home, they spent all their time in the children's house which included
bedrooms, classrooms, a dining room, and playrooms. This collectivistic system had been accepted as the normative form and only four old
kibbutzim preserved the familistic system. This situation remained unchanged until after the War of Liberation (1948-1949), when some
kibbutzim proposed the reintroduction of the familistic system. The
Federation fought a battle of delay and retreat against the innovation,
and during the years 1951-1963 it reluctantly agreed to the change of
system in the case of nine kibbutzim. In 1963 it decided to carry out
a comparative research on the two systems in order to discover whether
there was any association between the desired familistic system and certain attitudes considered to be negative from the point of view of dominant kibbutz values.

Shepher took a sample of matched pairs of kibbutzim, nine with
collectivistic and nine with familistic systems.[19] Within each kibbutz
he took a proportional random sample of couples numbering altogether
818 interviewees. He used a lengthy open schedule and he compared
the material collected through the questionnaire with the results of
observation.

Shepher found differences between the two systems in 68 percent

of his 153 variables, of which 65 percent were statistically significant.
Moreover, all the differences showed the same direction. Anti-collecti-
vistic attitudes were associated with the familistic system of housing
the children. Thus in the kibbutzim of the familistic system people
had a more positive attitude toward ecological concentration of parts
of the extended multigenerational family, and more people than in
the collectivistic system indicated that the emerging extended family
tended to appear as a political pressure group.

In the familistic system people wanted to shorten the woman's
workday by 33 percent or more. The division of labor in the home
of couples was more polarized in the familistic system and likewise
in the distribution of public activities. Whereas in both systems women
were less active than men, in the familistic system the few who were active
were concentrated in activities considered feminine, those that dealt
mainly with educational, social and cultural issues. Only 5.5 percent
of the women in the familistic system had typical masculine jobs
(general management of economy, planning, sport) as against 16.2
percent of the women who performed such jobs in the collectivistic
system. Furthermore, the general social activity was more intensive
in the collectivistic system in the case of both sexes, and the lag between the sexes was wider in the familistic system. Although the
legitimacy of the collective educational system in the familistic
kibbutzim was largely intact, women were prevented from participating in the social life of the kibbutz because the burden of caring
for the children during the evenings and mornings fell mainly on
them. The difference between the two systems was especially conspicuous in the sphere of collective consumption. The general tendency in the familistic kibbutz was more individualistic, with an
intention to abolish the collective social control of consumption.
Interestingly enough, the permissive attitude toward individualistic
tendencies in the familistic system did not create a higher level of
satisfaction. In both systems the general reward balance was essentially positive; only in the sphere of consumption were members of
familistic kibbutzim less content than those in the collectivistic
kibbutzim, probably because of higher levels of aspiration. The
theoretical conclusions of his research were summarized by the
author as follows:

Theoretically two interesting points emerge from the inquiry.
First, there is apparently some intrinsic tension between the
value system of the kibbutz and that of the family as a social
unit. In this stage of research, it seems to be impossible to
decide whether this tension is the result of the remnants of
the "Bund" period or whether it is caused by the present
organization of the kibbutz collectivism and direct democracy
requiring limitations on the functions of the family unit. . . .
Second, the development of the division of labor between
the sexes in the kibbutz emphasizes the necessity for developing a theoretical framework which would enable us to explain the emergence of different patterns of division of labor
between the sexes and their course of change. Elizabeth Bott's
theoretical proposal, that familism is positively associated with
polarized division of labor between the sexes, was corroborated
in our research. In contrast to most modern societies, the kibbutz community is moving from more equalitarian to more
polarized division of labor. The case of the kibbutz contains
important implications for a general theory of division of
labor between the sexes.[20]

THE SECOND GENERATION IN THE KIBBUTZ

The kibbutz, as an innovative social experiment, is especially
interested in its second generation. The main criterion of its survival as a form of living is the extent to which it will succeed in
socializing the second generation into the social structure of the
kibbutz while based on the special value system. Most of the ephe-
meral social and utopian experiments were phenomena of one generation; parents failed to transmit their values to their children, who
consequently left the settlement.[21]
No precise empirical data exist concerning the success or failure
of the absorption of the second generation in the kibbutz. Population registration is a recent phenomenon in the kibbutz; there
are almost no data on the first forty years of the kibbutz movement.
The only possible source of knowledge is the memory of the founders
and pioneers (Hebrew: *vatikim*).[22] Only one Federation collected

demographic material on the second-generation members who left
the kibbutz in all the years of its existence. In the Kibbutz Artsi
Federation, which came into existence after World War I, 16.1
percent of all the second generation born into the seventy-three
kibbutzim of this federation left the kibbutz for good, 2.1 percent
died (mostly they had fallen in the three wars: 1948-1949, 1956,
1967), and 11.3 percent left for other kibbutzim, mostly because
of marriage. Therefore, 70.5 percent of 2,904 second-generation
members born into this federation still lived in their kibbutz of
origin.[23] This is a surprisingly high percentage, a success of more than
80 percent in the kibbutz socialization process. There is no reason to
suppose that the data would be considerably different in the remaining three federations. There is some hope that a forthcoming comprehensive work will include authentic data concerning all the federations.[24]

    The first research project devoted to the second generation was
part of the comprehensive exploratory research of Talmon and was
written up by one of her assistants, M. Sarel.[25] He extended the
original sample of Talmon, in which there were only seventy second-
generation members in five kibbutzim, through the addition of four
kibbutzim which had an adult second-generation population, from
which he took a sample of seventy-five more interviewees out of
700 second-generation adolescents (in the 17-18 age group) from
practically all the kibbutzim of the federation.

    Sarel pointed out that the second generation in the kibbutz was
caught in a dilemma; socialization in a revolutionary movement
tended to transmit revolutionary values, but the transmission itself was conservative. If the second generation accepted the values
of the parents' generation, it was conservative; it retained the basic
values of the parents. If it revolted against those values, it had to
return to the individualistic-familistic values against which the
parents revolted, and its approach would then be morphologically
revolutionary but essentially conservative. There were, however,
two additional possibilities. Since the parents' generation underwent
a process of institutionalization during the very years of the socialization of the second generation, it was possible that the second
generation would accept a "militant conservatism" approach. That
is, it would be critical of the parents' compromises with the original
values. It was also possible that, in case of the failure of the sociali-

zation process, the second generation would abstain from taking
its own standpoint on questions of values or would even demand
deviant values.

Sarel investigated the attitude of the second generation to different values in the institutional spheres of family and economy
(work and consumption). He found that the second generation
took an intermediate position between the Bund-type revolutionary
young kibbutzim and the first generation of the older kibbutz communities. Thus, the attitude towards the crucial question of the
housing system for children took the form shown in Table 79.

TABLE 79
ATTITUDE TO HOUSING SYSTEM FOR CHILDREN (PERCENTAGE)

	For the collective system	For the familistic system	No Material
Bund Kibbutzim	64	26	10
Second-generation adolescents	67	25	8
Second-generation adults	58	34	8
First-generation in communities	44	46	10

Source: M. Sarel, *"Research Report on the Second Generation in the Kibbutz"*
(Jerusalem: Hebrew University, 1959): p. 27 (mimeographed in Hebrew).

The intermediate position of the adult second generation is clear
from this table. The adolescents were even more conservative (or
radical) than the Bund kibbutzim, although the difference was not
significant. This same intermediate position was revealed in all
questions investigated except one: the size of the family. Here the
second generation's attitude was one of "innovation," 47 percent
were for intermediate and 40 percent for large families, as compared
with 37 percent and 5 percent of the Bund type and 47 percent and
26 percent of the first generation, respectively. This apparent deviation from the general pattern was aptly explained by Sarel. The
problem of family size had a different meaning for the second generation. Whereas in the first phase of the existence of the kibbutz a
large family would have meant a lack of concern for the basic interests

of the still economically weak kibbutz, in the phase when the second
generation came of age, a large family was an asset for the kibbutz.
Therefore one cannot see in the positive attitude of the second generation towards a large family a deviation from the original reason of the
first generation to limit the family size: the constellation having changed,
the "conservative" approach (concern for the interests of the kibbutz)
would demand a larger family.

The future of the second generation in the kibbutz was not wholly
dependent on its attitude towards the basic kibbutz values. If members
of the second generation could not find suitable mates inside the kibbutz when they came of age and were attracted to exogamous partners,
there was greater probability that they would follow their spouses and
leave the kibbutz. Whereas theoretically endogamy was possible, it
seems that certain characteristic traits of the socialization process prevented endogamy within the educational peer group and limited it in
the second generation as a whole. Outside the second generation there
were different sorts of potential mates, partly within the kibbutz, partly
within social groups connected with the kibbutz and partly outside.

Talmon devoted her last article,[26] which is widely known and quoted
in the sociological literature, to this problem, and according to Young[27]
it is the most outstanding contribution to the theory of incest and
exogamy since the publication of Murdoch's famous book, *Social
Structure.*[28]

This article is too well-known to be commented upon more than
briefly here. Talmon selected a sub-sample of three kibbutzim from
her original sample and investigated the mate selection patterns of
125 couples. She was aware of the fact that her sample was not representative of even the Federation in which she worked, and that her
data on premarital affairs were scanty. The main value of the article
lay in the excellent functional analysis of the main patterns found by
Talmon in her three kibbutzim. Talmon explained that the function
of the delicate balance between the exogamous and endogamous
patterns was to maintain the boundary of the kibbutz as a social
system and at the same time to prevent its social isolation by con-
necting it with social groups of ideological propinquity in Israeli
society. Moreover, Talmon succeeded in offering a plausible explanation of the way in which the societal functions of mate selection
patterns were translated into motivational factors in the development

of the personalities of second-generation adolescents through the peculiar process of socialization. Thereby Talmon conformed successfully to the famous requirements of Merton's well-known article on functional analysis.[29]

Five years later, the subject was taken up by J. Shepher[30] who wanted to complete Talmon's research by providing data on premarital heterosexual behavior and by analyzing the marriage data of the entire second generation in the three big Kibbutz Federations.

In the first part of the research, the entire adolescent and adult second generation of one kibbutz was observed. No heterosexual partnerships were found between any two members of the same peer group who had been socialized together during their first ten years. Within this kibbutz, heterosexual relationships between members of different peer groups were exceedingly rare. Males tended to have sexual relationships with and marry women from outside the kibbutz, whereas females tended to find partners within the kibbutz.

The investigation of the socialization process in the kibbutz revealed that children of the same peer group spent most of their time together and that they frequently engaged in sexual play. This sexual activity was not interfered with by the significant adult figures, the nurse and the parents. Sexual shame first appeared at the ages of nine and ten. A period of three to four years of tension between the sexes in the peer group followed, and a warm friendly relationship characterized the peer group during adolescence.

Investigation of the marriage statistics of 211 kibbutzim revealed that among 2,769 marriages of the second generation in those kibbutzim not a single case had been found in which both partners had been together in the same peer group for more than three years, between infancy and age six. Interpeer group marriages varied inversely with the emphasis on group solidarity in the ideology of the kibbutz: the more emphasis on group solidarity the fewer interpeer group marriages. The marriages with partners from outside the second generation followed the pattern found in the one kibbutz; males tended to marry exogamously, females endogamously (the latter could marry men younger or older than they). There were more interpeer group marriages in kibbutzim with a familistic system of housing children than in those with a collective housing system. Marriages contracted before 1958 included fewer interpeer group

marriages than those contracted after 1959. Males who excelled
in the army tended to marry more interpeer group partners than did
the control group, males who did not excel in the army.

Although there are some differences between Talmon's data and
Shepher's, the latter do not disprove Talmon's basic arguments. The
comparison is given in Table 80.

TABLE 80
COMPARISON OF TALMON'S DATA (1964) WITH SHEPHER'S DATA
(1971) (PERCENTAGES)

	Talmon 1964 N = 125 %	Shepher 1971 Ichud Federation N = 905 %	Shepher 1971 All the Federations N = 2769 %
1. Intrapeer group marriage[1]	0	0	0
2. Interpeer group marriage[2]	3	16.27	18.28
3. Intrakibbutz marriage[3]	31	32.68	33.84
4. Interkibbutz marriage[4]	23	21.20	25.71
5. Intramovement marriage[5]	27	21.97	16.21
6. Extramovement marriage[6]	16	7.98	5.97
Total	100	100.00	100.00

[1] Marriages contracted between any two second-generation people, who were reared in the same peer group.
[2] Marriages between second-generation partners, reared in different peer groups.
[3] Marriages of second-generation adults with adults of their own kibbutz, who have not been socialized with the kibbutz during the first six years of their life, or at all.
[4] Marriages with members of kibbutzim other than the second-generation members' own.
[5] Marriages with partners who were, or are, members of youth movements affiliated to the Kibbutz Federations.
[6] All other partners.

The main differences are seen in the second and sixth rows. It is
plausible to suppose that they stem from the fact that Shepher's data
were obtained ten years later than Talmon's, since the kibbutz movements had become more endogamous during those ten years.

Shepher focused his interest on the intrapeer group and interpeer group marriages. Impressed by the universal lack of intrapeer group sexual relations and marriages, he argued that this phenomenon must be explained by a sort of negative imprinting. Consequently he claimed that the well-known controversy between Freud and Westermarck had to be seen in a different light, and he offered a new theoretical paradigm for the understanding of incest regulations. He explained his finding, that the rate of intrapeer group marriages varied inversely with the intensity of group solidarity, according to Young's theoretical proposal.[31]

Another aspect of the second generation of the kibbutz was investigated by Yehuda Amir of Bar-Ilan University. Amir[32] wanted to evaluate the efficiency of kibbutz youth as soldiers in the Israeli Defence Forces (IDF). Using official data of three age-groups, he compared kibbutz-born soldiers with kibbutz-educated soldiers[33] and with all the rest who had been educated in individualistic forms of living.

Amir used three criteria in evaluating the efficiency of kibbutz-born soldiers as compared with that of the control groups: (1) the extent of volunteering for specially difficult and dangerous tasks; (2) advancement in rank and job level; and (3) successful completion of military training courses. Before presenting these comparative data, Amir investigated the question whether the kibbutz-born children had a better "start" than the control groups, i.e., how did they compare with the control data in intelligence and educational level, in scores of personality, and in ethnic origin. He found, indeed, that kibbutz soldiers had a far better start than the control groups. They were, on the average, of higher intelligence, had a much higher educational level, possessed a better knowledge of the Hebrew language, scored higher marks in tests of personal suitability to army life and army demands, and were mostly of Western origin. When Amir investigated the three main criteria, he found that in all of them kibbutz-born soldiers excelled in comparison with the control groups; this of course could have been ascribed to their better background talents and personality traits. In order to eliminate the influence of the superior start, Amir held constant the background variables and even then found that kibbutz-born soldiers were superior to those of the control groups. Tables 81, 82 and 83 illustrate these findings.

TABLE 81
SUITABILITY FOR COMMAND POSITIONS
BY SUB-GROUP – HIGH HOMOGENEOUS GROUP ONLY
(PERCENTAGES)

Suitability score	Kibbutz-born	Kibbutz-bred	Others
High	65	52	54
Average	12	22	14
Low	23	26	32

Source: Yehuda Amir, "The Effectiveness of the Kibbutz Born Soldier in the Israeli Defense Forces," *Human Relations* (22, 1969): p. 340.

TABLE 82
FAILURE RATES IN OFFICER SCHOOL BY
HOMOGENEOUS SUB-GROUPS[1]

Homogeneous group	Kibbutz-born	Others
High	8%	19%
Low	22%	28%

[1] The kibbutz-bred group was not included here because of their small number in this comparison.

TABLE 83
IDF RECRUITS BY SUB-GROUP, GENERAL ABILITY INDEX,
AND ADVANCEMENT TO COMMAND POSITIONS[1]
(PERCENTAGES)

Ability index	Kibbutz-born	Others
1 (high)	69	23
2	45	24
3	32	19
4	26	6

[1] The kibbutz-bred group was not included here because of their small number in each cell.
Source: Yehuda Amir, "The Effectiveness of the Kibbutz Born Soldier in the Israeli Defense Forces," *Human Relations* (22, 1969): p. 341.

Although Amir did not pretend to give a satisfactory explanation of these findings, he pointed out that at least some of the differences between the groups might stem from the social structure of the kibbutz. He pointed especially to childrearing, and suggested that the special educational system of the kibbutz more successfully developed certain personality traits and motives which resulted in the relative excellence of the kibbutz-born children in the army. Another possible factor suggested by Amir was the group influence on kibbutz-born children.

Interestingly enough, Amir's research report, when first published in Hebrew, aroused tremendous controversy among the Israeli public. Several journalists fiercely attacked the research report and, without bothering about questions of validity and reliability, questioned his conclusions as to the relative superiority of kibbutz-born soldiers. They especially attacked the suggestion that higher rates of volunteering were indices of superiority. After the Six Day War, a new research on the connection between the system of kibbutz socialization and the excellence of the army was inaugurated by the Israel Institute of Applied Social Research, the results of which have not yet been published.

WORK AND PUBLIC ACTIVITY

One of the first questions occurring to an interested layman who visits a kibbutz for the first time is almost always "just why do kibbutz members take upon themselves public activity in their leisure time?" It is difficult for people who have been socialized and have experienced individual forms of living to understand how it is possible that people do their work without receiving any differential remuneration. Kibbutz members, of course, do not receive any salary from the kibbutz. Most of their economic rewards are given to them in kind, and there is absolutely no connection between the economic role and status which they enjoy in the kibbutz system, and the level of performance in their jobs and public activity on the one hand and the amount of eonomic rewards they receive from the kibbutz on the other. Thus the general manager of the economy or the head of the work branch receives the same rewards as any rank and file worker. The general secretary of the kibbutz does not receive greater economic rewards than does any member of one of the numerous committees which comprise the organizational structure of the kibbutz. The main question then is: What is the motivation to work, and how can the kibbutz system manipulate those rewards which make up the system of motivation?

Several investigations were devoted to this important question. Shepher,[34] Cohen,[35] and Rosner[36] emphasized that the most accentuated rewards in the system of motivation in the kibbutz were the relational rewards and identification with the work itself or with the values of the kibbutz. Since economic rewards were granted to the members of the kibbutz in complete equality, they were not given to manipulation and therefore the importance and significance of the relational rewards came into the foreground. Whereas, for instance, it was unimaginable that the head would reward a hard-working member of his branch by ordering the waiter in the communal dining room to give a double portion of meat to this successful worker, it was acceptable that he praise him for his good performance just as he could criticize and blame somebody else in the branch who neglected his work. Being the only form of manipulable reward, the relational reward was of tremendous importance in kibbutz life. The reaction of a co-member as the formal or informal expression of public opinion was almost the only acceptable form of prize or punishment in the kibbutz system of motivation. Therefore, kibbutz people were highly sensitive to the formal and informal expression of other people's reactions to their performance.

There were some differences between the reward systems for work and those for public activity. Everybody worked; everybody appeared in the daily work-assignment sheet, but not everybody had an additional job in public activity. Kibbutz administration included a few full-time jobs filled by functionaries such as the general secretary, the general manager of the economy and the treasurer, whose roles in the administration also constituted their daily work. All the other functionaries, such as chairmen and members of the different committees (economy, social affairs, education, health, culture, housing, planning, sport, etc.) were elected by the annual General Assembly for a year and did their work in their leisure time. The decisions of these committees and these functionaries greatly affected the daily life of every kibbutz member. The relational reward balance of these functionaries was highly ambivalent. Contrary to the situation in most modern social systems, kibbutz people did not strive to be elected to these jobs. They usually accepted their election somewhat reluctantly. This ambivalent reward balance was geared into the system of job rotation in the kibbutz system; thus, most of the functionaries were elected for one or two years only, and the value system emphasized the need of rotation in order to prevent the concentration of power in the hands of certain individuals. Of course, the kibbutz system had to pay a heavy price in order to maintain this system of rotation. It took quite a long time to reach efficiency in a highly complicated position like that of the general manager of the economy or the secretary or the treasurer; and as soon as the incumbent became expert, he was apt to be discharged from his job, which was then given to somebody else who had to start from the very beginning. The economic jobs especially were in a state of strain because of the high price which had to be paid for the system of rotation.

Eric Cohen[37] investigated the annual rotation in three sorts of jobs—in work, in public activity and in full-time management—during the four years between 1957 and 1961 in three federations, the Kibbutz Artzi Federation, the Ichud Federation and the Federation of Religious Kibbutzim. He found that stability was generally higher in work than in public activity or in full-time managerial jobs. Moreover, the rotation was higher in the Kibbutz Artzi and Ichud Federations and lower in the Religious Federation. Thus during the four years investigated the full-time managers rotated in the first two federations at a rate of 55 percent (this means that during four years 55 percent of the job-bearers were discharged from their positions and vacated their places for new appointees). In the Religious Federation the rate of rotation was only 38 percent. The rotation in public activity jobs was somewhat greater (57 percent and 58 percent in the first two Federations and 41 percent in the Religious Federation), whereas in work, the rotation was understandably less (42 percent in the Kibbutz Artzi Federation and 25 percent in the Ichud and Religious Federations respectively). Thus, the research revealed that the kibbutzim had to compromise with the severe requirements of rotation. In the most powerful jobs only about half of the job-bearers vacated their positions during the four years, which meant that, on the average only one in four managers rotated during the two-year period originally accepted as the term of office. This was a compromise which could be understood in the light of the rapid development and the sophistication of the kibbutz economy (and to a certain extent kibbutz society) which required more stability in management positions.

Etzioni[38] devoted a research project to the relations of different work branches with their "clientele." He compared agricultural branches with service branches, especially education and the kitchen. He found that the strategical importance of relational rewards showed itself in the differences between the reward systems of the agricultural branches and the service branches. The workers in the agricultural branches were usually active outside the kibbutz in the fields. There were no immediate controlling agents present. On the other hand, the clientele of the kitchen were present at least three times a day and therefore the possibility of negative reactions was higher. Then, too, the agricultural branches usually worked for an anonymous market. They did not meet their clientele physically and their clientele's reaction to the quality of the branch product was expressed solely through prices. The service branches, on the other hand, had a clientele within the kibbutz which was highly sensitive to their products, food and education. Moreover, the agricultural branches were protected by their high level of professionalism. Only those who were actually working in those branches understood the complicated processes of work and therefore only they could criticize them.

The situation was somewhat similar in the work of education, but since the parents were also involved in education they might be more critical of the work of the nurses and teachers. On the other hand, everybody seemed to be expert in food preparations, and so the most criticized work branch was the kitchen. The agricultural branches and the educational groups had institutional backing. A special committee (Committee of Economy, or Committee of Education) could be called upon to deal with the criticisms, which were therefore cooler and calmer than the criticism levelled against the kitchen, which enjoyed no institutional backing and where criticism was therefore fiercer and was expressed on the spot. Since the balance of relational rewards was the most significant, Etzioni hypothesised that he would find a higher stability in the agricultural jobs, a somewhat lower one in the educational jobs, and the lowest of all in the kitchen. This hypothesis

was later completely verified. If we take into account that most of
the workers in the service branches were women, we can readily understand that the reward balance of women in the kibbutz created severe
problems which in recent years have been dealt with by a steady improvement in technological equipment and by the rising level of
professionalism.

Shepher[39] investigated a special sort of public activity in the kibbutz.
Public activity outside the kibbutz was imposed upon a certain percentage of the working power of the kibbutz, jobs being occupied in the
Kibbutz Federations and the wider circles of Israeli society, in the
Israeli Parliament (Knesset), in the Government, in the Jewish Agency,
and in the General Federation of Labour (Histadrut). These people
were claimed by the federation for service lasting at least two years
and lived during the week in the big cities, especially in Tel Aviv where
the center of the federation was located. In spite of the fact that the
values of the solitary kibbutz were similar to those of the federation,
it nevertheless had its own interests. Highly qualified personnel in the
kibbutz were rare. The jobs within the kibbutz were numerous and
those members who were capable of doing these jobs were usually
also in demand by the federation. The person desired by the federation,
therefore, was caught in a role conflict. He owed allegiance first of all
to his own kibbutz, but he also had certain commitments to the federation. The process of recruitment was usually very long and tedious, and
the social norms required that the person wanted by the federation display no great enthusiasm for going out and work in the city.

Once the decision had been reached, however, the kibbutz member
left for the city and started to work in the federation or in some other
institution. During his term of office, he again had a serious role conflict which can be described as "less acute" and "more chronic." He
had to devote himself to his new job, but the kibbutz required of him
a devotion to its own special problems. He had to represent the kibbutz
to a certain extent in his new job. He also possessed somewhat more
"liquid funds"[40] than the usual kibbutz member, and since he had to
appease his children, who were relatively disadvantaged because of his
absence, he purchased little presents for them and could cause a certain amount of consternation in cases where the presents were too
unusual for a kibbutz child. He had furthermore to divide the time
he spent at his kibbutz home between rest and helping his spouse

(who was alone during the week and burdened with household work) and his friends in the kibbutz and his commitment to his public duties. Once in a while he also had to work, according to the corvée system,[41] in the kitchen or dining room. He had to participate in the meetings of the General Assembly and sometimes in those of a committee. When his term was near its end the kibbutz usually demanded his immediate return, while the federation as a rule asked for a prolongation of the term since the recruitment of a substitute was, as we have seen, very difficult. Thus he was again torn between two allegiances, his work and his kibbutz.

Accordingly, the reward balance of these outside workers was somewhat ambiguous. On the one hand, there were some economic rewards (the federation granted budget for expenses, the amount of which was very small; nevertheless it was "free income"—the outside worker was at liberty to save it or spend it on such "luxuries" as a book or going to a concert in the city). However, those outside workers, who took their jobs seriously, did not usually have time to enjoy these little amenities. Their work hours were usually unending, their leisure time short or nonexistent. They might also have some positive relational rewards, since the outside jobs enjoyed some prestige, especially in the higher echelons. On the other hand, his absence from the kibbutz might impair the outside worker's relations with his co-members in the kibbutz and sometimes with his family. In such a situation, only those who were highly identified with both the kibbutz and the federation were able to perform their duties in the outside job. Some of them were recalled again and again by the Federation, and built up a *curriculum vitae* which was an alternation between outside and inside jobs. Some of them, again, were so attracted by their high jobs outside the kibbutz that they actually severed their relations with the kibbutz altogether.

Sometimes public activity outside the kibbutz might be a solution for certain personal problems. People who had difficulties in adjusting to kibbutz life, some personal problems within the family, or problems of aging, might find temporary relief by being sent out for a while to engage in outside activity. These usually constituted a small amount (about 15 percent) of all the personnel working outside the kibbutz. Another small percentage, some 9 percent and usually in the higher age-group, settled down in their outside jobs

and remained in them for years. Their membership in the kibbutz
became somewhat fictitious. However, the majority, about 60
percent, succeeded in withstanding the difficulties of the job outside the kibbutz and solved the delicate problems of role conflict,
returned to their kibbutz, were reintegrated into its life, and might
return after some years to another term of public activity outside
the kibbutz.

SOCIAL PARTICIPATION AND DIRECT DEMOCRACY

The kibbutz is one of the few examples still existing of direct democracy in a highly sophisticated modern society. We are told that in some
small New England towns and some Cantons of Switzerland direct democracy is still working, but in these cases the General Assembly of the
residents or citizens is summoned once or twice a year and the questions
usually submitted are simple enough to be answered by an "aye" or "no"
vote. On the other hand, the General Assembly of the kibbutz is a very
active living institution. In most of the kibbutzim it meets once a week,
deals with all sorts of questions and, as we shall see, it is not merely a
legislative assembly but also has executive and judicial functions.

The General Assembly is the highest political institution of the
kibbutz community. In principle, every question may be brought before the General Assembly, which is also the highest institution of
appeal; a kibbutz member has the right to appeal against decisions
of any functionary or committee. Every member possesses the same
active and passive political rights, and the decisions in the General
Assembly are taken by a vote of all the members present. The General
Assembly elects the functionaries and the committees; these control
the main executive power of the kibbutz and are responsible to the
General Assembly for their activities. However, the General Assembly
itself sometimes adopts executive decisions.

In the light of the complete absence of a judiciary in the kibbutz
system, the General Assembly decides in any dispute between a
member and a committee, or between any two members, and acts
in serious cases of deviation by the most effective form of punishment—
the cancellation of membership. It also grants membership to new
applicants.

The political institutions of the kibbutz have a very interesting characteristic trait. There is an almost complete overlapping between three factors of the political process which are usually separate in modern societies: the legislative institution, the executive institution, and the clientele for whom the executive performs the service. Every kibbutz member is part of the legislative General Assembly, every member has his task in the executive organizational system, and everybody belongs to the clientele, receiving services from the executive organ, which works according to the decision of the legislative Assembly. It is this peculiar trait that makes very intensive social control of the executive possible.

Nevertheless, in the light of the social change which the kibbutz has undergone during the years of its existence, certain problems have arisen to which two research projects have been devoted. Rosner pointed out that, in the optimal conditions of the functioning of a direct democracy, the kibbutz General Assembly had been working satisfactorily over the years.[42] He laid down the following conditions for the existence of real democracy within a voluntary organization:

1) A relatively small scale for the society, allowing members to be in constant proximity to the decision-making center, and permitting an awareness of events through direct personal contact.
2) Active interest of the members in the events of organization and willingness to participate in the execution of its functions.
3) The existence of a non-formalized public opinion which functions together with, or even without, the formalized institutions of the political system.
4) A sizeable reserve of potential cadres—that is, a considerable number of members who have both the necessary talent and the experience to perform activities within the political system; this implies a rather high level of general education and intensive experience in the political system.
5) Basic equality in the living conditions of the functionaries and the (temporarily) politically inactive members of the society—that is, the absence of special privileges which eventually would motivate the office holders to hold on to their positions.

Rosner pointed out that since in the first decades of the existence of kibbutz society all five conditions were present, direct democracy worked smoothly and satisfactorily. During the last two decades, however, some important changes occurred in some of the kibbutzim. The population of some kibbutzim grew considerably, and this growing population became more complex and heterogeneous with regard to age, ethnic origin, and cultural and educational background. This meant that in some kibbutzim social and economic relations became more complex. The kibbutz economy underwent a real technical revolution; the work branches functioned at a high level of sophistication and brought about another important change. The degree of awareness on the part of members about the general life in the kibbutz declined. There were several things which the rank and file kibbutz member could not understand, especially those problems connected with sophisticated economic activities.

The organizational structure of the kibbutz adjusted itself to the new situation through developing a ramified, complex, almost bureaucratic system. This process of institutionalization had two aspects. First, there was an increase in the number of rules and codes, some of which were introduced by the national federations, while others were specific to particular kibbutzim. Second, the formal institutions regulating different aspects of life grew accordingly and contributed to the complexity of the kibbutz organizational structure. This increased complexity and the higher sophistication of most economic, educational, and social activities, required more specialized manpower. Whereas in the beginning a talented member was generally able to perform any public activity in the kibbutz, in recent years long and intensive special courses were necessary to train adequate personnel for such jobs as general manager of the economy, the secretary and the heads of agricultural work branches.

The population of the kibbutz movement has always been a selective one and generally of a higher educational level than the average in the surrounding society. However, due to certain processes after the War of Liberation, the acceptance into kibbutz membership became less selective, and the average educational level was lowered somewhat. On the other hand, the growing second generation had received the standard secondary education, a factor which restored the educational level.

However, the educational requirements for filling of new jobs rose tremendously. Therefore the direct involvement of the general population in the ongoing business of kibbutz economy and in the activities of the main functionaries gradually lessened. The participation in the

General Assembly, especially in larger kibbutzim, decreased. Some of the functions of the General Assembly were delegated to the committees. The introduction of a complicated system of communication using modern techniques became necessary. It was also felt that a steady improvement in the educational level of the general membership was urgently needed. The kibbutz tried to meet this need by intensified refresher courses, by setting up study circles, and by sending almost everybody to the district colleges and the country's few universities.

Peres[43] devoted his research to the actual changes in the functioning of the General Assembly in five kibbutzim. He pointed out that Enemy No. 1 of direct democracy in the kibbutz was the apathy of its members. The best index of this was the active participation by members in the General Assembly. Peres found that active participation in the General Assembly varied with the degree of institutionalization of the original Bund-form in the different kinds of community. The younger the kibbutz, the higher was the active participation of the majority of its members. In the Bund-type kibbutz of his sample, 71 percent of the members always participated in the assembly and 23 percent frequently participated, whereas in the older and larger kibbutz communities (where different compromises with original kibbutz values were present and where the process of institutionalization described above had taken place) less than half of the membership always participated in the General Assembly. Women usually tended to be more apathetic than men, while rank and file members tended to be more apathetic than active members in the different elites of the kibbutz. Furthermore, mere presence in the assembly did not necessarily mean real involvement. Active participation in the assembly was measured by the number of times people asked for the floor; the same differences were again evident between the various types of kibbutz. Peres found that, due to the process of institutionalization, certain functions of the General Assembly had been delegated to the committees, and that on the whole solidary and communicatory functions of the General Assembly had been gradually more emphasized. He recommended the following steps be taken by the kibbutz movement in order to raise the level of active participation in the General Assembly:

1) Explanatory information about the matters to be dealt with in

the General Assembly should be provided to the different strata
of the membership, according to their level of education and previous
contact with the subject.

2) Care should be taken that different points of view be considered
when any specific problem on the agenda was dealt with. For instance, if an economic problem were going to be discussed, then
the cultural and social implications of the problem should also be
presented.

3) Members who were reluctant to speak up in public should be
encouraged to do so.

4) Simple, understandable forms of democratic procedure should
be introduced.

5) The activity of the Assembly should be so directed that the
discussion could be comparatively quick and effective.

Etzioni[44] investigated the organizational structure of the kibbutz.
He compared the classical Weberian ideal of bureaucratic structure
with the kibbutz social structure and found that although the comprehensive and complicated social and economic activity of the kibbutz
justified and even necessitated the use of a bureaucratic structure,
certain qualities of kibbutz society prevented the simple application
of bureaucratic procedures to kibbutz life. Thus, one of the main
characteristics of a bureaucratic structure was hierarchy, a well-graded
ladder-like system of authority; yet one of the main values of kibbutz
society was the equality of every member. Authority, though given
to certain members, might be used only very specifically and in a
nonaccentuated form having the appearance of offering consulta-
tion rather than giving orders. Moreover, a bureaucrat was supposed
to see in his job a life career, whereas a kibbutz functionary was
elected to his job for a limited time and was not supposed to desire
to remain in his task. The social life of the kibbutz was very intensive. High departmentalization and rigid division of labor, integral
parts of a bureaucratic structure, were considered by kibbutz members
to be an unnecessary complication of matters and directed against highly
valued spontaneity and mutual help.

Nevertheless, Etzioni came to the conclusion that the kibbutz had
no choice but to introduce a well-organized bureaucratic structure with
basic lines of division of labor between large spheres of societal functions. Using the Parsonian system, Etzioni proposed four branches of

the organizational structure—the adaptive (professional), economic, social, and value spheres. He admitted that the adaptive (professional) and economic branches had to be pooled together under the direction of the Committee for Economic Affairs. Since this Committee was in charge of the social sphere, he proposed a new committee, which he called the Control Committee, as the head of the value sphere. The chairmen of these three principal committees would be members of the Secretariat, which would function at the highest level as the co-ordinator of executive power and would have the task of preparing the agenda of the General Assembly. There were also special committees that would take care of specific functions. To solve the problem of the integration of social life in the kibbutz, Etzioni proposed certain inter-linking committees that would deal with questions in which both economic and social considerations had to be taken into account. Etzioni also recommended an elaborate system of communication to activate the membership and inform it of the activities and decisions of the committees.

Etzioni's work met with severe criticism from the kibbutzim, which especially opposed his idea of creating a special Committee of Control to deal with value problems. The representatives of these kibbutzim argued that values penetrated the whole social life of the kibbutz and were omnipresent; therefore their departmentalization could only create a situation in which most of the members and committees would feel themselves free of the need to care for values, since a special committee had been set up in that sphere. Only a very few kibbutzim actually tried out Etzioni's system in its entirety, but many of them accepted the main idea of a synthetic Secretariat, meanwhile profiting from the understanding of the principal mechanisms at work in the organization in kibbutz society.

STRATIFICATION

To speak of stratification in kibbutz society is almost a contra-diction in terms. Kibbutz society claims to be a classless society based on complete economic equality between the members and lacking any differential system of economic remuneration. This very claim has long been a challenging factor to some American scientists who wanted to test the validity of the claim and therefore came to Israel quite early to conduct research, usually with a subconscious hope of discovering proof that this so-called classless society was in fact a more or less disguised stratified system. The most prominent example of this approach is certainly that of Eva Rosenfeld (1951, 1957).[45] Using the theoretical framework of Davies and Moore,[46] she came to the conclusion, after about a year's research in one of the kibbutzim, that in spite of the absence of economic differentiation, one could find in this kibbutz two clearly crystallized social strata. Although differences in rank were due to objectively defined attributes of managerial positions, leaders and managers were usually recruited from the sub-group of old-timers, and these constituted the upper stratum. The lower stratum, on the other hand, included both old-timers and newcomers. There was a discernible difference between the rewards of the two strata. Although Rosenfeld admitted that the managerial leadership positions did not carry any privileges of sustenance and comfort, she claimed that upper stratum members were privileged in regard to diversion, self-respect, and ego expansion. There were also some differences in living conditions; the higher stratum, usually made up of old-timers, had a somewhat higher standard of living, their apartments being sooner and better furnished,[47] and enjoyed a certain amount of independence from the communal institutions.

Talmon[48] devoted a special study to the conclusions of Rosenfeld and the problems of social differentiation in six collectives. She investigated the leader/manager elite of these kibbutzim and examined five aspects in order to determine whether they could be considered a distinguished stratum. The aspects were representation, patterns of rotation, formal and informal leadership, the pattern of inter-personal relations, and attitudes to basic ideological issues. She found that in none of the collectives were most of the elite positions monopolized by one group defined by seniority, ethnic origin, or former leadership in youth movements. The appointment was intended to assure the widest possible participation and representation; and whereas it was possible that a certain group, which had come to the kibbutz later than the founders, might penetrate the elite positions after years of adjustment and absorption into the system, there were several cross-cutting categories and a basic homogeneity as to the degree of indoctrination and the way of life which counteracted monopolization.

The system of rotation was another mechanism which prevented concentration of power in the hands of certain individuals belonging to one social group. The rate of turnover in elite positions was more rapid than in spheres of work and lower positions in the organizational structure. The turnover rates in the central committees rarely exceeded two years. The continuous tenure in all primary elite positions was less than two years, whereas the noncontinuous tenure (that is, election to a job, then some years of work without the job, and then return to the job) was 2.6 years. Although there was a certain trend towards bureaucratization reflected in the demand for more suitability in elite positions, this was countered by several mechanisms, among them the difficulty of recruitment, the intensive vocational training of new applicants, and the recruitment to elite positions outside the community. Nor was the elite the only monopolizer of social influence. There existed a very active informal leadership which exerted a pervasive influence without being part of the formal elite group.

In investigating the interpersonal relations, Talmon came to the conclusion that in most of the collectives there was a small clique (comprising some of the officeholders and a number of informal leaders) who met quite often and discussed community affairs, but in most cases this was an amorphous and unstable group. Family members and friends did not belong to the group itself, and most elite officeholders established their more intimate friendships with members of their own sub-group, who were not members of the elite. Thus the line dividing the elite from other members was not important from the point of view of interpersonal relations. What existed therefore was not a separate and exclusive status group, as the main ideological trends could be divided into conservative and innovative ideologies. Talmon surmised that although more conservatives could be found in the elite groups than in the rank and file, there were always innovators in the elite groups and in some collectives these innovators even constituted a majority. Whereas differences of opinion cut across the distinction between the various sub-groups (seniority, ethnic origin, youth movement background), these sub-groups were more homogeneous in their ideological approach than were the elite themselves. Thorough analysis of the reward balance of the elite groups revealed that this was highly ambiguous and produced considerable strain in at least some of the positions. This also could prevent most people from craving constant membership in the elite groups.

Shepher's research, along with that of Schwartz,[49] corroborates to a certain extent Talmon's findings, as does Cohen's previously mentioned survey of rotation in elite positions. Nevertheless, since stratification is probably the most sensitive point in the ongoing social change, more research is now needed to establish the facts of the present situation. As more than fifteen years have elapsed since the research of Rosenfeld and Talmon, and as the facts may be different today, a thorough investigation of the problem is not only necessary but would prove to be most rewarding.

VALUES

There is only one significant study on the value system of the kibbutz, Talmon's "Secular Asceticism—Patterns of Ideological Change."[50] This article was written by Talmon with the help of Mrs. Tsipora Stupp-Ben-Zimra. It dealt especially with values of consumption, but the underlying analysis of the value system of the kibbutz was so comprehensive and exhaustive that it embraced almost all the principal values of the kibbutz. Talmon pointed to an essential similarity between kibbutz values of consumption and the Protestant ethic described in Weber's famous article, "The Protestant Ethic and the Spirit of Capitalism." She found that both value orientations connected asceticism with a positive attitude to this worldliness, as compared with the asceticism in certain oriental religions which negated the life in this world and therefore adopted an attitude of contempt and negation to any satisfaction and pleasure in everyday life. Just as in the Protestant ethic, there were in the kibbutz ideology a high evaluation of work and a postponement of material satisfaction stemming from consumption. This attitude was highly integrated with the basic values of the kibbutz, nationalism, socialism, and the renaissance of the individual. The kibbutz was committed to the national values of Zionism—the creation of a sound national economy through voluntary return to agriculture and the natural life. The creation of a new Jewish farming society which would be the base of a normal, national economy, the colonization of a severely underdeveloped country without sufficient funds and without professional know-how, and the difficulties in the preparation of the soil, all demanded the acceptance of a very low standard of living throughout the first decades of the kibbutz movement. Work was regarded not only as a means of improving the economy but also as a value in itself. Devotion to work became the highest ritual expression of the individual and served as a symbol of his devotion to national values.

The connection between asceticism and socialistic values is somewhat problematic. Socialism does not oppose a rise in the standard of living. In fact, one of the aims of socialism is the improvement of the worker's standard of living, but the focusing of aspirations on improving the standard of living directs the energies in an undesirable way. Efforts should rather be focused on the long-term aim of creating a society based on social equality and communal living. Too much commitment to consumption causes the individual and the society to be concerned with trifles, while the real aims of socialism are apt to be neglected. On the other hand, a comparatively low standard of living also has the symbolic value of identification with the working class. Luxury symbolizes the bourgeoisie. Life in comparative poverty is an honorable symbol of those who belong to the small circle of pioneers. Moreover, a life of equality and communality is possible, at least in the first phases in the life of the kibbutz, only if the general standard of living is low. The interest of the individual is subordinated to the interests of the society as a whole. The higher the standard of living, the more differentiated it is, the more difficult is the maintenance of the system of equality and communal living. The kibbutz ideology claims that the new Jewish type is expected to find real liberty in being devoted to a life of values and not in being involved in the race after materialistic goals. A life devoted to the quest for pleasure is a life of anxiety, competition, and envy.

The original pioneer ideology could not be maintained during the first half-century of the existence of the kibbutz. To be sure, this ideology never encouraged the individual to practice asceticism. There are no signs of monastic attitudes. As we have mentioned earlier, the rise of the standard of living was embedded to a certain extent in the socialistic ideology. With the improvement of the economic situation of most of the kibbutzim, a new approach to the problem of asceticism developed. The feeling grew that the standard of living had to be set according to the economic capability of the kibbutz. If the kibbutz could afford a higher standard of living, it should not be

denied to the members. On the other hand, even in this situation the
stylistic-symbolic aspect of asceticism still remained. Even when the
standard of living rose, the kibbutz member was expected to choose
an aesthetic simplicity. With the establishment of the state, the whole
Israeli society underwent a major social change. Instead of the spon-
taneous volunteering, on which the pre-state society was based, the
new state emphasized the enforcement of universal laws and used
bureaucratic systems of state administration and the organization of
the General Federation of Labour (Histadrut). The strategic position
of the kibbutz movement as the main factor in the realization of
societal aims was questioned. The dimensions of the new goals were
beyond the capability of kibbutz society, which was less than 4 percent of the total population. The high prestige of the "elite of implementation" ceased to be effective. Other social groups in Israeli
society gradually affected the kibbutz members as reference groups.
Why should kibbutz members accept a lower standard of living than
comparable social groups of workers in the cities and in the towns?
Consumption-oriented attitudes started to appear in some kibbutzim.

Talmon found that in the total population of her research there
was an equally divided distribution of the attitudes to the problem
of asceticism. About one-third of the population accepted the original ascetic attitude, another third was consumption-oriented, and
the remaining third of the population chose an attitude of compromise. One part of this compromise stressed the stylistic-symbolic
approach and another the situational approach. Talmon hypothesized
that she would find in the so-called Bund-type kibbutzim the highest
support for the original ascetic attitude, while in communities with
an economic emphasis the compromise attitudes would be dominant
and in the fully developed consumption-oriented communities most
of the members would reject the original ascetic ideology.

This hypothesis, however, was not verified. The greatest support
for the original ascetic approach was found in the economically
oriented communities, while the Bund-type kibbutzim were closer
to the consumption-oriented communities. The explanation of this
curious finding was discovered through a cross-analysis of the data
to lie in the seniority of the kibbutzim. Since most of the Bund-type
kibbutzim were established after the founding of the state, their members' attitude was influenced by that prevailing in Israeli society, where-

as the economically oriented communities were established at a time
when the original ascetic ideology still prevailed and their members'
attitude was still influenced by those original values when their resis-
tance to change was more powerful.

An interesting aspect of the problem was revealed by an analysis
of the attitudes of the central functionaries of the kibbutzim. It was
found that those attitudes were influenced by two main factors, viz.
the sphere in which the functionary fulfilled his social role and the
general attitude of the entire membership of his kibbutz. Roughly, the
central elite of any kibbutz could be divided into three sub-groups:
the ideological cultural elite, the economic elite and the elite of service
branches. Talmon found that the first elite group possessed the most
outspoken ascetic ideology, the second tended to accept the compromise attitudes (the stylistic-symbolic and situational), while the
service elite was very close to the consumptional pole. This distribution was crossed by the general attitude of the members of the
kibbutz in which the functionary lived. Generally, the elite accepted
the prevailing ideological attitude in its kibbutz. Thus in the economically oriented communities where the ascetic ideology prevailed the
elite as a whole accepted that ideology to a great extent. Since Talmon
did not use multivariate analysis in any refined statistical sense, further analysis must be made in order to determine which factor was
more active in the creation of the attitude of the elite.

Talmon compared the attitudes of males and females and found
that the attitude of females was generally more consumption-oriented than was that of the males. However, the difference between
the sexes was much more accentuated in those kibbutzim where the
prevailing attitude was ascetic, and insignificant in the consumption-
oriented kibbutzim. The second generation, as in most value-oriented
attitudes, also took an intermediate position between the original
ascetic values and the innovating consumption oriented values, and
emphasized especially the stylistic-symbolic approach.

Summarizing her findings, Talmon emphasized that the research
on ideological change presented an exceptional picture of a great
effort to maintain original value orientations in a changing social
situation. The attitude of the kibbutz member was affected not only
by the general attitude in his kibbutz but by the slowly crystallizing
characteristic attitude of the Kibbutz Federation and the general

social atmosphere of the surrounding Israeli society. Talmon also emphasized that her research was entirely conducted on an ideological level of social attitudes, and that her other data revealed that in their practical behavior they were in fact still very economic.

THE KIBBUTZ AND THE SURROUNDING ISRAELI SOCIETY

Amazingly, no special research has yet been devoted to the interesting problem of the kibbutz in Israeli society. Several researchers touched the problem marginally. Shepher,[51] for instance, analyzed the public activity of kibbutz members in the different elite groups of Israeli society without, however, giving an exhaustive analysis of the interaction between the two systems. Talmon emphasized the impact of Israeli society on kibbutz attitudes to the values of consumption.

Voluminous ideological literature has dealt with the problem of the interaction between the two systems. One can discern two basic approaches in these ideological writings. The first one was a sense of *mission*: according to this attitude, the kibbutz was expected to volunteer for the most difficult social tasks of Israeli society. If in the beginning the principal aim was colonization, the creation of an underground army and the establishment of a new farmer class with a revived Jewish-Hebrew culture, the main goals after the establishment of the state were different. In the early 1950s there was a battle for food; in the first five years of the state the population of Israel more than doubled and enormous efforts were needed to provide the necessary food for this rapidly-growing population. The absorption of the new immigrants and the mingling of the returning exiles from different diasporas demanded great efforts in integrating the new immigrants into the existing kibbutzim and, for those who refused to join the kibbutz (an overwhelming majority), in volunteering to go out to their settlements—mostly Moshav co-operatives— and teach them the ways of agriculture, cooperation and Hebrew culture. With the advent of the 1960s the need for accelerating industrialization appeared. The kibbutz had to take its part in this effort.

The second approach discerned in the ideological literature sees the role of the kibbutz as serving an example for the whole of society. Its influence and impact on society, according to this view, were to be seen in the adoption of its socialistic and nationalistic values. The main efforts accordingly had to be directed to the steady improvement of the functioning of the social system. The kibbutz had done its job in the heroic era of pioneering and now it had to direct its efforts inwards. The ideological dispute about the role of the kibbutz in Israeli society was still proceeding, and there was a discussion in Israeli society about what place the kibbutz had to take in the country's social structure. The kibbutz population was highly overrepresented in the different national elites, especially in the political sphere, and several political groups, especially right wing ones, repeatedly argued that this overrepresentation was unjustified. The political scientist Arian[52] has devoted a short article to this problem of political representation in which he gives authentic data on the extent of this overrepresentation without, however, exhausting the subject.

SUMMARY

We have tried to survey the scientific research literature on the kibbutz. We do not claim that our selection of the research surveyed is in any way representative of the voluminous literature available. We have merely surveyed what we regard as a selection of the most important topics of research in the limited space at our disposal. A great deal of research is still going on, dealing with new problems such as the absorption of the second generation into the social system, the motivation of the youth movement groups organized in a special unit of the army (*Nachal*—literally: pioneer fighting youth) in joining the kibbutz, the process of industrialization, the effects of different forms of group therapy on kibbutz problems, and the part played by kibbutz socialization in the success of second-generation kibbutz members in the army. It may be expected that research literature on the kibbutz will grow considerably in the years to come.

NOTES

1. Only about half of these publications are scientific research reports

and articles; the rest are mostly journalistic. The bibliography is certainly not exhaustive and is unfortunately full of mistakes. One should consult it with the utmost care. A better bibliography but not up-to-date is that of Eric Cohen, *Bibliography of the Kibbutz.* (Giv'at Ha'viva, 1964) (in Hebrew). One is due to appear in the United States. Albert Rabin, *Kibbutz Studies* (East Lansing, Michigan, 1970, mimeographed).

2. Bruno Bettelheim, "Does Communal Education Work?" *Commentary* (33, 1962): pp. 117-125; Bruno Bettleheim, *The Children of the Dream.* (New York and London: MacMillan, 1969).

3. Albert I. Rabin, *Growing Up in the Kibbutz.* (New York: Springer, 1965).

4. Melford E. Spiro, *Kibbutz: Venture in Utopia.* (Cambridge: Harvard University Press, 1956); Melford E. Spiro, *Children of the Kibbutz.* (Cambridge: Harvard University Press, 1958).

5. Richard D. Schwartz, "Functional Alternatives to Inequality," *American Sociological Review* (20, 1955): pp. 424-430.

6. Eva Rosenfeld, "The American Social Scientist in Israel: A Case Study in Role Conflict," *American Journal of Orthopsychiatry* (28, 1958): pp. 563-571.

7. Yonina Garber-Talmon, "Differentiation in Collective Settlements," *Scripto Hierosolymitana* (3, 1956): pp. 153-178; Yonina Garber-Talmon, "Mate Selection in Collective Settlements," *American Sociological Review* (29, 1964): pp. 491-508; Joseph Shepher, "Self-Imposed Incest and Exogamy in Second Generation Kibbutz Adults. (Unpublished doctoral dissertation, Rutgers University, New Brunswick, New Jersey, 1971).

8. Yonina Garber-Talmon, *The Individual and the Group in the Kibbutz.* (Jerusalem: Magnes Press, 1970) (in Hebrew).

9. There are four Kibbutz Federations in Israel: Hakkibutz Hame'uhad,

Ichud Hakkibutzim Vehakebutzot, Hakkibutz Ha'artsi and Hakkibutz Hadati.

10. Herman Schmalenbach, "The Sociological Category of Communion," in T. Parsons *et al.* (eds.), *Theories of Society.* (New York: The Free Press, 1961), pp. 331-348.

11. This is so for the great majority of kibbutzim; however, in some the children do sleep with their parents.

12. Melford E. Spiro, *Kibbutz: Venture in Utopia.* (Cambridge: Harvard University Press, 1956).

13. There are several methods for distributing clothing. Originally most kibbutzim used the communal or "organic" system of distribution, according to which nobody owned any clothing but obtained the necessary garments from the communal store. This system was abandoned by most kibbutzim in the late thirties, when two systems of rationing were accepted, the quantitative and the qualitative. In the former, each member was provided with a certain quantity of clothes each year; in the latter, new clothing was provided when the old became worn-out. In the late forties, the so-called individual budget was introduced in one of the federations. In this system, each member was granted a budget and he was free to decide what garments to order from the communal store. This system, however, did not remain individual but immediately became a family budget with the authority usually given to the wife to spend the money as she saw fit. A kibbutz joke reflected this important change: "Not an individual budget but the budget of my wife" (Hebrew: *lo takziv ishi, ki im takziv ishti).*

14. Menachem Rosner, "Women in the Kibbutz: Changing Status and Concepts," *Asian and African Studies* (3, 1967): pp. 35-68; Menachem Rosner, *Research Report on the Status of the Women in the Kibbutz.* (Giv'at Ha'viva, 1966) (in Hebrew).

15. Yonina Garber-Talmon, "Differentiation in Collective Settlements," *Scripto Hierosolymitana* (3, 1956): pp. 153-178.

16. The three big Kibbutz Federations were affiliated with three

political parties to which the traditional left-right continuum could have been applied before the Six Day War. Since then the political differences between both the federations and the parties have become blurred.

17. Menachem Rosner, "Women in the Kibbutz: Changing Status and Concepts," *Asian and African Studies* (3, 1967): pp. 35-68.

18. Joseph Shepher, *The Reflections of the Housing System of the Children in the Social Structure of the Kibbutz*. (Tel Aviv: Ichud, 1967) (in Hebrew); Joseph Shepher, "Familism and Social Structure: The Case of the Kibbutz," *Journal of Marriage and the Family* (31, 1969): pp. 567-573.

19. According to the following variables: size of total population, size of working population, age structure, seniority of the members in Israel, seniority in the kibbutz, country of origin of most members, and economic situation.

20. Joseph Shepher, "Familism and Social Structure: The Case of the Kibbutz," *Journal of Marriage and the Family* (31, 1969): p. 573.

21. One of the numerous examples is Oneida. See especially Pierrepont Noyes, *My Father's House and Oneida Boyhood*. (New York: 1937).

22. When the parents of those second-generation members who have left the kibbutz are still present in the kibbutz, the problem is not serious; but sometimes the parents have died or left the kibbutz themselves, and in these cases it is hard to find somebody who remembers these second-generation members.

23. "Survey of Deserters of the Kibbutz from the Second Generation and from the Internees." (Giv'at Ha'viva, 1969) (in Hebrew).

24. In 1968-1969, the three large Kibbutz Federations carried out a comprehensive census of their entire populations. These data are being processed now and will probably be published within a year.

25. Moshe Sarel, *Research Report on the Second Generation in the*

Kibbutz. (Jerusalem: Hebrew University, 1959) (mimeographed in Hebrew).

26. Yonina Garber-Talmon, "Mate Selection in Collective Settlements," *American Sociological Review* (29, 1964): pp. 491-508.

27. Frank W. Young, "Incest Taboos and Social Solidarity," *American Journal of Sociology* (72, 1967): pp. 589-600.

28. George R. Murdoch, *Social Structure.* (New York: MacMillan, 1949).

29. Robert K. Merton, *Social Theory and Social Structure.* (Glencoe, Ill.: The Free Press, 1949), pp. 73-138.

30. Joseph Shepher, "Self Imposed Incest and Exogamy in Second Generation Kibbutz Adults." (Unpublished doctoral dissertation, Rutgers University, New Brunswick, New Jersey, 1971).

31. *Idem.*

32. Yehuda Amir, "Adjustment and Promotion of Soldiers from Kibbutzim (Communal Settlements)," *Megamot* (15, 1967): pp. 250-258 (in Hebrew); Yehuda Amir, "The Effectiveness of the Kibbutz Born Soldier in the Israeli Defense Forces," *Human Relations* (22, 1969): pp. 333-344.

33. Amir's definition of kibbutz-born soldiers is somewhat different from that of Talmon and Shepher. He includes in this category all those persons who joined the kibbutz before the age of ten, whereas in the category of kibbutz-educated soldiers he includes those who joined the kibbutz after the age of ten.

34. Joseph Shepher, "Motivation Work and Social Activity in Kibbutz Society," *Proceedings of the International Symposium of Cooperative Rural Communities.* (Tel Aviv, 1968) Vol. I, pp. 205-207.

35. Eric Cohen, "Changes in the Social Structure of Work in the Kibbutz," *Economic Quarterly* (Riv'on Lekalkala) (10, 1963): pp. 378-388 (in Hebrew).

36. Menachem Rosner, "Difficulties and Rewards in the Role of Branch Manager," *Hedim* (46, 1963) (in Hebrew).

37. Eric Cohen, *Bibliography of the Kibbutz*. (Giv'at Ha'viva, 1964) (in Hebrew).

38. Amitai Etzioni, *The Crystalization of Solidary Work Groups in the Kibbutz*. (Jerusalem: Hebrew University, 1956) (mimeographed in Hebrew). Amitai Etzioni, "Solidaric Work-Groups in Collective Settlements (Kibbutzim)," *Human Organization* (16, 1957): pp. 2-6.

39. Joseph Shepher, "Public Activity Outside the Kibbutz," *Niv Hakvutzah* (15, 1966): pp. 39-59 (in Hebrew).

40. The allowance for living costs is, to be sure, very low, about one dollar for a work-day. Not the size of this allowance is important but the almost symbolic fact that these people have comparatively more "free income" than their fellow members at home and that at least theoretically they can decide not ot eat, save the money and bring the presents. Today, this advantage is almost nonexistent. Certainly less so than in 1957, when the research was conducted.

41. Certain jobs, which are considered unpleasant and inconvenient, are performed in turns (corvée system). These are waiting at table, dishwashing, nightwatching, etc.

42. Menachem Rosner, "Direct Democracy in the Kibbutz," *New Outlook* (8, 1965): pp. 29-41.

43. Yohanan Peres, "The General Assembly in 'the Kibbutz'," *Oranim* (3, 1962): pp. 105-197 (in Hebrew).

44. Amitai Etzioni, "The Organizational Structure of the Kibbutz." (Unpublished doctoral dissertation, Berkeley, University of California, 1958).

45. Eva Rosenfeld, "Social Stratification in a 'Classless' Society," *American Sociological Review* (16, 1951): pp. 766-774; Eva Rosen-

feld, "Institutional Change in the Kibbutz," *Social Problems* (5, 1957): pp. 110-136.

46. Kingsley Davis and Wilbert E. Moore, "Some Principles of Stratification," *American Sociological Review* (10, 1945): pp. 242-249.

47. Furniture is provided on the basis of seniority; so is housing.

48. Yonina Garber-Talmon, "Differentiation in Collective Settlements," *Scripto Hierosolymitana* (3, 1956): pp. 153-178.

49. *Idem.* and Schwartz, *op. cit.*

50. Yonina Garber-Talmon, "Ascetism-Patterns of Ideological Change," (with Tsipora Stupp) in Wurm, S. H. (ed.), *Sefer Bussel.* (Tel Aviv: Tarbut Ve'Ichud, 1960), pp. 149-190.

51. Joseph Shepher, "Public Activity outside the Kibbutz," *Niv Hakvutzah* (15, 1966): pp. 39-59 (in Hebrew).

52. A. Arian, "Utopia and Politics: The Case of the Israeli Kibbutz," *Journal of Human Relations* (14, 1967): pp. 391-403.

9

Conclusion

Sociology in Israel is certainly not an ivory tower discipline. The basic problems of Israeli society have been studied, as evidenced by the research on immigration, education, and inter-group relations. Yet it would be misleading to conclude that the only concern is with the Israeli scene. Many sociologists have made significant contributions to general sociology, but in this work only research done on Israeli society has been cited.

The principal finding that emerges is that one factor separates the population, whether it be in academic achievement, criminality, prostitution, social class, mobility, family size, intrafamily relationships, or religiosity. There is always the dichotomy of Jews of Eastern descent *vs.* Jews of Western descent. While we have sometimes used the shorthand terminology, "Eastern Jews" and "Western Jews," we prefer the more cumbersome notation, Jews of Eastern (or Oriental or Asian-African) descent and Jews of Western (or European) descent. For Jews born in Israel to parents born abroad or even for Jews living in Israel who were born abroad, the appellation Eastern Jew or Western Jew is somewhat misleading. Be that as it may, we are confronted with consistent findings in every area of sociological research that not only do Eastern Jews differ from Western Jews, but the difference is virtually always to the detriment of the former.

Very often the researcher did not ferret out class effects. That is, when comparing Jews of Eastern descent to Jews of Western descent,

comparisons were not made among those of the same social class. Since
the majority of Eastern Jews are found in the lower social class and the
majority of the Western Jews in the middle social class, the failure to
take account of this ethnic-social class overlap may easily lead to a
false interpretation where the findings are attributable solely to the
influence of ethnicity. The reason why many investigators did not
hold social class constant is undoubtedly due to the difficulty of
locating the proper comparison group. Lower-class Eastern Jews can
easily be located for a study, but a comparable group of lower-class
Western Jews is more difficult to find. I can testify to this from my
own research, in which first grade pupils were studied. Having located
lower-class children of Eastern origin, we had great difficulty finding
such children of Western origin despite the fact that we deliberately
chose schools in "mixed" neighborhoods. Conversely, while middle-
class Western children were easily accessible, it was not easy to locate
Eastern children of similar background.

    Still, the demonstrated differences are only in part disguised class
differences. The investigators who considered the joint effects of
social class and ethnicity point to the independent impact of the
latter, although the extent of its effect is still be to determined. This
is a question of significance for those educators who are seeking to
isolate the causes of Eastern children's failure in school.

    Another factor which has not received sufficient treatment is
the differences within the Eastern group. Most research has regret-
fully lumped sample members whose geographic origin is Asia or
Africa into one grouping, "Eastern." This is justified on the grounds
that the differences within the Asian-African group are smaller than
the differences between it and the Western group (the lumping of
Jews from all parts of Europe into one category is not a problem, as
ethnic communities did not exist in Europe in the same sense as they
did in Asia or Africa). While there may be a large degree of similarity among many Eastern groups, some of them do differ, and these
variations are often slighted. The Yemenites are a marked case, and
indeed in one study by the author and a colleague on perception, it
was shown that Yemenite children resembled Western children while
differing from other Eastern children. If children of two different
Eastern groups have difficulties in school, the reasons may not be the
same, and yet, few studies, before making comparison between

"Easterners" and "Westerners," first demonstrated that there were no differences among the various Eastern groups comprising the sample. Perhaps most disappointing is the failure to investigate the etiology of these ethnic differences. A recent exception was a study on birth-order, where the authors attempted to show how country of birth, a reflection of varying socialization patterns and cultural values, differentially affected the volunteering for officer candidacy in the Israeli army. In addition, excellent studies, mostly of an anthropological sort, were undertaken of several ethnic communities in the early 1950s. There have also been several studies in the field of education that related the home background of the child to his success or failure in school. Nevertheless, the vast majority of studies have been content to demonstrate ethnic differences and not to explain them.

It is to be remembered that many of the studies dealt with second- and third-generation Oriental Jews who were born in Israel, went to Israeli schools, and served in the army. Many of them, it appears, are still not "making it" in Israeli society. It is not known in which specific ways the old world still influences them.

We wish to restate a point made in the introduction. Israel is a country which less than twenty-five years ago comprised only 650,000 Jews, 85 percent of Western origin. Somewhat less than a quarter of a century after, the country consists of over two and a half million Jews, approximately 50 percent from Levantine societies representing a wide cultural heterogeneity. When one speaks of integration into Israeli society, it is not clear what this Israeli society is.

The fact that ethnic origin has been the dominant research theme has been attributed to the large social gap between the two ethnic communities which sociologists naturally enough wished and felt obligated to investigate. In addition, Easterners, due to their less successful adjustment, are beset by more problems, such as delinquency and poverty. There may also be another reason. Virtually all Israeli social scientists are of Western origin, and they may well have been intrigued by their fellow Jews who were so different. This may be a parallel phenomenon to the many American-Jewish sociologists who for many years studied the blacks, but until recently displayed little interest in the Jewish community. Whatever the reason, one effect of the plethora of studies on the Eastern community has been a neglect of Jews of European descent and their problems. While there are exceptions (the studies of middle-class delinquency, for example), the fact is that there have been relatively few studies on such topics as social class (aside from those on mobility), problems of the "western" family, and the effects of the concentration camps on survivors and their children.

The second major social problem facing Israel, less serious than the first, is the cleavage between the religious and the non-religious. In Israel, "religious" and "non-religious" are recognized social categories which influence the daily lives of the people. Although a minority, the religious party, desired as a coalition partner by the major political party, has been successful in passing legislation with which the majority of the population would probably not agree. The ban of public transportation on Saturday (except in Haifa), seriously affects the nonreligious population, particularly since Sunday is a regular workday. Similarly, movies and other entertainments are closed on the Sabbath.

One might then expect to find a fair amount of research on the religious factor. Yet there have been relatively few studies of religion as it affects daily life, attitudes, expectations, and behavior. What stereotypes do the religious and nonreligious hold of one another? To what extent is there enmity towards the religious? These and similar questions have not been investigated. Since most Israeli sociologists are not religious, perhaps there was simply less interest in this topic; or perhaps, given a choice of problems, they chose to focus their attention on the most pressing subject of ethnicity. We note that several researchers indicate that the religious do differ from the nonreligious on a number of attitudinal measurements, and that the middle group, called the "traditionalist," showed no consistent pattern. It is this group particularly that warrants further research.

One major problem which has received little attention has been the effect of the prolonged war on the citizens, particularly the youth. When Israel fought its War of Independence, few outsiders thought she would succeed. Besides an inequality of numbers (about half a million Jews to more than one hundred million Arabs), the Arabs had ample arms. From 1948 until 1956 (the period of the Sinai War), infiltrators from Arab countries entered Israel and attacked the civilian population. From 1956 to 1967, Israel's political and military situations improved and relative quiet prevailed on the borders. The standard of living improved. Concomitantly, a problem developed which had been hitherto largely unknown here. Until the Sinai War youth were engaged; they were aware that the very existence of Israel depended on them. Many were active in youth movements, most of which were ideologically oriented, calling for settlement in a kibbutz (these youth movements exist today, but have lost their momentum, partly because today's urban youth are not attracted to the kibbutz way of life and the prestige of the kibbutz has waned). After 1956, for perhaps the first time, Israeli youth began to feel bored. We emphasize that this was the beginning of a trend.

Immediately after the 1967 War, it was hoped that peace had finally arrived. Moshe Dayan, the country's Minister of Defense, stated at that time that he was waiting for a call from the Arabs—which never came. Not long after, the war of attrition was started by the Arabs. Due to a shortage of manpower the period of compulsory military service was raised from two and a half to three years for males. During that period Israeli youths were being killed every week; high school graduates knew that some of their friends would never be seen again. For the first time in Israeli society, the country's leaders began to lecture in the high schools, particularly to the seniors. This group, not the college students who had been in the army, became the critical one, for upon graduation they would enter the army.

How all these factors affect Israeli youth and the entire society is a matter which certainly deserves much more attention.

The natural social science laboratory of Israel has barely been exploited due to the small number of sociologists (in absolute terms) and limited funds for research. Whole areas of enquiry have received minimal attention and those subjects which have been examined have not been intensively investigated. This is true for every area reviewed. Furthermore, many of the studies were conducted ten, fifteen, or even twenty years ago, and the findings may be outdated; consider that the only study on intergenerational mobility was conducted in 1955. Finally, the topic which has without doubt received the most attention—ethnicity—is only at its beginning stage, as explanations for the differences have not been sought.

The burden of the work lies ahead.

Bibliography

Adar, Leah and Adler, Chaim, *Education for Values in Schools for Immigrant Children in Israel.* (Jerusalem: School of Education of the Hebrew University, 1965) (in Hebrew).

Adar, Leah, "A Study on the Scholastic Difficulties of Immigrant Children," *Megamot* (7, 1956): pp. 139-180 (in Hebrew).

Adar, Zvi, "An Education Examination of Modern Teaching Methods," *Megamot* (14, 1966): pp. 74-77 (in Hebrew).

Adiel, S., "Reading Ability of Culturally Deprived First Graders," *Megamot* (15, 1968): pp. 345-356 (in Hebrew).

Adjustment to the Physical and Social Environment in a Development Settlement–Kiryat Malachi. (Jerusalem: Ministry of Housing, 1965) (mimeographed).

Adler, Chaim, *et al., Youth in the Morasha Neighborhood.* (Office of the Prime Minister, 1965) (mimeographed, in Hebrew).

Amir, Yehuda, "Adjustment and Promotion of Soldiers from Kibbutzim (Communal Settlements)," *Megamot* (15, 1967): pp. 250-258 (in Hebrew).

Amir, Yehuda, Sharan, Shlomo and Kovarsky, Yakov, "Birth Order, Family Structure and Avoidance Behavior," *Journal of Personality and Social Psychology* (10, 1968): pp. 271-278.

Amir, Yehuda, "The Effectiveness of the Kibbutz Born Soldier in the Israeli Defense Forces," *Human Relations* (22, 1969): pp. 333-344.

Antonovsky, Aaron and Katz, David, "Factors in the Adjustment to Israeli Life of American and Canadian Immigrants," *Jewish Journal of Sociology* (12, 1970): pp. 77-87.

Antonovsky, Aaron, "Israeli Social-Political Attitudes," *Amot* (6, 1963): pp. 11-22 (in Hebrew).

Arian, A., "Utopia and Politics: The Case of the Israeli Kibbutz," *Journal of Human Relations* (14, 1964): pp. 391-403.

Bachi, Roberto and Matras, Judah, "Contraception and Induced Abortion Among Jewish Maternity Cases in Israel," *Milbank Memorial Fund Quarterly* (40, 1962): pp. 207-229.

Bachi, Roberto and Matras, Judah, "Family, Size, Preferences of Jewish Maternity Cases in Israel," *Milbank Memorial Fund Quarterly* (42, 1964): pp. 9-37.

Bar-Yosef, Rivkah and Padan, Dorit, "Eastern Ethnic Communities in the Class Structure of Israel," *Molad* (22, 1964): pp. 504-516 (in Hebrew).

Bar-Yosef, Rivkah, "The Moroccans: Background of the Problem," *Molad* (17, 1959): pp. 247-251 (in Hebrew).

Bar-Yosef, Rivkah, "Role Differentiation in the Urban Family in Israel," in Bar-Yosef, R. and Shelach, I. (eds.), *The Family in Israel.* (Jerusalem: Academon, 1969), pp. 167-182 (in Hebrew).

Bar-Yosef, Rivkah and Shelach, Ilana, "The Position of Women in Israel," in Eisenstadt, S. N., *et al.* (eds.), *Stratification in Israel* (Jerusalem: Academon, 1968), pp. 414-454.

Bar-Yosef, Rivkah, "The Type of the Moroccan Community," *The Oriental Ethnic Communities in Israeli Society*. (Jerusalem: Ministry of Education and Culture, 1957), pp. 50-62.

Bart, Cilly, "Group Discussions with Teachers in Schools for Backward Children," *Megamot* (6, 1955): pp. 305-310 (in Hebrew).

Ben-David, Joseph (ed.) *Agricultural Planning and Village Community in Israel.* (Paris: Unesco, 1964).

Ben-David, Joseph, "Ethnic Differences or Social Change?" in C. Frankenstein (ed.), *Between Past and Future*. (Jerusalem: Szold Foundation, 1953), pp. 33-52.

Ben-David, Joseph, "Professions and Unions in Israel," *Industrial Relations* (5, 1965/1966): pp. 48-66.

Ben-David, Joseph, "Scientific Endeavor in Israel and the United States," *American Behavioral Scientist* (1962): pp. 12-16.

Ben-David, Joseph and Collins, R., "Social Factors in the Origins of a New Science: The Case of Psychology," *American Sociological Review* (31, 1966): pp. 451-465.

Bentwich, J., "Examinations and Evaluation in Secondary Schools," *Megamot* (12, 1963): pp. 203-219 (in Hebrew).

Bentwich, J. and Schubert, Y., "The Pedagogical Division in the Secondary School," *Megamot* (6, 1955): pp. 113-129 (in Hebrew).

Berman, I., "Drug Abuse Among Israeli Youth: A Survey " (Jerusalem: Ministry of Social Welfare, 1969) (in Hebrew).

Bettelheim, Bruno, *The Children of the Dream*. (New York and London: MacMillan, 1969).

Bettelheim, Bruno, "Does Communal Education Work?" *Commentary* (33, 1962): pp. 117-125.

Bier, Fanny, "Value Conflicts in Immigrant Children–Reflections of a Ma'abara Teacher," *Megamot* (5, 1954): pp. 386-391 (in Hebrew).

Bolotin-Kobovi, Dvorah, "Individual Counselling to Teachers in School for Backward Children," *Megamot* (6, 1955): pp. 298-304 (in Hebrew).

Bott, Elizabeth, *Family and Social Network.* (London: Tavistock, 1957).

Brill, Moses, "Retarded Children and Adult Learning," *Education* (11, 1938): pp. 110-122 (in Hebrew).

Chen, Michael, "Patterns of Application to High School from Tel Aviv Elementary School Graduates," *Megamot* (11, 1961): pp. 388-396 (in Hebrew).

Chen, Michael, Schifenbauer, David and Doron, Rina, "Uniformity and Diversity in Leisure Activities of Secondary School Students in Israel," *Megamot* (13, 1964): pp. 188-199 (in Hebrew).

Christiansen, C., "Industrialization and Urbanization in Relation to Crime and Juvenile Delinquency," *International Review of Criminal Policy* (1960): pp. 3-8.

Cloward, Richard A. and Jones, James J., "Social Class; Educational Attitudes and Participation," in Passow, A. Harry (ed.), *Education in Depressed Areas.* (New York: Teachers College, Columbia University, 1963): pp. 190-216.

Cloward, Richard A. and Ohlin, Lloyd H., *Delinquency and Opportunity.* (New York: The Free Press, 1960).

Cohen, Eric and Leinman, Elazar, *Survey of Social Activity in Three Kibbutz Federations.* (Jerusalem: The Hebrew University, 1964-65) (in Hebrew).

Cohen, Eric, *Bibliography of the Kibbutz.* (Giv'at Ha'viva, 1964) (in Hebrew).

Cohen, Eric, "Changes in the Social Structure of Work in the Kibbutz," *Economic Quarterly* (Riv'on Lekalkala) (10, 1963): pp. 378-388 (in Hebrew).

Cohen, Eric, "Mixed Marriages in an Israeli Town," *Jewish Journal of Sociology* (11, 1969): pp. 41-50.

Cohen, Eric, "Social Images in an Israeli Development Town," *Human Relations* (21, 1968): pp. 163-176.

Cohen, Haim I., "A Look at the Education of Oriental Communities," *Molad* (23, 1966): pp. 208-210 (in Hebrew).

Cohen, Percy S., "Alignments and Allegiances in the Community of Sha'arayim in Israel," *Jewish Journal of Sociology* (4, 1962): pp. 14-38.

Cohen, Percy S., "Ethnic Group Differences in Israel," *Race* (9, 1968): pp. 303-310.

Cohen, Percy S., "Ethnic Hostility in Israel," *New Society* (February 28, 1963).

Cohen, Peretz, "Community and Stability in an Immigrant Town," in *Immigrants in Israel,* Lissak, M., Barelly, M., and Ben-David, O. (eds.). (Jerusalem: Academon, 1969), pp. 217-233 (in Hebrew).

Coster, John H., "Some Characteristics of High School Pupils from Three Income Groups," *Journal of Educational Psychology* (50, 1959): pp. 55-62.

Davis, Kingsley, and Moore, E. Wilbert, "Some Principles of Stratification," *American Sociological Review* (10, 1945): pp. 242-249.

Dayan, Shmuel, *Moshav Ovdim in the Land of Israel.* (Tel Aviv: Palestine Pioneer Library, No. 6) (in Hebrew).

Department of Absorption, *Sixteen Years of Immigrant Absorption in Israel.* (Jerusalem: Jewish Agency, 1964).

Deshen, Shlomo, "A Case of Breakdown of Modernization in an Israeli Immigrant Community," *Jewish Journal of Sociology* (7, 1965): pp. 63-91.

Deshen, Shlomo, "Conflict and Social Change: The Case of an Israeli Village," *Sociologia Ruralis* (VI, 1966), pp. 31-55.

Deshen, Shlomo, *Immigrant Voters in Israel: Parties and Congregations in a Local Election Campaign.* (Manchester: Manchester University Press, 1971).

Deshen, Shlomo, "Modern Leadership in a Traditional Village," with D. Jaeger, *Bi'tefutzot Ha'gola* (VIII, 1966): pp. 108-115 (in Hebrew); revised English version in O. Shapiro (ed.), *Rural Settlements of New Immigrants in Israel.* (Rehovot: Settlement Study Centre, 1971), pp. 125-138.

Deshen, Shlomo, "Non-Conformists in an Israeli Immigrant Community," *Mankind Quarterly* (IX, 1969): pp. 166-177.

Deshen, Shlomo, "The Ethnic Factor in a Local Election Campaign," in A. Arian (ed.), *The 1969 General Election Campaign in Israel.* (Jerusalem: Academic Press, 1972).

Deshen, Shlomo, "The Ethnic Synagogue: A Pattern of Religious Change in Israel," in S. N. Eisenstadt (ed.), *The Integration of Immigrants from Different Countries of Origin.* (Jerusalem: Magnes Press, 1969), pp. 63-73.

Deshen, Shlomo, "The Process of Absorption and Social Struggle in a New Moshav," *Bi'tefutzot Ha'gola* (VI, 1964): pp. 108-117 (in Hebrew).

Dimona: Social-Economic Development. (Jerusalem: Ministry of Housing, 1969) (mimeographed in Hebrew).

Don, Yehuda, Hovav, Hagit and Weller, Leonard, *Social and Economic Adjustment in Towns in Israel.* (Ramat Gan: Bar-Ilan University, 1970) (mimeographed in Hebrew).

Drapkin, T. and Landau, S., "Drug Offenders in Israel," *British Journal of Criminology* (6, 1966): pp. 376-391.

Eisenstadt, S. N., *The Absorption of Immigrants* (London: Routledge and Kegan Paul, Ltd., 1954), chs. 2, 3, 4.

Eisenstadt, S. N., "Breakdown of Modernization," *Economic Development and Cultural Change* (13, 1964): pp. 345-367.

Eisenstadt, S. N., "Communication Processes Among Immigrants in Israel," *Public Opinion Quarterly* (16, 1952): pp. 42-58.

Eisenstadt, S. N., "Evaluation of the Adjustment of Immigrants," *Megamot* (1, 1950): pp. 335-346 (in Hebrew).

Eisenstadt, S. N., "Israeli Identity: Problems in the Development of the Collective Identity of an Ideological Society," *The Annals of the American Academy of Political and Social Science* (March 1967): pp. 16-23.

Eisenstadt, S. N., *Israeli Society*. (London: Weildenfeld and Nicolson, 1967).

Eisenstadt, S. N., "The Oriental Jews in Israel," *Jewish Social Studies* (12, 1950): pp. 199-222.

Eisenstadt, S. N., "The Place of Elites and Primary Groups in the Process of Absorption of New Immigrants in Israel," *American Journal of Sociology* (57, 1951): pp. 222-231.

Eisenstadt, S. N., "Problems of Leadership Training Among New Immigrants," *Megamot* (4, 1953): pp. 182-191 (in Hebrew).

Eisenstadt, S. N., "The Process of Absorption of New Immigrants and Institutionalization of Immigrant Behavior," *Human Relations* (5, 1952): pp. 223-246.

Eisenstadt, S. N., "Institutionalization of Immigrant Behavior," *Human Relations* (5, 1952): pp. 373-395.

Eisenstadt, S. N., "The Social Significance of Education in the Absorption of Immigrants," *Megamot* (3, 1952): pp. 330-341 (in Hebrew).

Eisenstadt, S. N., "Sociological Approach to Education," *Megamot* (12, 1963): pp. 295-301 (in Hebrew).

Eisenstadt, S. N., "Sociological Aspects of the Economic Adaptation of Oriental Immigrants in Israel: A Case Study in the Process of Modernization," *Economic Development and Cultural Change* (4, 1956): pp. 269-278.

Englard, I., "The Relationship Between Religion and State in Israel," *Scripto Hierosolymitana* (16, 1966): pp. 254-275.

Enoch, Chanan, "Early School Leavers in the Municipal Schools of Tel Aviv," *Megamot* (2, 1950): pp. 34-51 (in Hebrew).

Erikson, Erik H., *Childhood and Society.* (New York: Norton, 1950), pp. 98-140.

Etzioni, Amitai, *The Crystalization of Solidary Work Groups in the Kibbutz.* (Jerusalem: Hebrew University 1956) (mimeographed in Hebrew).

Etzioni, Amitai, *The Organizational Structure of the Kibbutz.* (Unpublished doctoral dissertation, Berkeley, University of California, 1958).

Etzioni, Amitai, "Solidaric Work-Groups in Collective Settlements (Kibbutzim)," *Human Organization* (16, 1957): pp. 2-6.

Faulshouk, Z. and S. Halevi, "The Ethnic Factor in Abortion and Premature Deliveries," *Harephu* (68:1965): pp. 219-294 (in Hebrew).

Feitelson, Dina, "Aspects of the Social Life of the Kurdish Jews," *Jewish Journal of Sociology* (1, 1959): pp. 201-216.

Feitelson, Dina, "Causes of Scholastic Failure in First Graders—Part One," *Megamot* (4, 1952): pp. 37-63 (in Hebrew).

Feitelson, Dina, "Causes of Scholastic Failure in First Graders—Part Two," *Megamot* (4, 1953): pp. 123-173 (in Hebrew).

Feitelson, Dina, "Education of Pre-School Children in Kurdistan Communities," *Megamot* (5, 1954): pp. 95-109 (in Hebrew).

Feitelson, Dina, "Some Changes in the Educational Patterns of the Kurdish Community in Israel," *Megamot* (6, 1955): pp. 275-297 (in Hebrew).

Festinger, Leon, *A Theory of Cognitive Dissonance.* (Stanford, California: Stanford University Press, 1957).

Feuerstein, Reuven and Richelle, M. *Children of the Mellah.* (Jerusalem: Jewish Agency and Szold Foundation, 1953).

Feuerstein, Reuven, and Richelle, M., "Perception and Drawing Ability Among North African Jewish Children," *Megamot* (9, 1958): pp. 156-162 (in Hebrew).

Feuerstein, Reuven, and Shalom Haim, "Learning Potential Assessment of Culturally and Socially Disadvantaged Children," *Megamot* (15, 1967): pp. 174-187 (in Hebrew).

Frankenstein, Carl, "The Problem of Ethnic Differences in the Absorption of Immigrants," in Frankenstein, Carl, *Between Past and Future.* (Jerusalem: Szold Foundation, 1963), pp. 13-32.

Friedman, Irit and Peer, Ilana, "Drug Addiction Among Pimps and Prostitutes in Israel," *International Journal of Addictions* (3, 1968): pp. 271-300.

Goldman, E., *Religious Issues in Israel's Political Life.* (Jerusalem: Jewish Agency, 1964).

Gorer, Geoffrey, *Death, Grief, and Mourning*. (Garden City: Doubleday, 1965), pp. 72, 112-113.

Goshen-Gottestein, Esther R., "Courtship, Marriage and Pregnancy in 'Geula'," *The Israel Annuals of Psychiatry and Related Disciplines* (4, 1966): pp. 43-66.

Goshen-Gottestein, Esther R., *Marriage and First Pregnancy–Cultural Influence on Attitudes of Israeli Women*. (London: Tavistock, 1966).

Government of Israel Yearbook, 1950-1951 (Jerusalem, 1951).

Hanoch, Giora, "Income Differences in Israel," *Falk Center for Economic Research in Israel* (Report for the year No. 5, 1959/1960) (Jerusalem, 1961) (in Hebrew).

Havighurst, Robert J., *Growing-Up in River City*. (New York: John Wiley and Sons, 1962).

Havighurst, Robert J., "Social Class and the American School System," in George Bereday, Z. F. Luigi and T. V. Volpicelli, (eds.), *Public Education in America*. (New York: Harper, 1958).

Hollingshead, August B., *Elmtown's Youth*. (New York: John Wiley and Sons, 1949).

Isaac, Harold R., *American Jews in Israel*. (New York: John Day, 1967).

Jaffe, Emmanuel and Smilansky, Moshe, "The Extent and Causes of Early School Leaving," *Megamot* (9, 1958): pp. 275-285 (in Hebrew).

Janowsky, Oscar I., *Foundations of Israel*. (Princeton, New Jersey: D. Van Nostrand, 1959).

Katz, Elihu and Denet, Brenda, "Petitions and Persuasive Appeals: A Study of Official Client Relations," *American Sociological Review* (31: 1966): pp. 811-822.

Katz, Elihu and Eisenstadt, S. N., "Some Sociological Observations on the Response of Israeli Organizations to New Immigrants," *Administrative Science Quarterly* (5, 1960): pp. 113-133.

Katz, Elihu and Zloczower, Avraham, "Ethnic Continuity in the Second Generation: A Report on Yeminites and Ashkenazim (European Jews) in a Small Israeli Town," *Megamot* (9, 1958): pp. 187-200 (in Hebrew).

Kirschenbaum, Allen and Cumay, Y., "Components of Attraction to New Towns: Preliminary Results," *Environmental Planning* (19-20: 1972): pp. 85-92.

Kohls, Margot, "Culture Patterns and Adjustment Processes of Morocco Immigrants from Rural Areas," *Megamot* (7, 1956): pp. 345-376 (in Hebrew).

Landis, J. R., Dinitz, S. and Reckless, W. C., "Implementing Two Theories of Delinquency: Value Orientation and Awareness of Limited Opportunity," *Sociology and Social Research* (47, 1963): pp. 408-416.

Lipset, Seymour Martin and Bendix, Reinhard, *Social Mobility in Industrial Society.* (Berkeley: University of California Press, 1959): pp. 19-21.

Lissak, Moshe, "Expectations of Social Mobility and Occupational Choice Amongst Urban Youth in Israel," *Bahistadrut* (1965-1966): pp. 2-40 (in Hebrew).

Lissak, Moshe, "Factors Underlying Occupational Preferences: Theoretical Model and Hypotheses for Research," *Megamot* (13, 1965): pp. 321-330 (in Hebrew).

Lissak, Moshe, "Patterns of Change in Ideology and Class Structure in Israel," *Jewish Journal of Sociology* (7, 1965): pp. 46-62.

Lissak, Moshe, *Social Mobility in Israeli Society.* (Jerusalem: Israel Universities Press, 1969).

Lissak, Moshe, "Stratification Models and Mobility Aspiration: Sources of Mobility Motivation," *Megamot* (15, 1967): pp. 66-82 (in Hebrew).

Maller, O., "Psychopathological Problems of Modern Immigration," *Niv Harofe,* (12, 1962): pp. 77-86 (in Hebrew).

Mannheim, Bilha, and Rim, Yehoshua, "Attitudes of Managers and Union Representatives to Issues in Labor Relations," *Israel Economic Quarterly* (40, 1963): pp. 367-377.

Mannheim, Bilha, and Rim, Yehoshua, "Factors Related to Attitudes of Management and Union Representatives," *Personnel Psychology* (17, 1964): pp. 149-165.

Mannheim, Bilha, Rim, Yehoshua, and Grinberg, Geula, "Instrumental Status of Supervisors as Related to Workers' Perceptions and Expectations," *Human Relations* (20, 1967).

Mannheim, Bilha, "Pressure Groups in Organization," *Organization and Administration* (13, 1967): pp. 3-14.

Mannheim, Bilha, "Wadi-Salib; Social Considerations in Slum Rehabilitation," in Soen, Dan (ed.), *Social Problems in Urban Renewal; A Symposium* (Ramat Gan: Bar-Ilan University, 1969): pp. 71-104.

Mannheim, Bilha, and Samuel, Yitzhak, "A Multi-Dimensional Approach Toward a Typology of Bureaucracy," *Administrative Science Quarterly* (15, 1970): pp. 216-229.

Mannheim, Bilha, "Attitudes of Older Industrial Workers Toward Retirement" in Miller, L. (ed.), *Mental Health in Rapid Social Change.* (Jerusalem: Academic Press, 1971): pp. 253-264.

Matras, Judah, "Religious Observance and Family Formation in Israel: Some Intergenerational Changes," *American Journal of Sociology* (69, 1964): pp. 464-475.

Matras, Judah, *Social Change in Israel.* (Chicago: Aldine, 1965).

Matras, Judah, "The Social Strategy of Family Formation: Some Variations in Time and Space," *Demography* (2, 1965): pp. 349-362.

Matras, Judah and Auerbach, C., "On Rationalization of Family Formation in Israel," *Milbank Memorial Fund Quarterly* (42, 1962).

Merton, Robert K., *Social Theory and Social Structure* (Glencoe, Ill.: The Free Press, 1949), pp. 73-138.

Minkovitz (Shokeid), Moshe, "Extended Families' Adjustment to the Moshav," *Megamot* (7, March .1963): pp. 281-284 (in Hebrew).

Minkovitz (Shokeid), Moshe, "Immigration and Factionalism: An Analysis of Factions in Rural Israeli Communities of Immigrants," *The British Journal of Sociology* (19, December 1968): pp. 385-406.

Minkovitz (Shokeid), Moshe, "Moshav Sela: Frustration and Crisis in the Process of Absorption," in O. Shapiro (ed.), *Rural Settlements of New Immigrants in Israel.* (Rehovot: Settlement Study Centre, 1971), pp. 103-123.

Minkovitz (Shokeid), Moshe, *Nevatim: A Village in Crisis.* (Beersheba: Jewish Agency Settlement Department, 1963) (in Hebrew).

Minkovitz (Shokeid), Moshe, "Old Conflicts in a New Environment: A Study of a Moroccan Atlas Community Transplanted in Israel," *Jewish Journal of Sociology* (9, 1967): pp. 191-208.

Minkovitz (Shokeid), Moshe, "Social Networks and Innovation in the Division of Labor Between Men and Women in the Family and in the Community: A Study of Moroccan Immigrants in Israel," *Canadian Review of Sociology and Anthropology* (8, February 1971): pp. 1-12. An earlier version appeared in Hebrew, *Megamot* (17, November 1970): pp. 241-253.

Minkovitz (Shokeid), Moshe, *The Dual Heritage: Immigrants from the Atlas Mountains in an Israeli Village.* (Manchester: Manchester University Press, 1971).

Morris, Terrence, *The Criminal Area.* (London: Routledge and K. Paul, 1957).

Murdoch, George, *Social Structure.* (New York: MacMillan, 1949).

Muhsam, H. V., "Mode of Life and Longevity in Israel," *Jewish Journal of Sociology* (8, 1966): pp. 39-48.

Nadad, Abraham, "The Village of Shalem—Image of a Poor Neighborhood," *Megamot* (7, 1956): pp. 5-40 (in Hebrew).

Noyes, Pierrepont, *My Father's House and Oneida Boyhood.* (New York, 1937).

Ortar, Gina and Frankenstein, Carl, "How to Develop Abstract Thinking in Immigrant Children from Oriental Countries," *Megamot* (2, 1951): pp. 361-384 (in Hebrew).

Ortar, Gina, "A Way to Avoid Cultural Retardation of the Young Child," *Megamot* (14, 1966): pp. 78-86, (in Hebrew).

Ortar, Gina, "The Diagnostic Significance of the Wechsler-Bellevue Test at Different Intelligence Levels," *Megamot* (4, 1953): pp. 199-216 (in Hebrew).

Ortar, Gina, "Differences in the Structure of Intelligence—A Comparative Analysis of Ethnic Sub-Groups," *Megamot* (4, 1953): pp. 107-122 (in Hebrew).

Ortar, Gina, "The Eighth Grade Survey of 1955," *Megamot* (7, 1956): pp. 76-85 (in Hebrew).

Ortar, Gina, "Educational Achievements as Related to Socio-Cultural Background of Primary School Graduates in Israel," *Megamot* (15, 1967): pp. 220-230 (in Hebrew).

Ortar, Gina, "Elementary School Graduates: Their Scholastic Aspirations and Achievements," *Megamot* (8, 1957): pp. 56-70 (in Hebrew).

Ortar, Gina, "Improving Test Validity by Coaching," *Megamot* (11, 1960): pp. 33-37 (in Hebrew).

Ortar, Gina, "The Influence of Some Environment Factors on Bible Study in Elementary School," *Megamot* (7, 1956): pp. 265-273 (in Hebrew).

Ortar, Gina, "On the Validity of Certain School Entrance Tests—A Follow-Up Study," *Megamot* (3, 1951): pp. 375-379 (in Hebrew).

Ortar, Gina, "The Predictive Value of the Eighth Grade Survey Tests," *Megamot* (10, 1960): pp. 209-221.

Ortar, Gina, "Principles of Transfer of Psychological Tests from One Culture to Another," *Megamot* (11, 1961): pp. 338-344 (in Hebrew).

Ortar, Gina, "Standardization in Israel of the Wechsler Test for Children," *Megamot* (4, 1952): pp. 87-100 (in Hebrew).

Ortar, Gina, "Thirteen Years of the Eighth Grade Survey," *Megamot* (15, 1967): pp. 220-230 (in Hebrew).

Ortar, Gina, "The Validity in Israel of Certain Intelligence Tests for Children at the Age of Six," *Megamot* (1, 1950): pp. 206-223 (in Hebrew).

Ortar, Gina, "Verbal and Performance Tests: Their Relative Value as Tools for Inter-Cultural Comparison," *Megamot* (9, 1958): pp. 207-227 (in Hebrew).

Palgi, Phyllis, "The Adaptability and Vulnerability of Types in the Changing Israeli Society," in Jarus, A., Marcus, J., Oren, J. and Rapaport, C. (eds.), *Children and Families in Israel: Some Mental Health Perspectives.* (Jerusalem: Szold Foundation, 1970), pp. 97-135.

Parsons, Talcott, "General Theory in Sociology," in Merton, R. K., Broom. L. and Cottrell, L. S., Jr., (eds.), *Sociology Today.* (New York: Basic Books, 1959), pp. 3-38.

Parsons, Talcott, *The Social System.* (Glencoe, Ill.: The Free Press, 1951), chapters 7 & 10.

Peres, Yohanan, *Ethnic Identity and Inter-Ethnic Relations.* (Unpublished doctoral dissertation, Hebrew University, 1968).

Peres, Yohanan, "The General Assembly in 'the Kibbutz'," *Oranim* (3, 1963): pp. 105-197 (in Hebrew).

Population and Housing Census (Jerusalem: Central Bureau of Statistics: 1961) (in Hebrew).

Porterfield, A. L., "Delinquency and Its Outcome in Court and College," *American Journal of Sociology* (49, 1948): pp. 199-208.

Preale, Ilana, Amir, Yehuda and Sharan, Shlomo, "Perceptual Articulation and Task Effectiveness in Several Israeli Subcultures," *Journal of Personality and Social Psychology* (15, 1970): pp. 190-195.

Rabin, Albert I., *Growing Up in the Kibbutz.* (New York: Springer, 1965).

Rabin, Albert I., *Kibbutz Studies.* (East Lansing, Michigan, mimeographed, 1970).

Reckless, Eyon and Reckless, Walter, "Companionship of Delinquency Onset," *British Journal of Criminology* (1961): pp. 162-170.

Rieger, Hagit, "Some Aspects of the Acculturation of Yemenite Youth Immigrants," in Frankenstein, C. (ed.), *Between Past and Future.* (Jerusalem: Szold Foundation, 1953), pp. 82-108.

Rieger, Hagit, "Problems of Adjustment of Yemenite Children in Israel," *Megamot* (3, 1951): pp. 259-291.

Rim, Y., and Kurzweil, Z. E., "A Note on Attitudes to Risk-Taking of Observant and Non-Observant Jews," *Jewish Journal of Sociology* (7, 1965): pp. 238-245.

Ritterband, Paul, *The Non-Returning Foreign Student: The Israeli Case.* (New York: Columbia University, Bureau of Applied Social Research, 1968) (mimeographed).

Rogof, Natalie, "Local Social Structure and Educational Selection," in Halsey, H. A., *et al.* (eds.), *Education Economy and Society.* (New York: The Free Press, 1961), pp. 241-251.

Rosenfeld, Eva, "The American Social Scientist in Israel: A Case Study in Role Conflict," *American Journal of Orthopsychiatry* (28, 1958): pp. 563-571.

Rosenfeld, Eva, "Institutional Change in the Kibbutz," *Social Problems* (5, 1957): pp. 110-136.

Rosenfeld, Eva, "Social Stratification in a 'Classless' Society," *American Sociological Review* (16, 1951): pp. 766-774.

Rosenstein, Eliezer, "Histradut Search for a Participation Program," *Industrial Relations* (9, 1970): pp. 170-186.

Rosenstein, Eliezer and Strauss, G., "Worker's Participation: A Critical Review," *Industrial Relations* (9, 1970): pp. 197-214.

Rosenstein, Eliezar and Rosenfeld, J. "Toward a Conceptual Framework for the Study of Parent Absent Familes," *Journal of Marriage and the Family* (36, 1973).

Rosner, Menachem, "Difficulties and Rewards in the Role of Branch Manager," *Hedim* (46, 1963) (in Hebrew).

Rosner, Menachem, "Direct Democracy in the Kibbutz," *New Outlook* (8 [6], 1965): pp. 29-41.

Rosner, Menachem, *Research Report on the Status of the Women in the Kibbutz.* (Gi'vat Ha'viva, 1966) (in Hebrew).

Rosner, Menachem, "Women in the Kibbutz: Changing Status and Concepts," *Asian and African Studies* (3, 1967): pp. 35-68.

Rubin, Nissan, *Change of Funeral Practices in the Period of the Talmud.* (Unpublished M.A. dissertation, Hebrew University, 1971).

Sacher, Harry, *Israel: The Establishment of a State.* (London: George Weidenfield and Nicholson, 1952).

Sarel, Moshe, *Research Report on the Second Generation in the Kibbutz.* (Jerusalem: Hebrew University, 1959) (mimeographed in Hebrew).

Schachter, Stanley, *The Psychology of Affiliation: Experimental Studies of the Sources of Gregariousness.* (Stanford, California: Stanford University Press, 1959).

Schmalenbach, Herman, "The Sociological Category of Communion," in Parsons, T., Shils, E., Naegele, K. D., Pitts, J.R. (eds.), *Theories of Society.* (New York: The Free Press, 1961), pp. 331-348.

Schwartz, Richard D., "Functional Alternatives to Inequality," *American Sociological Review* (20, 1955): pp. 424-430.

Sewell, William H., Haller, Archie O. and Strauss, Murray A., "Social Status and Educational and Occupational Aspirations," *American Sociological Review* (22, 1957): pp. 67-73.

Sharan, Shlomo, Amir, Yehuda and Kovarsky, Yacov, "Birth Order and Level of Task Performance: A Cross Cultural Comparison," *Journal of Social Psychology* (78, 1969): pp. 157-163.

Sharan, Shlomo and Weller, Leonard, "Classification Patterns in Underprivileged Children in Israel," *Child Development* (42, 1971): pp. 581-594.

Shaw, C. and McKay, R., *Juvenile Delinquency and Urban Areas.* (Chicago: University of Chicago Press, 1942).

Shepher, Joseph, "Familism and Social Structure: The Case of the Kibbutz," *Journal of Marriage and the Family* (31, 1969): pp. 567-573.

Shepher, Joseph, "Motivation to Work and Social Activity in Kibbutz Society," *Proceedings of the International Symposium of Cooperative Rural Communities.* (Tel Aviv, 1968), Vol. I, pp. 205-207.

Shepher, Joseph, "Public Activity Outside the Kibbutz," *Niv Hakvutzah* (15, 1966): pp. 39-59 (in Hebrew).

Shepher, Joseph, *The Reflections of the Housing System of the Children in the Social Structure of the Kibbutz.* (Tel Aviv: Ichud, 1967) (in Hebrew).

Shepher, Joseph, *Self Imposed Incest and Exogamy in Second Generation Kibbutz Adults.* (Unpublished doctoral dissertation, Rutgers University, New Brunswick, New Jersey, 1971).

Shoham, Shlomo, "The Application of the Culture Conflict Hypothesis and the Criminality of Immigrants in Israel," *Journal of Criminal Law, Criminology and Police Science* (53, 1962).

Shoham, Shlomo, "The Culture Conflict Hypothesis and the Criminality of Immigrants in Israel," *Journal of Criminal Law, Criminology and Police Science* (53, 1952): pp. 202-214.

Shoham, Shlomo, Erez, Ruth and Reckless, Walter C., "Value Orientation and Awareness of Differential Opportunity of Delinquent and Non-Delinquent Boys in Israel," *British Journal of Criminology* (5, 1965): pp. 325-332.

Shoham, Shlomo and Hovav, Meir, "Bnei Tovim—Middle and Upper Class Delinquency in Israel," *Sociology and Social Research* (48, 1964): pp. 454-468.

Shoham, Shlomo and Hovav, Meir, "Social Factors, Aspects of Treatment and Patterns of Criminal Career Among the Bnei-Tovim," *Human Relations* (19, 1966): pp. 47-56.

Shoham, Shlomo, Kaufman, Yaron and Menaker, Michal, "The Tel-Mond Follow-Up Research Project," *Houston Law Review* (5, 1967): pp. 36-62.

Shoham, Shlomo, *The Mark of Cain, the Stigma Theory of Crime and Deviation.* (Chicago: University of Chicago Press, 1968).

Shoham, Shlomo, "Psychopathology as Social Stigma: A Myth Revisited," *Journal of Corrective Psychology and Social Therapy* (13, 1967): pp. 21-41.

Shoham, Shlomo, and Rahav, Giora, "Social Stigma and Prostitution," *International Annals of Criminology* (6, 1967): pp. 479-513.

Shoham, Shlomo, Shavit, G. and Keren, R., "Pimps and Prostitutes," reported in Shoham, Shlomo and Rahav, Giora, "Social Stigma and Prostitution," *British Journal of Sociology* (15, 1968): pp. 402-412.

Shoham, Shlomo and Sandberg, Moshe, "Suspended Sentences in Israel: An Evaluation of the Preventive Efficacy of Prospective Imprisonment," *Crime and Delinquency* (50, 1964): pp. 74-83.

Shoham, Shlomo, "Sentencing Policy of Criminal Courts in Israel," *Journal of Criminal Law, Criminology and Police Science* (50, 1959): pp. 327-337.

Shoham, Shlomo and Shaskolsky, Leon, "An Analysis of Delinquents and Non-Delinquents in Israel: A Cross Cultural Perspective," *Sociology and Social Research* (53, 1969): pp. 333-343.

Shoham, Shlomo, Shoham, Nahum and Aba-El-Razak, "Immigration, Ethnicity and Ecology as Related to Juvenile Delinquency in Israel," *The British Journal of Criminology* (5, 1966): pp. 391-409.

Shoham, Shlomo, "Social Stigma and the Criminal Group," *The Irish Jurist* (7, 1968): pp. 1-23.

Shuval, Judith T., "Class and Ethnic Correlates of Causal Neighboring," *American Sociological Review* (21, 1956): pp. 453-458.

Shuval, Judith T., "Emerging Patterns of Ethnic Strain in Israel," *Social Forces* (40, 1962): pp. 323-330.

Shuval, Judith T., "Factors Related to Identification With Place of Residence in New Immigrant Settlement," *Megamot* (11, 1960): pp. 66-72 (in Hebrew).

Shuval, Judith T., *Immigrants on the Threshold*. (New York: Atherton, 1963).

Shuval, Judith T., "The Micro-Neighborhood: An Approach to Ecological Patterns of Ethnic Groups," *Social Problems* (9, 1961): pp. 272-280.

Shuval, Judith T., "Parental Pressure and Career Commitments," *Megamot* (13, 1964): pp. 33-39 (in Hebrew).

Shuval, Judith T., "Patterns of Inter-Group Tension and Affinity," *International Social Science Bulletin* (8, 1956): pp. 75-123.

Shuval, Judith T., "The Role of Class in Structuring Inter-Group Hostility," *Human Relations* (10, 1957): pp. 61-75.

Shuval, Judith T., "The Role of Ideology as a Predisposing Frame of Reference for Immigrants," *Human Relations* (12, 1959): pp. 51-63.

Shuval, Judith T., "Self-Rejection Among North African Immigrants to Israel," *The Israel Annals of Psychiatry and Related Disciplines* (4, 1966): pp. 101-110.

Shuval, Judith T., "Some Persistent Effects of Trauma: Five Years after the Nazi Concentration Camps," *Social Problems* (5, 1957): pp. 230-243.

Shuval, Judith T., "Value Orientations in Israel," *Sociometry* (26, 1963): pp. 247-259.

Sicron, Moshe, *Immigration to Israel: 1948-1953*, (2 vols.), (Jerusalem: Israel Central Bureau of Statistics, Special Series No. 60, 1957).

Simon, Aryeh, "On the Scholastic Achievements of Immigrant Children in the Lower Elementary Grades," *Megamot* (8, 1957): pp. 343-368 (in Hebrew).

Smilansky, Moshe, Burg, Blanca and Kreiger, Thehila, "Regional Enrichment Centers for Disadvantaged Children in the Grades of Elementary School," *Megamot* (14, 1966): pp. 200-212 (in Hebrew).

Smilansky, Moshe and Parnas, Tikvah, "Educational and Vocational Guidance in Israel: A Follow-up Study," *Megamot* (10, 1960): pp. 242-270 (in Hebrew).

Smilansky, Moshe, "Outlines for a Reform in Secondary Education," *Megamot* (11, 1961): pp. 364-372 (in Hebrew).

Smilansky, Moshe, "The Social Implications of the Educational Structure in Israel," *Megamot* (8, 1957): pp. 227-338 (in Hebrew).

Smilansky, Moshe and Yam, Yosef, "The Relationship Between Family Size, Ethnic Origin, Father's Education and Student's Achievements," *Megamot* (16, 1966): pp. 248-273 (in Hebrew).

Smilansky, Sara, "Children Who Fail in the First Elementary Grades and Their Parents," *Megamot* (8, 1957): pp. 430-445 (in Hebrew).

Smilansky, Sara, "The Effect of Certain Learning Conditions on Disadvantaged Children of Pre-School Age," *Megamot* (14, 1966): pp. 213-224 (in Hebrew).

Smilansky, Sara, "The Kindergarten as a Means of Promoting Intellectual Development in Underprivileged Children," *Megamot* (9, 1958): pp. 163-180. (in Hebrew).

Spiegel, Erika, *New Towns in Israel.* (Stuttgart: Kramer, 1966).

Spiro, Melford, E., *Children of the Kibbutz.* (Cambridge: Harvard University Press, 1958).

Spiro, Melford E., "Is the Family Universal?" *American Anthropologist* (56, 1954): pp. 839-846.

Spiro, Melford E., *Kibbutz: Venture in Utopia.* (Cambridge: Harvard University Press, 1956).

Statistical Abstracts of Israel (No. 16, 1966).

Statistical Abstracts of Israel (No. 21, 1970).

"Survey of Deserters of the Kibbutz from the Second Generation and from the Internees" (Giv'at Ha'viva, 1969) (in Hebrew).

Tabb, J. Y. and Goldfarb, A. Workers' Participation in Management Expectations and Experience (London: Pergamon Press, 1970).

Tabb, J. Y. and Mannheim, Bilha, *The Human Factor in Production* (Tel Aviv: Dvir and Am-Oved, 1965) (in Hebrew).

Talmon-Garber, Yonina, "Asceticism-Patterns of Ideological Change," (with Tsipora Stupp) in Wurm, S. H. (ed.), *Sefer Bussel.* (Tel Aviv: Tarbut Ve'Ichud, 1960), pp. 149-190.

Talmon-Garber, Yonina, 'Differentiation in Collective Settlements," *Scripto Hierosolymitana* (3, 1956): pp. 153-178.

Talmon-Garber, Yonina, *The Individual and the Group in the Kibbutz.* (Jerusalem: Magnes Press, 1970) (in Hebrew).

Talmon-Garber, Yonina, "Mate Selection in Collective Settlements," *American Sociological Review* (29, 1964): pp. 491-508.

Talmon-Garber, Yonina, "Report on Division of Labor in the Kibbutz." (Jerusalem: The Hebrew University, 1956) (mimeographed in Hebrew).

Talmon-Garber, Yonina, "Social Differentiation in Co-operative Communities," *British Journal of Sociology* (3, 1952): pp. 339-357.

Viscount Samuel, "Where Did Israel Put Its Million Jewish Immigrants," *Jewish Journal of Sociology* (8, 1966): pp. 81-91.

Weinberg, Abraham Albert, *Immigration and Belonging.* (The Hague: Martinus Nijhoff, 1961).

Weingrod, Alex, "Administered Communities: Some Characteristics of New Immigrant Villages in Israel," *Economic Development and Cultural Change* (11, 1962): pp. 69-84.

Weingrod, Alex, "Change and Continuity in a Moroccan Immigrant Village in Israel," *Middle East Journal* (14, 1960): pp. 277-291. Also appears in Hebrew, *Megamot* (10, 1960): pp. 322-355.

Weingrod, Alex, *Israel: Group Relations in a New Society.* (London: Pall Mall Press, 1965).

Weingrod, Alex, "Moroccan Jewry in Transition," *Megamot* (10, 1960): pp. 193-208 (in Hebrew).

Weingrod, Alex, "Reciprocal Change: A Case Study of a Moroccan Immigrant Village in Israel," *American Anthropologist* (64, 1962): pp. 115-131.

Weintraub, Dov and Lissak, Moshe, "The Absorption of North African Immigrants in Agricultural Settlements in Israel," *Jewish Journal of Sociology* (3, 1961): pp. 29-54.

Weintraub, Dov, *Patterns of Social Change in New Immigrants' Smallholders' Co-operative Settlements.* (Unpublished doctoral dissertation, Hebrew University, Jerusalem, 1962) (in Hebrew).

Weintraub, Dov and Shapiro, Miriam, "The Traditional Family in Israel in the Process of Change—Crisis and Continuation," in Bar-Yosef, R. and Shelach, I. (eds.), *The Family in Israel.* (Jerusalem: Academon, 1969), pp. 215-228.

Weintraub, Dov, "A Study of New Farmers in Israel," *Sociologia Ruralis* (4, 1964): pp. 3-51.

Weller, Leonard and Sharan, Shlomo, "Articulation of the Body Concept Among First-Grade Israeli Children," *Child Development* (42, 1971): pp. 1553-1559.

Weller, Leonard and Tabory, Ephraim, "Religiosity of Nurses and their Orientation to Patients," in H. Z. Hirschberg, Y. Don and L. Weller (eds.), *Memorial to H. M. Shapiro* (Ramat Gan: Bar-Ilan University, 1972), pp. 97-110.

Weller, Leonard *et al.*, "Authoritarianism and Degree of Religiosity," (mimeographed, 1973).

Weller, Leonard, "The Effects of Class, Ethnicity, Age and Sex on Delayed Gratification" (in preparation).

Weller, Leonard, Glanz, Israel and Klein, Iris, "Personality Characteristics of First Time Offenders and Recidivists, Property and Violent Offenders," in Shoham, Shlomo (ed.), *Israel Studies in Criminology*, vol. 2 (Jerusalem: Academic Press, 1973): pp. 113-125.

Weller, Leonard, "The Adjustment of American Immigrants in Israel," (Department of Sociology, Bar-Ilan University, 1968, mimeographed).

Willner, Dorothy and Kohls, Margot, "Jews in the High Atlas Mountain of Morocco: A Partial Reconstruction," *Jewish Journal of Sociology* (4, 1962): pp. 207-241.

Willner, Dorothy, "Politics and Change in Israel: The Case of Land Settlements," *Human Organization* (24, 1965): pp. 65-79.

Wilson, Alan B., "Residential Segregation of School Classes and Aspirations of High School Boys," *American Sociological Review* (24, 1950): pp. 836-845.

Witkin, H. A., Dyk, R. B., Paterson, H. F., Goodenough, D. R. and Darp, S. A., *Psychological Differentiation.* (New York: Wiley, 1962).

Yaari, Hayim, "Unsuccess in Absorption From Affluent Countries," *Davar* (January 1, 1966) (in Hebrew).

Yaari, Hayim, "Why Do American Immigrants Fail in Business?" *Davar* (February 4, 1966) (in Hebrew).

Young, Frank W., "Incest Taboos and Social Solidarity," *American Journal of Sociology* (72, 1967): pp. 589-600.

Zadik, Baruch, "Field Dependence-Independence Among Oriental and Western School Children," *Megamot* (16, 1968): pp. 51-58 (in Hebrew).

Index

307